CASENOTE® Legal Briefs®

INTERNATIONAL LAW

Keyed to Courses Using

Damrosch and Murphy's
International Law: Cases and Materials
Seventh Edition

Authored by: Publisher's Editorial Staff

Wolters Kluwer

Published by Wolters Kluwer in New York.

Wolters Kluwer Legal & Regulatory U.S. serves customers worldwide with CCH, Aspen Publishers, and Kluwer Law International products. (www.WKLegaledu.com)

To contact Customer Service, e-mail customer.service@wolterskluwer.com, call 1-800-234-1660, fax 1-800-901-9075, or mail correspondence to:

Wolters Kluwer
Attn: Order Department
P.O. Box 990
Frederick, MD 21705

Printed in the United States of America.

1 2 3 4 5 6 7 8 9 0

ISBN 978-1-5438-1335-7

SUSTAINABLE FORESTRY INITIATIVE Certified Sourcing www.sfiprogram.org SFI-00756

About Wolters Kluwer Legal & Regulatory U.S.

Wolters Kluwer Legal & Regulatory U.S. delivers expert content and solutions in the areas of law, corporate compliance, health compliance, reimbursement, and legal education. Its practical solutions help customers successfully navigate the demands of a changing environment to drive their daily activities, enhance decision quality, and inspire confident outcomes.

Serving customers worldwide, its legal and regulatory portfolio includes products under the Aspen Publishers, CCH Incorporated, Kluwer Law International, ftwilliam.com, and MediRegs names. They are regarded as exceptional and trusted resources for general legal and practice-specific knowledge, compliance and risk management, dynamic workflow solutions, and expert commentary.

Format for the Casenote® Legal Brief

Nature of Case: This section identifies the form of action (e.g., breach of contract, negligence, battery), the type of proceeding (e.g., demurrer, appeal from trial court's jury instructions) or the relief sought (e.g., damages, injunction, criminal sanctions).

Fact Summary: This is included to refresh your memory and can be used as a quick reminder of the facts.

Rule of Law: Summarizes the general principle of law that the case illustrates. It may be used for instant recall of the court's holding and for classroom discussion or home review.

Facts: This section contains all relevant facts of the case, including the contentions of the parties and the lower court holdings. It is written in a logical order to give you a clear understanding of the case. The plaintiff and defendant are identified by their proper names throughout and are always labeled with a (P) or (D).

Issue: The issue is a concise question that brings out the essence of the opinion as it relates to the section of the casebook in which the case appears. Both substantive and procedural issues are included if relevant to the decision.

Palsgraf v. Long Island R.R. Co.

Injured bystander (P) v. Railroad company (D)

N.Y. Ct. App., 248 N.Y. 339, 162 N.E. 99 (1928).

NATURE OF CASE: Appeal from judgment affirming verdict for plaintiff seeking damages for personal injury.

FACT SUMMARY: Helen Palsgraf (P) was injured on R.R.'s (D) train platform when R.R.'s (D) guard helped a passenger aboard a moving train, causing his package to fall on the tracks. The package contained fireworks which exploded, creating a shock that tipped a scale onto Palsgraf (P).

RULE OF LAW

The risk reasonably to be perceived defines the duty to be obeyed.

FACTS: Helen Palsgraf (P) purchased a ticket to Rockaway Beach from R.R. (D) and was waiting on the train platform. As she waited, two men ran to catch a train that was pulling out from the platform. The first man jumped aboard, but the second man, who appeared as if he might fall, was helped aboard by the guard on the train who had kept the door open so they could jump aboard. A guard on the platform also helped by pushing him onto the train. The man was carrying a package wrapped in newspaper. In the process, the man dropped his package, which fell on the tracks. The package contained fireworks and exploded. The shock of the explosion was apparently of great enough strength to tip over some scales at the other end of the platform, which fell on Palsgraf (P) and injured her. A jury awarded her damages, and R.R. (D) appealed.

ISSUE: Does the risk reasonably to be perceived define the duty to be obeyed?

HOLDING AND DECISION: (Cardozo, C.J.) Yes. The risk reasonably to be perceived defines the duty to be obeyed. If there is no foreseeable hazard to the injured party as the result of a seemingly innocent act, the act does not become a tort because it happened to be a wrong as to another. If the wrong was not willful, the plaintiff must show that the act as to her had such great and apparent possibilities of danger as to entitle her to protection. Negligence in the abstract is not enough upon which to base liability. Negligence is a relative concept, evolving out of the common law doctrine of trespass on the case. To establish liability, the defendant must owe a legal duty of reasonable care to the injured party. A cause of action in tort will lie where harm, though unintended, could have been averted or avoided by observance of such a duty. The scope of the duty is limited by the range of danger that a reasonable person could foresee. In this case, there was nothing to suggest from the appearance of the parcel or otherwise that the parcel contained fireworks. The guard could not reasonably have had any warning of a threat to Palsgraf (P), and R.R. (D) therefore cannot be held liable. Judgment is reversed in favor of R.R. (D).

DISSENT: (Andrews, J.) The concept that there is no negligence unless R.R. (D) owes a legal duty to take care as to Palsgraf (P) herself is too narrow. Everyone owes to the world at large the duty of refraining from those acts that may unreasonably threaten the safety of others. If the guard's action was negligent as to those nearby, it was also negligent as to those outside what might be termed the "danger zone." For Palsgraf (P) to recover, R.R.'s (D) negligence must have been the proximate cause of her injury, a question of fact for the jury.

ANALYSIS

The majority defined the limit of the defendant's liability in terms of the danger that a reasonable person in defendant's situation would have perceived. The dissent argued that the limitation should not be placed on liability, but rather on damages. Judge Andrews suggested that only injuries that would not have happened but for R.R.'s (D) negligence should be compensable. Both the majority and dissent recognized the policy-driven need to limit liability for negligent acts, seeking, in the words of Judge Andrews, to define a framework "that will be practical and in keeping with the general understanding of mankind." The Restatement (Second) of Torts has accepted Judge Cardozo's view.

Quicknotes

FORESEEABILITY A reasonable expectation that change is the probable result of certain acts or omissions.

NEGLIGENCE Conduct falling below the standard of care that a reasonable person would demonstrate under similar conditions.

PROXIMATE CAUSE The natural sequence of events without which an injury would not have been sustained.

Party ID: Quick identification of the relationship between the parties.

Concurrence/Dissent: All concurrences and dissents are briefed whenever they are included by the casebook author.

Analysis: This last paragraph gives you a broad understanding of where the case "fits in" with other cases in the section of the book and with the entire course. It is a hornbook-style discussion indicating whether the case is a majority or minority opinion and comparing the principal case with other cases in the casebook. It may also provide analysis from restatements, uniform codes, and law review articles.

Holding and Decision: This section offers a clear and in-depth discussion of the rule of the case and the court's rationale. It is written in easy-to-understand language and answers the issue presented by applying the law to the facts of the case. When relevant, it includes a thorough discussion of the exceptions to the case as listed by the court, any major cites to the other cases on point, and the names of the judges who wrote the decisions.

Quicknotes: Conveniently defines legal terms found in the case.

Note to Students

Wolters Kluwer Legal & Regulatory U.S. is proud to offer *Casenote® Legal Briefs*—continuing thirty years of publishing America's best-selling legal briefs.

Casenote® Legal Briefs are designed to help you save time when briefing assigned cases. Organized under convenient headings, they show you how to abstract the basic facts and holdings from the text of the actual opinions handed down by the courts. Used as part of a rigorous study regimen, they can help you spend more time analyzing and critiquing points of law than on copying bits and pieces of judicial opinions into your notebook or outline.

Casenote® Legal Briefs should never be used as a substitute for assigned casebook readings. They work best when read as a follow-up to reviewing the underlying opinions themselves. Students who try to avoid reading and digesting the judicial opinions in their casebooks or online sources will end up shortchanging themselves in the long run. The ability to absorb, critique, and restate the dynamic and complex elements of case law decisions is crucial to your success in law school and beyond. It cannot be developed vicariously.

Casenote® Legal Briefs represents but one of the many offerings in Legal Education's Study Aid Timeline, which includes:

- *Casenote® Legal Briefs*
- *Emanuel® Law Outlines*
- Emanuel® *Law in a Flash* Flash Cards
- Emanuel® *CrunchTime®* Series

Each of these series is designed to provide you with easy-to-understand explanations of complex points of law. Each volume offers guidance on the principles of legal analysis and, consulted regularly, will hone your ability to spot relevant issues. We have titles that will help you prepare for class, prepare for your exams, and enhance your general comprehension of the law along the way.

To find out more about our law school tools for success, visit us at *www.WKLegaledu.com* or email us at *legaledu@wolterskluwer.com*. We'll be happy to assist you.

How to Brief a Case

A. Decide on a Format and Stick to It

Structure is essential to a good brief. It enables you to arrange systematically the related parts that are scattered throughout most cases, thus making manageable and understandable what might otherwise seem to be an endless and unfathomable sea of information. There are, of course, an unlimited number of formats that can be utilized. However, it is best to find one that suits your needs and stick to it. Consistency breeds both efficiency and the security that when called upon you will know where to look in your brief for the information you are asked to give.

Any format, as long as it presents the essential elements of a case in an organized fashion, can be used. Experience, however, has led *Casenote® Legal Briefs* to develop and utilize the following format because of its logical flow and universal applicability.

NATURE OF CASE: This is a brief statement of the legal character and procedural status of the case (e.g., "Appeal of a burglary conviction").

There are many different alternatives open to a litigant dissatisfied with a court ruling. The key to determining which one has been used is to discover *who is asking this court for what.*

This first entry in the brief should be kept as *short as possible.* Use the court's terminology if you understand it. But since jurisdictions vary as to the titles of pleadings, the best entry is the one that addresses who wants what in this proceeding, not the one that sounds most like the court's language.

RULE OF LAW: A statement of the general principle of law that the case illustrates (e.g., "An acceptance that varies any term of the offer is considered a rejection and counteroffer").

Determining the rule of law of a case is a procedure similar to determining the issue of the case. Avoid being fooled by red herrings; there may be a few rules of law mentioned in the case excerpt, but usually only one is *the* rule with which the casebook editor is concerned. The techniques used to locate the issue, described below, may also be utilized to find the rule of law. Generally, your best guide is simply the chapter heading. It is a clue to the point the casebook editor seeks to make and should be kept in mind when reading every case in the respective section.

FACTS: A synopsis of only the essential facts of the case, i.e., those bearing upon or leading up to the issue.

The facts entry should be a short statement of the events and transactions that led one party to initiate legal proceedings against another in the first place. While some cases conveniently state the salient facts at the beginning of the decision, in other instances they will have to be culled from hiding places throughout the text, even from concurring and dissenting opinions. Some of the "facts" will often be in dispute and should be so noted. Conflicting evidence may be briefly pointed up. "Hard" facts must be included. Both must be *relevant* in order to be listed in the facts entry. It is impossible to tell what is relevant until the entire case is read, as the ultimate determination of the rights and liabilities of the parties may turn on something buried deep in the opinion.

Generally, the facts entry should not be longer than three to five *short* sentences.

It is often helpful to identify the role played by a party in a given context. For example, in a construction contract case the identification of a party as the "contractor" or "builder" alleviates the need to tell that that party was the one who was supposed to have built the house.

It is always helpful, and a good general practice, to identify the "plaintiff" and the "defendant." This may seem elementary and uncomplicated, but, especially in view of the creative editing practiced by some casebook editors, it is sometimes a difficult or even impossible task. Bear in mind that the *party presently* seeking something from this court may not be the plaintiff, and that sometimes only the cross-claim of a defendant is treated in the excerpt. Confusing or misaligning the parties can ruin your analysis and understanding of the case.

ISSUE: A statement of the general legal question answered by or illustrated in the case. For clarity, the issue is best put in the form of a question capable of a "yes" or "no" answer. In reality, the issue is simply the Rule of Law put in the form of a question (e.g., "May an offer be accepted by performance?").

The major problem presented in discerning what is *the* issue in the case is that an opinion usually purports to raise and answer several questions. However, except for rare cases, only one such question is really the issue in the case. Collateral issues not necessary to the resolution of the matter in controversy are handled by the court by language known as *"obiter dictum"* or merely *"dictum."* While dicta may be included later in the brief, they have no place under the issue heading.

To find the issue, ask *who wants what* and then go on to ask *why did that party succeed or fail in getting it.* Once this is determined, the "why" should be turned into a question.

The complexity of the issues in the cases will vary, but in all cases a single-sentence question should sum up the issue. *In a few cases,* there will be two, or even more rarely, three issues of equal importance to the resolution of the case. Each should be expressed in a single-sentence question.

Since many issues are resolved by a court in coming to a final disposition of a case, the casebook editor will reproduce the portion of the opinion containing the issue or issues most relevant to the area of law under scrutiny. A noted law professor gave this advice: "Close the book; look at the title on the cover." Chances are, if it is Property, you need not concern yourself with whether, for example, the federal government's treatment of the plaintiff's land really raises a federal question sufficient to support jurisdiction on this ground in federal court.

The same rule applies to chapter headings designating sub-areas within the subjects. They tip you off as to what the text is designed to teach. The cases are arranged in a casebook to show a progression or development of the law, so that the preceding cases may also help.

It is also most important to remember to *read the notes and questions* at the end of a case to determine what the editors wanted you to have gleaned from it.

HOLDING AND DECISION: This section should succinctly explain the rationale of the court in arriving at its decision. In capsulizing the "reasoning" of the court, it should always include an application of the general rule or rules of law to the specific facts of the case. Hidden justifications come to light in this entry: the reasons for the state of the law, the public policies, the biases and prejudices, those considerations that influence the justices' thinking and, ultimately, the outcome of the case. At the end, there should be a short indication of the disposition or procedural resolution of the case (e.g., "Decision of the trial court for Mr. Smith (P) reversed").

The foregoing format is designed to help you "digest" the reams of case material with which you will be faced in your law school career. Once mastered by practice, it will place at your fingertips the information the authors of your casebooks have sought to impart to you in case-by-case illustration and analysis.

B. Be as Economical as Possible in Briefing Cases

Once armed with a format that encourages succinctness, it is as important to be economical with regard to the time spent on the actual reading of the case as it is to be economical in the writing of the brief itself. This does not mean "skimming" a case. Rather, it means reading the case with an "eye" trained to recognize into which "section" of your brief a particular passage or line fits and having a system for quickly and precisely marking the case so that the passages fitting any one particular part of the brief can be easily identified and brought together in a concise and accurate manner when the brief is actually written.

It is of no use to simply repeat everything in the opinion of the court; record only enough information to trigger your recollection of what the court said. Nevertheless, an accurate statement of the "law of the case," i.e., the legal principle applied to the facts, is absolutely essential to class preparation and to learning the law under the case method.

To that end, it is important to develop a "shorthand" that you can use to make marginal notations. These notations will tell you at a glance in which section of the brief you will be placing that particular passage or portion of the opinion.

Some students prefer to underline all the salient portions of the opinion (with a pencil or colored underliner marker), making marginal notations as they go along. Others prefer the color-coded method of underlining, utilizing different colors of markers to underline the salient portions of the case, each separate color being used to represent a different section of the brief. For example, blue underlining could be used for passages relating to the rule of law, yellow for those relating to the issue, and green for those relating to the holding and decision, etc. While it has its advocates, the color-coded method can be confusing and time-consuming (all that time spent on changing colored markers). Furthermore, it can interfere with the continuity and concentration many students deem essential to the reading of a case for maximum comprehension. In the end, however, it is a matter of personal preference and style. Just remember, whatever method you use, underlining must be used sparingly or its value is lost.

If you take the marginal notation route, an efficient and easy method is to go along underlining the key portions of the case and placing in the margin alongside them the following "markers" to indicate where a particular passage or line "belongs" in the brief you will write:

N (NATURE OF CASE)
RL (RULE OF LAW)
I (ISSUE)
HL (HOLDING AND DECISION, relates to the RULE OF LAW behind the decision)
HR (HOLDING AND DECISION, gives the RATIONALE or reasoning behind the decision)
HA (HOLDING AND DECISION, applies the general principle(s) of law to the facts of the case to arrive at the decision)

Remember that a particular passage may well contain information necessary to more than one part of your brief, in which case you simply note that in the margin. If you are using the color-coded underlining method instead of marginal notation, simply make asterisks or checks in the margin next to the passage in question in the colors that indicate the additional sections of the brief where it might be utilized.

The economy of utilizing "shorthand" in marking cases for briefing can be maintained in the actual brief writing process itself by utilizing "law student shorthand" within the brief. There are many commonly used words and phrases for which abbreviations can be substituted in your briefs (and in your class notes also). You can develop abbreviations that are personal to you and which will save you a lot of time. A reference list of briefing abbreviations can be found on page x of this book.

C. Use Both the Briefing Process and the Brief as a Learning Tool

Now that you have a format and the tools for briefing cases efficiently, the most important thing is to make the time spent in briefing profitable to you and to make the most advantageous use of the briefs you create. Of course, the briefs are invaluable for classroom reference when you are called upon to explain or analyze a particular case. However, they are also useful in reviewing for exams. A quick glance at the fact summary should bring the case to mind, and a rereading of the rule of law should enable you to go over the underlying legal concept in your mind, how it was applied in that particular case, and how it might apply in other factual settings.

As to the value to be derived from engaging in the briefing process itself, there is an immediate benefit that arises from being forced to sift through the essential facts and reasoning from the court's opinion and to succinctly express them in your own words in your brief. The process ensures that you understand the case and the point that it illustrates, and that means you will be ready to absorb further analysis and information brought forth in class. It also ensures you will have something to say when called upon in class. The briefing process helps develop a mental agility for getting to the *gist* of a case and for identifying, expounding on, and applying the legal concepts and issues found there. The briefing process is the mental process on which you must rely in taking law school examinations; it is also the mental process upon which lawyers rely in serving their clients and in making a living.

Abbreviations for Briefs

acceptance ... acp
affirmed ... aff
answer ... ans
assumption of risk ... a/r
attorney ... atty
beyond a reasonable doubt ... b/r/d
bona fide purchaser ... BFP
breach of contract ... br/k
cause of action ... c/a
common law ... c/l
Constitution ... Con
constitutional ... con
contract ... K
contributory negligence ... c/n
cross ... x
cross-complaint ... x/c
cross-examination ... x/ex
cruel and unusual punishment ... c/u/p
defendant ... D
dismissed ... dis
double jeopardy ... d/j
due process ... d/p
equal protection ... e/p
equity ... eq
evidence ... ev
exclude ... exc
exclusionary rule ... exc/r
felony ... f/n
freedom of speech ... f/s
good faith ... g/f
habeas corpus ... h/c
hearsay ... hr
husband ... H
injunction ... inj
in loco parentis ... ILP
inter vivos ... I/v
joint tenancy ... j/t
judgment ... judgt
jurisdiction ... jur
last clear chance ... LCC
long-arm statute ... LAS
majority view ... maj
meeting of minds ... MOM
minority view ... min
Miranda rule ... Mir/r
Miranda warnings ... Mir/w
negligence ... neg
notice ... ntc
nuisance ... nus
obligation ... ob
obscene ... obs
offer ... O
offeree ... OE
offeror ... OR
ordinance ... ord
pain and suffering ... p/s
parol evidence ... p/e
plaintiff ... P
prima facie ... p/f
probable cause ... p/c
proximate cause ... px/c
real property ... r/p
reasonable doubt ... r/d
reasonable man ... r/m
rebuttable presumption ... rb/p
remanded ... rem
res ipsa loquitur ... RIL
respondeat superior ... r/s
Restatement ... RS
reversed ... rev
Rule Against Perpetuities ... RAP
search and seizure ... s/s
search warrant ... s/w
self-defense ... s/d
specific performance ... s/p
statute ... S
statute of frauds ... S/F
statute of limitations ... S/L
summary judgment ... s/j
tenancy at will ... t/w
tenancy in common ... t/c
tenant ... t
third party ... TP
third party beneficiary ... TPB
transferred intent ... TI
unconscionable ... uncon
unconstitutional ... unconst
undue influence ... u/e
Uniform Commercial Code ... UCC
unilateral ... uni
vendee ... VE
vendor ... VR
versus ... v
void for vagueness ... VFV
weight of authority ... w/a
weight of the evidence ... w/e
wife ... W
with ... w/
within ... w/i
without ... w/o
without prejudice ... w/o/p
wrongful death ... wr/d

Table of Cases

CHAPTER 1

Nature of International Law

Quick Reference Rules of Law

Legality of the Threat or Use of Nuclear Weapons

[Parties not identified.]

I.C.J., Advisory Opinion, 1996 I.C.J. 226

NATURE OF CASE: Advisory opinion examining whether the threat or use of nuclear weapons is permitted under international law.

FACT SUMMARY: [The International Court of Justice was asked by the U.N. General Assembly for an advisory opinion as to whether States are permitted to use nuclear weapons under international law.]

RULE OF LAW

In determining whether States are "permitted" to use nuclear weapons under international law, it is not relevant to the disposition of that question whether the independence of States to act is restricted by the principles and rules of international law, as well as whether permissibility to use nuclear weapons depends on whether authorization can be found in a treaty provision or customary international law.

FACTS: [The International Court of Justice was asked by the U.N. General Assembly for an advisory opinion as to whether States are permitted to use nuclear weapons under international law.]

ISSUE: In determining whether States are "permitted" to use nuclear weapons under international law, is it relevant to the disposition of that question whether the independence of States to act is restricted by the principles and rules of international law, as well as whether permissibility to use nuclear weapons depends on whether authorization can be found in a treaty provision or customary international law?

HOLDING AND DECISION: [Judge not stated in casebook excerpt.] No. In determining whether States are "permitted" to use nuclear weapons under international law, it is not relevant to the disposition of that question whether the independence of States to act is restricted by the principles and rules of international law, as well as whether permissibility to use nuclear weapons depends on whether authorization can be found in a treaty provision or customary international law. Some States criticized the use of the word "permitted" in the question posed, on the grounds such use implied the threat of the use of nuclear weapons would only be permissible if authorization could be found in a treaty or customary international law. These States argue such an implication is incompatible with the core principles of sovereignty and consent, and States are free to use nuclear weapons absent a prohibition on such use in a treaty or customary international law. Support for this contention comes from dicta in the *Lotus* case [*The Case of the S.S. "Lotus" (France v. Turkey)* 1927 P.C.I.J. (ser. A) No. 10], which indicates that "restrictions upon the independence of States cannot . . . be presumed" and that States have "a wide measure of discretion which is only limited in certain cases by prohibitive rules." Other States rejected these arguments as inapposite, since the *Lotus* case dealt with the possession of arms, rather than their use. However, it was not disputed that States' independence to act is restricted by principles and rules of international law, and with regard to the use of nuclear weapons, by humanitarian law. Accordingly, arguments based on the use of the word "permitted" in the question posed are without much relevance to the disposition of the issues before the Court. Having said that, however, neither customary international law nor any treaties expressly authorize the use of nuclear weapons, nor is there any principle or rule that makes the legality of such use dependent on a specific authorization. State practice shows that the illegality of the use of certain weapons does not arise from the absence of authorization but is based on express prohibitions.

ANALYSIS

The notion, urged by some States in response to the question posed to the Court, that there are no rules in international law other than those rules that are accepted by a State, as in a treaty, has been criticized in the area of nuclear weapons on the grounds that nuclear weapons by their very nature violate the sovereignty of other States who have in no way consented to the intrusion upon their sovereign rights that is implicit in the use of nuclear weapons. Judge Weeramantry, in dissent, also argued that it would be completely inconsistent with the progressive development of international law to interpret *Lotus* as meaning that a State could do whatever it pleased so long as it had not bound itself to the contrary.

Quicknotes

INTERNATIONAL LAW The body of law applicable to dealings between nations.

Accordance with International Law of the Unilateral Declaration of Independence in Respect of Kosovo

[Parties not identified.]

I.C.J., Advisory Opinion, 2010 I.C.J. 403

NATURE OF CASE: Advisory opinion addressing whether Kosovo's unilateral declaration of independence from Serbia was in accordance with international law.

FACT SUMMARY: [The Court of International Justice was asked for an advisory opinion as to whether Kosovo's unilateral declaration of independence from Serbia was in accordance with international law.]

RULE OF LAW

The question—of whether a political entity's unilateral declaration of independence from another political entity is in accordance with international law—is markedly different from the question of whether international law confers a right on a political entity to secede from another political entity.

FACTS: [The Provisional Institutions of Self-Government of Kosovo (Kosovo) unilaterally declared independence from Serbia. The U.N. General Assembly asked the International Court of Justice for an advisory opinion as to whether that declaration was in accord with international law.]

ISSUE: Is the question—of whether a political entity's unilateral declaration of independence from another political entity is in accordance with international law—markedly different from the question of whether international law confers a right on a political entity to secede from another political entity?

HOLDING AND DECISION: [Judge not stated in casebook excerpt.] Yes. The question—of whether a political entity's unilateral declaration of independence from another political entity is in accordance with international law—is markedly different from the question of whether international law confers a right on a political entity to secede from another political entity. In Canada, the Supreme Court of that country had before it the question of whether international law gave Quebec the right to secede from Canada. In other words, the Canadian Supreme Court had to decide whether international law conferred a positive entitlement on Quebec's political bodies to effect secession. Here, the question is whether Kosovo's declaration of independence was "in accordance with" international law. The answer to this question turns on whether international law prohibited such declaration. Thus, the task before the Court is to determine whether the declaration violated international law, not whether international law conferred an entitlement on Kosovo to unilaterally break away from Serbia.

ANALYSIS

By distinguishing its task from that of the Canadian Supreme Court, the Court here was able to focus its inquiry only on whether international law prohibited Kosovo from making a unilateral declaration of independence. As the Court pointed out, it is entirely possible for a particular act such as Kosovo's declaration of independence not to be in violation of international law without necessarily constituting the exercise of a right conferred by international law. The Court ultimately opined, by a vote of 10 to 4, that Kosovo's declaration of independence did not violate general international law, because international law does not contain a prohibition on declarations of independence.

Quicknotes

INTERNATIONAL LAW The body of law applicable to dealings between nations.

UNILATERAL One-sided; involving only one person.

CHAPTER 2

Sources: Customary International Law

Quick Reference Rules of Law

		PAGE
1.	*The Paquete Habana.* Coastal fishing vessels, with their cargoes and crews, are exempt from capture as prizes of war.	*6*
2.	*The Case of the S.S. "Lotus" (France v. Turkey).* (1) There is no rule of international law that limits a nation's criminal jurisdiction to acts that have occurred only within the nation's territory. (2) A State whose flag is flown on a vessel does not have exclusive jurisdiction over everything that occurs on board that vessel on the high seas. (3) Under international law, criminal proceedings arising from collisions at high sea are not within the exclusive jurisdiction of the State whose flag is flown.	*7*
3.	*North Sea Continental Shelf Cases (Federal Republic of Germany v. Denmark; Federal Republic of Germany v. Netherlands).* Delimitation must be the object of an equitable agreement between the States involved.	*9*
4.	*Case Concerning Military and Paramilitary Activities in and Against Nicaragua (Nicaragua v. United States).* A court may look to rules in multilateral conventions, and parties' agreements thereto and views thereof, in determining whether customary law rules independently parallel the rules in the conventions.	*10*
5.	*Legality of the Threat or Use of Nuclear Weapons.* United Nations General Assembly resolutions that affirm the illegality of the use of nuclear weapons do not signify the existence of a rule of customary international law that prohibits recourse to such weapons.	*12*
6.	*Questions Relating to the Obligation to Prosecute or Extradite (Belgium v. Senegal).* A nation is obligated to prosecute crimes under international customary law only to the extent the crimes occurred after the nation obligated itself by treaty or convention to prosecute such crimes.	*13*
7.	*Jurisdictional Immunities of the State (Germany v. Italy: Greece Intervening).* There is no conflict between the *jus cogens* rules forming part of the law of armed conflict, and between rules of jurisdictional immunity.	*14*

The Paquete Habana

Country at war (P) v. Fishermen (D)

175 U.S. 677 (1900)

NATURE OF CASE: Appeal from judgment condemning two fishing vessels and their cargoes as prizes of war.

FACT SUMMARY: The owners (D) of fishing vessels seized by officials of the United States (P) argued that international law exempted coastal fishermen from capture as prizes of war.

RULE OF LAW

Coastal fishing vessels, with their cargoes and crews, are exempt from capture as prizes of war.

FACTS: The owners (D) of two separate fishing vessels brought this appeal of a district court decree condemning two fishing vessels and their cargoes as prizes of war. Each vessel was a fishing smack, running in and out of Havana, sailing under the Spanish flag, and regularly engaged in fishing on the coast of Cuba. The cargoes of both vessels consisted of fresh fish that had been caught by their respective crews. Until stopped by the blockading United States squadron (P), the owners (D) had no knowledge of the existence of a war or of any blockage. The owners (D) had no arms or ammunition on board the vessels and had made no attempt to run the blockade after learning of its existence. The owners (D) did not offer any resistance at the time of capture, and the district court of the United States for the Southern District of Florida condemned the vessels and their cargoes as prizes of war. On appeal, the owners (D) argued that both customary international law and the writings of leading international scholars recognized an exemption from seizure at wartime of coastal fishing vessels.

ISSUE: Are coastal fishing vessels, with their cargoes and crews, exempt from capture as prizes of war?

HOLDING AND DECISION: (Gray, J.) Yes. Coastal fishing vessels, pursuing their vocation of catching and bringing in fresh fish, have been recognized as exempt, with their cargoes and crews, from capture as prizes of war. The doctrine that exempts coastal fishermen, with their vessels and cargoes, from capture as prizes of war, has been familiar to the United States from the time of the War of Independence, and has been recognized explicitly by the French and British governments. Where there are no treaties and no controlling executive or legislative acts or judicial decisions, as is the case here, resort must be had to the customs and usages of civilized nations, and, as evidence of these, to the works of jurists and commentators, who are well acquainted with the field. Such works are resorted to by judicial tribunals, not for the speculations of their authors concerning what the law ought to be, but for trustworthy evidence of what the law really is. At the present time, by the general consent of the civilized nations of the world, and independently of any express treaty or other public act, it is an established rule of international law that coastal fishing vessels, with their implements and supplies, cargoes, and crews, unarmed and honestly pursuing their peaceful calling of catching and bringing in fresh fish, are exempt from capture as prizes of war. Reversed.

ANALYSIS

In a dissenting opinion, which was not published in the main body of this casebook, Chief Justice Fuller argued that the captured vessels were of such a size and range as to not fall within the exemption. The Chief Justice also contended that the exemption in any case had not become a customary rule of international law but was only an "act of grace" that had not been authorized by the President.

Quicknotes

BLOCKADE When one country prevents materials or persons from entering or leaving another.

CUSTOM Generally any habitual practice or course of action repeated under like circumstances.

INTERNATIONAL LAW The body of law applicable to dealings between nations.

The Case of the S.S. "Lotus" (France v. Turkey)

Country of citizen (P) v. Country claiming jurisdiction (D)

P.C.I.J. (ser. A) No. 10 (1927)

NATURE OF CASE: Action to determine the validity of the exercise of criminal jurisdiction by one nation over the citizen of another nation.

FACT SUMMARY: France (P) contended that Turkey (D) violated international law by asserting jurisdiction over a French citizen who had been the first officer of a ship that collided with a Turkish ship on the high seas.

RULE OF LAW

(1) There is no rule of international law that limits a nation's criminal jurisdiction to acts that have occurred only within the nation's territory.
(2) A State whose flag is flown on a vessel does not have exclusive jurisdiction over everything that occurs on board that vessel on the high seas.
(3) Under international law, criminal proceedings arising from collisions at high sea are not within the exclusive jurisdiction of the State whose flag is flown.

FACTS: On August 2, 1926, just before midnight, a collision occurred between the French (P) mail steamer *Lotus*, which was captained by Demons, a French citizen, and the Turkish (D) collier *Boz-Kourt*, captained by Hassan Bey. The *Boz-Kourt*, which was cut in two, sank, and eight Turkish (D) nationals, who were on board, perished. After having done everything possible to help the shipwrecked persons, the *Lotus* continued its course to Constantinople, where it arrived on August 3. On August 5, Lieutenant Demons was requested by the Turkish (D) authorities to go ashore to give evidence. The examination led to the placing under arrest of Lieutenant Demons, without previous notice being given to the French (P) Consul-General. Although Demons argued that the Turkish (D) courts lacked jurisdiction over him, Demons was convicted of negligent conduct in allowing the accident to occur. France (P) and Turkey (D) then agreed to submit to the Permanent Court of International Justice (P.C.I.J.) the question of whether the exercise of Turkish (D) criminal jurisdiction over Demons for an incident that occurred on the high seas violated international law.

ISSUE:

(1) Is there a rule of international law that limits a nation's criminal jurisdiction to acts that have occurred only within the nation's territory?
(2) Does a State whose flag is flown on a vessel have exclusive jurisdiction over everything that occurs on board that vessel on the high seas?
(3) Under international law, are criminal proceedings arising from collisions at high sea within the exclusive jurisdiction of the State whose flag is flown?

HOLDING AND DECISION: [Judge not stated in casebook excerpt.]

(1) No. There is no rule of international law that limits a nation's criminal jurisdiction to acts that have occurred only within the nation's territory. The Court need not consider the contention that a State cannot punish offenses committed abroad by a foreigner merely because the victim is a national of that State. This is because the issue here is whether international law forbids a State from taking into consideration that the effects of a foreigner's acts have occurred in a place assimilated into that State's territory—as here, where the effects were manifested on the Turkish vessel. However, there is no rule or principle of international law whereby States have agreed to limit their criminal jurisdiction to the place where the perpetrator happens to be at the time of the offense. To the contrary, most States exercise criminal jurisdiction over perpetrators of crimes notwithstanding the perpetrator happens to be in another country when the offense occurs, if the effects of the offense have occurred within the State or its territory. Thus, once it is acknowledged that the effects here were produced on the Turkish vessel, it is impossible to hold that there is a rule of international law that prohibits Turkey (D) from prosecuting Demons merely because he happened to be aboard the French vessel at the time of the incident.
(2) No. A State whose flag is flown on a vessel does not have exclusive jurisdiction over everything that occurs on board that vessel on the high seas. While it is true that in most instances the state whose flag is flown has exclusive jurisdiction, international law provides some exceptions. A State may in its own territory exercise jurisdiction over acts that have occurred on board a foreign ship on the high seas. Although a vessel flying the flag of a State is akin to a territory of that State, there is nothing in international law that supports the claim that the rights of the State under whose flag the vessel sails may go farther than the rights the State exercises in its own territory. Thus, if a crime or offense is committed on the high seas aboard a vessel flying the flag of a nation, and the crime or offense produces effects on a vessel flying the flag of a different nation, the principles to be applied are the same ones that would be applied if the territories of the two nations

Continued on next page.

were involved. Applying these principles, there is no rule of international law that prohibits the State of the "victim" vessel from regarding the offense as having been committed in its territory and prosecuting the perpetrator accordingly. Moreover, a rule of customary law to the contrary has not conclusively been shown to exist. Neither scholars, nor the precedents from the judiciaries of various nations, establish such a contrary rule. And, in fact, many scholars conclude the general rules of each legal system regarding crimes committed abroad are applicable, and there is some precedent that involves concurrent jurisdiction of two nations to prosecute crimes committed on the high seas, thus refuting the principle of exclusive jurisdiction of the country whose flag the vessel flies. Additionally, conventions that reserve exclusive jurisdiction relate to specific maritime matters, but not to common-law offenses and crimes, and, in any event, such conventions relate to single ships, not to two ships of two different nations. For all these reasons, the Court rejects France's (P) exclusive jurisdiction argument and concludes this argument does not establish the existence of a rule of international law prohibiting Turkey (D) from prosecuting Demons.

(3) No. Under international law, criminal proceedings arising from collisions at high sea are not within the exclusive jurisdiction of the State whose flag is flown. France (P) argues that questions of jurisdiction in collision cases are rarely presented in criminal courts, and prosecutions only occur before the courts of the State whose flag is flown, thus demonstrating a tacit adherence by States to a rule of positive international law barring prosecutions by other States. This argument is rejected. First, States may be merely abstaining from instituting criminal proceedings, not necessarily believing they are obligated to do so. Case law from municipal tribunals cuts both ways, supporting on the one hand exclusive jurisdiction, while also supporting concurrent jurisdiction on the other. Moreover, in two cases where criminal jurisdiction was exercised by States whose flags were not flown, France and Germany, respectively, had failed to protest such exercise—thus demonstrating these countries did not believe such exercise was a violation of international law. For all these reasons, there is no rule of international law in regard to collision cases that confers exclusive jurisdiction in criminal proceedings on the State whose flag is flown. Based on the analysis of all the issues, it is determined that this is a case of concurrent jurisdiction, and Turkey (D) has not acted in a manner contrary to the principles of international law, so no damages are owing to Demons for its prosecution of him.

ANALYSIS

The six dissenting judges in this opinion argued, inter alia, that the judgment's basic premise—restrictions upon the freedom of States cannot be presumed, and international law permits all that it does not prohibit—was wrong. They contended the question should have been whether international law authorized Turkey (D) to exercise jurisdiction under the particular circumstances of the case, and they concluded customary law did not authorize a country to exercise criminal jurisdiction over a foreigner for an act committed in a foreign territory or in a vessel flying the flag of another nation on the high seas.

Quicknotes

CONCURRENT JURISDICTION Authority by two or more different courts over the subject matter of a proceeding; the case may be heard and determined by either.

North Sea Continental Shelf Cases (Federal Republic of Germany v. Denmark; Federal Republic of Germany v. Netherlands)

State not a party (D) v. Parties to Geneva Convention (P)

1969 I.C.J. 3

NATURE OF CASE: Action to determine national boundaries.

FACT SUMMARY: Denmark (P) and the Netherlands (P) contended that customary rules of international law determined the boundaries of areas located on the continental shelf between those countries and the Federal Republic of Germany (D).

RULE OF LAW

Delimitation must be the object of an equitable agreement between the States involved.

FACTS: Denmark (P) and the Netherlands (P) contended that the boundaries between their respective areas of the continental shelf in the North Sea, and the area claimed by the Federal Republic of Germany (Germany) (D), should be determined by the application of the principle of equidistance set forth in Article 6 of the Geneva Convention of 1958 on the Continental Shelf, which by January 1, 1969, had been ratified or acceded to by 39 States, but to which Germany (D) was not a party. Denmark (P) and the Netherlands (P) contended that Germany (D) was bound to accept delimitation on an equidistance basis because the use of this method was not merely a conventional obligation, but was a rule that was part of the corpus of general international law and like other rules of general or customary international law was binding automatically on Germany (D), independent of any specific assent, direct or indirect, given by Germany (D).

ISSUE: Must delimitation be the object of an equitable agreement between the States involved?

HOLDING AND DECISION: [Judge not stated in casebook excerpt.] Yes. Delimitation must be the object of an equitable agreement between the States involved. The equidistance principle, as stated in Article 6 of the Geneva Convention, is not part of customary international law. Article 6 is of the type of articles under which reservations may be made by any State on signing or ratifying the Convention, so that the State is not necessarily bound in all instances by that article. A general or customary law has equal force for all members of the international community and cannot be unilaterally abrogated. Article 6 has not been accepted as part of the general corpus of international law by the *opinio juris,* so as to have become binding even for countries that have never and do not become parties to the Convention. Rather than giving the principle of equidistance a fundamental norm-creating character, which is necessary to the formation of a general rule of law, Article 6 makes the obligation to use the equidistance method a secondary one, which comes into play only in the absence of an agreement between the parties. The delimitation here is to be executed by equitable agreement, taking into account the relevant circumstances.

DISSENT: (Lachs, J.) The principles and rules enshrined in the Convention, including the equidistance rule, have been accepted not only by those States that are parties to the Convention on the Continental Shelf, but also by those that have subsequently followed it in agreements, or in their legislation, or have acquiesced in it when faced with legislative acts of other States affecting them. This can be viewed as evidence of a practice widespread enough to satisfy the criteria for a general rule of law.

ANALYSIS

The dissent's analysis of the concept of *opinio juris* is in accord with the position taken by some legal scholars who maintain that *opinio juris* may be presumed from uniformities of practice regarding matters viewed normally as involving legal rights and obligations. A contrary position maintains that the practice of States must be accompanied by or consist of statements that something is law before it can become law.

Quicknotes

GENEVA CONVENTION International agreement that governs the conduct of warring nations.

OPINIO JURIS An "opinion of law," or belief certain conduct must occur due to legal obligation.

Case Concerning Military and Paramilitary Activities in and Against Nicaragua (Nicaragua v. United States)

State (P) v. Militarily intervening state (D)

1984 I.C.J. 14

NATURE OF CASE: Determination of jurisdiction in proceedings before the International Court of Justice alleging unlawful military and paramilitary acts.

FACT SUMMARY: Nicaragua (P) brought proceedings in the International Court of Justice (I.C.J.), complaining the United States (U.S.) (D) was conducting unlawful military and paramilitary operations in its territory. The U.S. (D) asserted the I.C.J. did not have jurisdiction over the matter.

RULE OF LAW

A court may look to rules in multilateral conventions, and parties' agreements thereto and views thereof, in determining whether customary law rules independently parallel the rules in the conventions.

FACTS: Nicaragua (P) brought proceedings in the International Court of Justice (I.C.J. or "the Court"), complaining the United States (U.S.) (D) was conducting unlawful military and paramilitary activities in and against Nicaragua (P). Although in 1946 the U.S. (D) accepted the I.C.J.'s jurisdiction in a declaration, that declaration contained a reservation that I.C.J. jurisdiction would not apply to disputes under a multilateral treaty unless all the treaty parties were parties to the case. Accordingly, the I.C.J. determined it could not rule on whether the U.S. (D) had violated the United Nations (U.N.) Charter. Nevertheless, the I.C.J. ruled it had jurisdiction to determine whether the actions of the U.S. (D) violated use of force norms of customary international law. The issue thus became whether the use of rules in the U.N. Charter also existed separately as customary law.

ISSUE: May a court look to rules in multilateral conventions, and parties' agreements thereto and views thereof, in determining whether customary law rules independently parallel the rules in the conventions?

HOLDING AND DECISION: [Judge not stated in casebook excerpt.] Yes. A court may look to rules in multilateral conventions, and parties' agreements thereto and views thereof, in determining whether customary law rules independently parallel the rules in the conventions. Norms in treaties, and identical norms in customary law, are nevertheless separate expressions of the same norms. Thus, it is possible to have two rules of the same content that are subject to separate treatment, depending on whether they are treaty rules or customary rules. Here, although the Court has no jurisdiction to determine whether the U.S. (D) breached the Charter of the U.N. or that of the Organization of American States, it must take those into account in determining whether the U.S. (D) breached customary law. In addition, the views of the parties may be considered. There is evidence that there is considerable agreement between the parties as to customary rules of the non-use of force and non-intervention. Notwithstanding such agreement, the Court must ascertain for itself what rules are applicable as a matter of general practice, and the Court must satisfy itself that the rule exists in the *opinio juris* of States as confirmed by practice. In determining customary law, it is relevant that the parties are bound by these rules, both in treaties and through customary law, and have expressed their recognition of the rules' validity. Moreover, in determining the existence of these rules in customary law, the practice of nations does not have to rigorously conform therewith; instead, it is sufficient that States' conduct is, in general, consistent with the rules. Also, instances of conduct inconsistent with a given rule should generally have been treated as breaches of that rule, rather than as indications of the recognition of a new rule. The U.S. (D) argues that, because the customary rules regarding the lawfulness of the use of force in inter-State relations are identical to those in the U.N. Charter, the Court should be prevented from applying customary law. This argument is rejected. However, even if it is true, as the U.S. (D) posits, that Nicaragua (P) holds the same view, this merely shows that principles relating to the use of force expressed by the Charter correspond to customary law and constitute an expression of those principles. The Court, however, must still be satisfied such views reflect an *opinio juris* as to the binding nature of these rules. Such an *opinio juris* may be deduced from the parties' views and the attitude of the parties and the attitude of other States towards certain General Assembly resolutions, and particularly resolution 2625 (XXV) entitled "Declaration on Principles of International Law concerning Friendly Relations and Co-operation among States in accordance with the Charter of the United Nations." The effect of consent to the text of such resolutions cannot be understood as merely that of a "reiteration or elucidation" of the treaty commitment undertaken in the Charter. On the contrary, it may be understood as an acceptance of the validity of the rule or set of rules declared by the resolution by themselves. The principle of non-use of force, for example, may thus be regarded as a principle of customary international law, not as such conditioned by

Continued on next page.

provisions relating to collective security, or to the facilities or armed contingents to be provided under Article 43 of the Charter. It seems, therefore, that the attitude referred to expresses an *opinio juris* respecting such rule (or set of rules), to be treated separately from the provisions, especially those of an insti-tutional kind, to which it is subject on the treaty-law plane of the Charter.

ANALYSIS

In parts of the opinion not covered by the casebook excerpt, the I.C.J. found the United States (D) was "in breach of its obligations under customary international law not to use force against another State," and "not to violate its sovereignty," among other things. The United States (D) refused to participate after the I.C.J. rejected its argument that the I.C.J. lacked jurisdiction to hear the case, and later blocked enforcement by the Security Council, making Nicaraguan (P) attempts at obtaining compliance futile. The Nicaraguan government (P) finally withdrew the complaint from the Court in September 1991.

Quicknotes

OPINIO JURIS An "opinion of law," or belief certain conduct must occur due to legal obligation.

SOVEREIGNTY The absolute power conferred to the State to govern and regulate all persons located and activities conducted therein.

Legality of the Threat or Use of Nuclear Weapons

[Parties not identified.]

I.C.J., Advisory Opinion, 1996 I.C.J. 226

NATURE OF CASE: Advisory opinion examining whether the threat or use of nuclear weapons is permitted under international law.

FACT SUMMARY: [The International Court of Justice was asked by the United Nations General Assembly for an advisory opinion as to whether States are permitted to use nuclear weapons under international law.]

RULE OF LAW

United Nations General Assembly resolutions that affirm the illegality of the use of nuclear weapons do not signify the existence of a rule of customary international law that prohibits recourse to such weapons.

FACTS: [The International Court of Justice (I.C.J.) was asked by the United Nations (U.N.) General Assembly for an advisory opinion as to whether States are permitted to use nuclear weapons under international law. In answering this question, the Court, inter alia, inquired into whether a series of U.N. resolutions demonstrated a prohibition in customary international law on the use of nuclear weapons. In particular, the Court focused on General Assembly resolution 1653, entitled "Declaration on the Prohibition of the Use of Nuclear and Thermo-nuclear Weapons," which declared that the use of nuclear and thermo-nuclear weapons is a violation of the U.N. Charter; exceeds the scope of war in its resulting indiscriminate suffering and destruction to mankind and civilization; is contrary to the rules of international law and humanity; is directed against mankind in general; and is a crime against mankind and civilization. The resolution also sought a special conference for signing a convention on the prohibition on the use of nuclear and thermo-nuclear weapons (G.A. Res. 1653 (XVI), paras. 1-2 (Nov. 24, 1961)).]

ISSUE: Do United Nations General Assembly resolutions that affirm the illegality of the use of nuclear weapons signify the existence of a rule of customary international law that prohibits recourse to such weapons?

HOLDING AND DECISION: [Judge not stated in casebook excerpt.] No. United Nations General Assembly resolutions that affirm the illegality of the use of nuclear weapons do not signify the existence of a rule of customary international law that prohibits recourse to such weapons. The nations themselves diverge as to this issue. Some States urge that the resolutions merely confirmed an existing rule of customary law applicable to means or methods of warfare that overstep the bounds of what is acceptable, whereas other States point to the non-binding nature of the resolutions, and that the resolutions did not meet with approval of many States. The States that consider the use of nuclear weapons illegal argue that because the resolutions merely applied existing rules to the use of nuclear weapons, it is irrelevant that the resolutions did not gain approval of all States, since negative votes on a resolution cannot have the effect of eliminating existing customary rules. Although such resolutions may provide evidence of the existence of a rule, or the emergence of an *opinio juris*, in this case the evidence falls of short of establishing an *opinio juris* on the illegality of the use of nuclear weapons, primarily because they have been adopted with many negative votes and abstentions. The resolutions, at most, signify a clear sign of deep concern regarding the problem of nuclear weapons. Moreover, the history of the resolutions, which shows that the General Assembly applied general rules of customary law to the particular case of nuclear weapons, indicates the General Assembly did not believe there was a specific rule of customary law that prohibited the use of nuclear weapons; if such a rule had existed, the General Assembly could simply have referred to it. In sum, there is still a deep tension in the international community between the desire to prohibit the use of nuclear weapons, on the one hand, and to permit them for the purposes of deterrence, on the other.

ANALYSIS

Although the Court was unable to find an *opinio juris* that nuclear weapons are illegal, the Court did conclude the threat or use of nuclear weapons would violate existing principles of humanitarian law that require States to refrain from using weapons that are incapable of distinguishing between civilian and military targets, or that would inflict useless suffering. The Court, however, was unable to reach a conclusion as to the legality or illegality of the use of nuclear weapons by a State for self-defense where the State's very existence was threatened.

Quicknotes

OPINIO JURIS An "opinion of law," or belief certain conduct must occur due to legal obligation.

Questions Relating to the Obligation to Prosecute or Extradite (Belgium v. Senegal)

Claimant nation (P) v. Respondent nation (D)

2012 I.C.J. 422

NATURE OF CASE: Proceedings brought by one State to have another State prosecute or extradite an individual alleged to have committed crimes of torture and crimes against humanity.

FACT SUMMARY: Belgium (P) brought proceedings in the International Court of Justice to have Senegal (D) either prosecute or extradite Habre, who was accused of terrorist crimes and crimes against humanity.

RULE OF LAW

A nation is obligated to prosecute crimes under international customary law only to the extent the crimes occurred after the nation obligated itself by treaty or convention to prosecute such crimes.

FACTS: Belgium (P) instituted proceedings in the International Court of Justice (I.C.J.) against Senegal (D) to have Senegal (D) comply with its obligation to either prosecute Habre, the former President of the Republic of Chad, or to extradite him to Belgium (P) for the purposes of criminal proceedings. Habre was accused of terrorist crimes and crimes against humanity. Belgium (P) based its claims on the United Nations Convention against Torture and Other Cruel, Inhuman or Degrading Treatment or Punishment of 10 December 1984 (hereinafter "the Convention against Torture" or "the Convention"), as well as on customary international law. Belgium (P) asserted that by failing to prosecute Habre, Senegal (D) had breached its obligations under the Convention, to which Senegal (D) became a party on June 26, 1987.

ISSUE: Is a nation obligated to prosecute crimes under international customary law only to the extent the crimes occurred after the nation obligated itself by treaty or convention to prosecute such crimes?

HOLDING AND DECISION: [Judge not stated in casebook excerpt.] Yes. A nation is obligated to prosecute crimes under international customary law only to the extent the crimes occurred after the nation obligated itself by treaty or convention to prosecute such crimes. The prohibition of torture is part of customary international law and it has become a peremptory norm (*jus cogens*). That prohibition is grounded in widespread international practice and on the *opinio juris* of States, and it appears in numerous international instruments of universal application. However, the obligation to prosecute the alleged perpetrators of acts of torture under the Convention applies only to facts that have occurred after a State has become a party to the Convention. Such an understanding is required by Article 28 of the Vienna Convention on the Law of Treaties, which reflects customary law on the matter. The Vienna Convention provides in pertinent part that: "Unless a different intention appears from the treaty or is otherwise established, its provisions do not bind a party in relation to any act or fact which took place or any situation which ceased to exist before the date of the entry into force of that treaty with respect to that party." Additionally, nothing in the Convention against Torture reveals an intention to require a State party to criminalize, under Article 4, acts of torture that took place prior to its entry into force for that State, or to establish its jurisdiction over such acts in accordance with Article 5. Accordingly, Senegal (D) was obligated to prosecute Habre only for acts that occurred after June 26, 1987. Because the complaints against Habre included numerous serious offenses allegedly committed after that date, Senegal (D) was obligated to prosecute those offenses and breached its obligations under the Convention for failing to do so. Judgment for Belgium (P).

ANALYSIS

Some of the sources the I.C.J. relied on for its finding that the prohibition of torture has become *jus cogens* included: the Universal Declaration of Human Rights of 1948; the 1949 Geneva Conventions for the protection of war victims; the International Covenant on Civil and Political Rights of 1966; and General Assembly resolution 3452/30 of 9 December 1975 on the Protection of All Persons from Being Subjected to Torture and Other Cruel, Inhuman or Degrading Treatment or Punishment. The Court also noted this prohibition had been introduced into the domestic law of almost all States, and acts of torture are regularly denounced within national and international fora.

Quicknotes

JUS COGENS Any principle of law that is recognized by the entire international community as essential to the preservation of human values and is therefore observed by all governments except outlawed governments.

OPINIO JURIS An "opinion of law," or belief certain conduct must occur due to legal obligation.

PEREMPTORY Final; conclusive; not subject to review.

Jurisdictional Immunities of the State (Germany v. Italy: Greece Intervening)

Perpetrator of atrocities in World War II (P) v. Former ally (D)

2012 I.C.J. 99

NATURE OF CASE: Proceedings before the International Court of Justice alleging violation by one nation of another nation's jurisdictional immunity.

FACT SUMMARY: Germany (P) claimed Italy (D) violated Germany's (P) jurisdictional immunity by permitting Italian citizens to bring claims in Italy against Germany (P) for atrocities committed by the German Third Reich in Italy during World War II.

RULE OF LAW

There is no conflict between the *jus cogens* rules forming part of the law of armed conflict, and between rules of jurisdictional immunity.

FACTS: In June 1940, Italy (D) entered World War II as an ally of the German Third Reich. In September 1943, following the removal of Italy's leader, Mussolini, from power, Italy (D) surrendered to the Allies and, the following month, declared war on Germany (P). German forces then occupied much of Italian territory and, between October 1943 and the end of the War, perpetrated many atrocities against the population of that territory, including massacres of civilians and the deportation of large numbers of civilians for use as forced labor. In addition, German forces took prisoner, both inside Italy (D) and elsewhere in Europe, several hundred thousand members of the Italian armed forces. Most of these prisoners (the "Italian military internees") were denied the status of prisoner of war and deported to Germany (P) and German-occupied territories for use as forced labor. Starting in 1998, Italian courts permitted Italian claimants to file suits against Germany (P) seeking reparations for the atrocities committed by the Third Reich. Italian courts also declared enforceable in Italy (D) decisions of Greek courts rendered against Germany (P) on the basis of German acts similar to those that gave rise to the claims brought before Italian courts (Greece was, for this reason, a non-party intervenor in the case). Italy (D) further took measures of constraint against Villa Vigoni, German State property located in Italy (D). Based on these acts of various Italian organs, Germany (P) brought proceedings in the International Court of Justice (I.C.J. or "the Court") alleging that Italy (D) had violated Germany's (P) jurisdictional immunity. The Court determined the acts of the Third Reich had been taken in the State's public capacity, and, therefore, were generally entitled to immunity, and the Court also rejected Italy's (D) argument under the territorial tort principal that immunity should be denied because the acts were committed in the territory of the forum State. The Court considered Italy's (D) argument that the *jus cogens* status of the rules that were violated by the Third Reich precluded immunity.

ISSUE: Is there a conflict between the *jus cogens* rules forming part of the law of armed conflict, and between rules of jurisdictional immunity?

HOLDING AND DECISION: [Judge not stated in casebook excerpt.] No. There is no conflict between the *jus cogens* rules forming part of the law of armed conflict, and between rules of jurisdictional immunity. Italy's (D) argument rests on the premise there is a conflict between *jus cogens* rules forming part of the law of armed conflict, and between according immunity to Germany (P). Italy's (D) argument is that since *jus cogens* rules always prevail over any inconsistent rule of international law, whether contained in a treaty or in customary international law, and since the rule that accords one State immunity before the courts of another does not have the status of *jus cogens*, the rule of immunity must give way. However, the premise of this argument, which rests on the conflict between rules, fails, as no such conflict exists. Even assuming, arguendo, the rules of the law of armed conflict that prohibit the murder of civilians in occupied territory, the deportation of civilian inhabitants to slave labor and the deportation of prisoners of war to slave labor are rules of *jus cogens*, there is no conflict between those rules and the rules on State immunity. The two sets of rules address different matters. The rules of State immunity are procedural in character and are confined to determining whether or not the courts of one State may exercise jurisdiction in respect of another State. They do not bear upon the question whether or not the conduct in respect of which the proceedings are brought was lawful or unlawful. They merely govern where proceedings for illegal acts may be brought. Similarly, focusing on the duty of the wrongdoing State to make reparation, rather than upon the original wrongful act, does not change the conclusion that there is no conflict of rules in this case. The duty to make reparation is a rule that exists independently of those rules that concern the means by which it is to be affected, and the law of State immunity concerns only the latter. Further, for the last century it has been the practice of the international community, as reflected in treaties, to not require the payment of reparations or the use of lump sum settlements and setoffs to fully compensate each individual victim of breaches of international law. Rejected, too, is the argument that no

Continued on next page.

rule that is not of the status of *jus cogens* may be applied if to do so would hinder the enforcement of a *jus cogens* rule, even in the absence of a direct conflict. A *jus cogens* rule is one from which no derogation is permitted, but the rules that relate to jurisdictional immunity and jurisdictional matters do not derogate from those substantive rules that possess *jus cogens* status, nor is there anything inherent in the concept of *jus cogens* that would require their modification or would displace their application. There is precedent for such an approach, notwithstanding that such an approach effectively means that a process by which a *jus cogens* rule might be enforced is rendered unavailable. Further, the argument that this approach has *jus cogens* displacing the law of State immunity has been rejected by various national and international courts. For all these reasons, even on the assumption that the proceedings in the Italian courts involved violations of *jus cogens* rules, the applicability of the customary international law on State immunity was not affected. Judgment for Germany (P).

DISSENT: (Trindade, J.) The majority proceeds from the wrong premise, i.e., that no conflict exists, or can exist, between the substantive rules of *jus cogens* and rules of jurisdictional immunity. The majority's assumption is tautological. There is in fact a conflict; it is a material conflict, even though a formalist one may not be discernible. The majority's deconstruction of *jus cogens* is to the detriment not only of the individual victims of grave violations of human rights and of international humanitarian law, but also of contemporary international law itself. This is because there can be no prerogative or privilege of State immunity in cases of international crimes, such as massacres of the civilian population, and deportation of civilians and prisoners of war to subjection to slave labor: these are grave breaches of absolute prohibitions of *jus cogens*, for which there can be no immunities.

ANALYSIS

The Court explained that because there was no conflict between *jus cogens* rules relating to war atrocities and the rules relating to jurisdictional immunity was why the application of the contemporary law of State immunity to proceedings concerning events that occurred in 1943-1945 did not infringe the principle that law should not be applied retrospectively to determine matters of legality and responsibility. The Court also explained that, for the same reason, recognizing the immunity of a foreign State in accordance with customary international law did not amount to recognizing as lawful a situation created by the breach of a *jus cogens* rule, or rendering aid and assistance in maintaining that situation, and so could not contravene the principle in Article 41 of the International Law Commission's Articles on State Responsibility.

Quicknotes

JUS COGENS Any principle of law that is recognized by the entire international community as essential to the preservation of human values and is therefore observed by all governments except outlawed governments.

CHAPTER 3

Law of Treaties

Quick Reference Rules of Law

Maritime Delimitation and Territorial Questions (Qatar v. Bahrain)

Sovereign (P) v. Sovereign (D)

1994 I.C.J. 112

NATURE OF CASE: Territorial dispute between sovereigns.

FACT SUMMARY: Qatar (P) filed a claim in the International Court of Justice against Bahrain (D) to settle a dispute involving sovereignty over certain islands, sovereign rights over certain shoals, and delimitation of a maritime boundary. Bahrain (D) disputed the Court's jurisdiction.

RULE OF LAW

Meeting minutes and exchanges of letters can constitute an international agreement creating rights and obligations for the signatories.

FACTS: Qatar (P) and Bahrain (D) sought for over 20 years to resolve a dispute concerning sovereignty over certain islands and shoals, and delimitation of a maritime boundary. In the process, they exchanged some letters, which were accepted by the respective parties' heads of State. A Tripartite Committee was created, consisting of representatives from Qatar (P), Bahrain (D), and Saudi Arabia "for the purpose of approaching the International Court of Justice (I.C.J.). . . ." The committee met several times but failed to produce an agreement on the specific terms for submitting the dispute to the Court. Eventually, the meetings culminated in "Minutes," which reaffirmed the process and stipulated that the parties "may" submit the dispute to the I.C.J. after giving the Saudi King six months to resolve the dispute. Qatar (P) filed a claim in the I.C.J., and Bahrain (D) disputed the Court's jurisdiction.

ISSUE: Can meeting minutes and exchanges of letters constitute an international agreement creating rights and obligations for the signatories?

HOLDING AND DECISION: [Judge not stated in casebook excerpt.] Yes. Meeting minutes and exchanges of letters can constitute an international agreement creating rights and obligations for the signatories. The parties agree that the letters constitute an international agreement with binding force, but Bahrain (D) argues that the Minutes were only a record of negotiations, and therefore could not serve as a basis for the I.C.J.'s jurisdiction. International agreements can take many forms under the Vienna Convention on the Law of Treaties, and the I.C.J. has enforced that rule in the past. The Minutes in this case are not only a record of the meetings; they contain reaffirmation of obligations previously agreed to, agreement to allow the King of Saudi Arabia to try to find a solution to the dispute during a six-month period, and indication of the possibility of the involvement of the I.C.J. The Minutes set forth commitments to which the parties agreed, thereby creating rights and obligations in international law. They are therefore an international agreement. The Foreign Minister of Bahrain's (D) argument that no agreement exists because he never intended to enter an agreement fails, because he signed the document creating rights and obligations for his country. And Qatar's (P) six-month delay in applying to the United Nations Secretariat does not indicate that Qatar (P) never considered the Minutes to be an international agreement, as Bahrain (D) argues. In any event, registration or non-registration with the Secretariat does not have any effect on the validity of the agreement.

ANALYSIS

No doubt the language used in various writings will influence a court's decision as to whether an agreement has been entered into, and in this case, the language was the main focus of the I.C.J., and it was the contents of the Minutes that persuaded the I.C.J. to reject the Bahrain foreign minister's (D) claim that he did not intend to enter into an agreement. Compare this to general U.S. contract law, where a claim by one of the parties that no contract existed because there was no meeting of the minds might cause a U.S. court to consider whether a contract existed with more care and thought than the I.C.J. gave the foreign minister of Bahrain's (D) claim.

Quicknotes

INTERNATIONAL LAW The body of law applicable to dealings between nations.

JURISDICTION The authority of a court to hear and declare judgment in respect to a particular matter.

SOVEREIGN A State or entity with independent authority to govern its affairs.

Reservations to the Convention on Genocide

I.C.J., Advisory Opinion, 1951 I.C.J. 15

NATURE OF CASE: Advisory opinion regarding the effect of reservations to the U.N. Convention on the Prevention and Punishment of the Crime of Genocide.

FACT SUMMARY: Several signatory States to the U.N. Convention on the Prevention and Punishment of the Crime of Genocide effected reservations to various provisions therein.

RULE OF LAW

A State may effect a reservation to the U.N. Convention on the Prevention and Punishment of the Crime of Genocide and still be considered a signatory thereto.

FACTS: In 1951, the United Nations (U.N.) unanimously adopted the Convention on the Prevention and Punishment of the Crime of Genocide ("the Convention"). Several States made reservations to one or more of its provisions. The International Court of Justice (I.C.J. or "the Court") was asked to render an opinion as to whether a party could express reservations and still be considered a signatory.

ISSUE: May a State effect a reservation to the U.N. Convention on the Prevention and Punishment of the Crime of Genocide and still be considered a signatory thereto?

HOLDING AND DECISION: [Judge not stated in casebook excerpt.] Yes. A State may effect a reservation to the U.N. Convention on the Prevention and Punishment of the Crime of Genocide and still be considered a signatory thereto. A reservation is permitted in a multilateral treaty as long as the reservation does not defeat the purpose of the treaty. It has been argued that any State may effect any reservation by virtue of its sovereignty. Such a rule would lead to a complete disregard for the object and purpose of a convention. Here, since numerous reservations were made by different States, the validity of each must be examined on a case-by-case basis. [The Court also held that a State objecting to a reservation could, if it desired, consider the reserving State not to be a party to the Convention.]

ANALYSIS

As is often the case, politics played a role in the decision here. Historically, international law usually held that reservations to a multilateral treaty had to be accepted by all other parties. Such a rule here would have made unanimous acceptance of the Convention impossible. The Court was undoubtedly determined to facilitate such unanimity.

Quicknotes

ADVISORY OPINION A decision rendered at the request of an interested party of how the court would rule should the particular issue arise.

INTERNATIONAL LAW The body of law applicable to dealings between nations.

Application of the Convention on the Prevention and Punishment of the Crime of Genocide (Bosnia and Herzegovina v. Serbia and Montenegro)

State (P) v. State (D)

2007 I.C.J. 191

NATURE OF CASE: Case brought in the International Court of Justice to determine whether a State committed a violation of the Convention on the Prevention and Punishment of the Crime of Genocide.

FACT SUMMARY: Bosnia and Herzegovina (P) initiated a case in the International Court of Justice (I.C.J.) against Serbia and Montenegro (D) following the genocide of Bosnian Muslims, asserting that those States—in contradistinction from their nationals—had violated the Convention on the Prevention and Punishment of the Crime of Genocide.

RULE OF LAW

The contracting parties to the Convention on the Prevention and Punishment of the Crime of Genocide ("the Convention") are bound by the obligation under the Convention not to commit, through their organs or persons or groups whose conduct is attributable to them, genocide and the other acts enumerated in Article III.

FACTS: Bosnia and Herzegovina (P) initiated a case in the International Court of Justice (I.C.J.) in 1993 against the Federal Republic of Yugoslavia (Serbia and Montenegro) (D) under the Convention on the Prevention and Punishment of the Crime of Genocide ("the Convention"). Bosnia and Herzegovina (P) claimed that Serbia and Montenegro (D) breeched the Convention by committing genocide against Bosnia's (P) Muslim population. Bosnia and Herzegovina (P) based jurisdiction on Article IX, which provides that "Disputes between the Contracting Parties relating to the interpretation, application or fulfilment of the present Convention, including those relating to the responsibility of a State for genocide or for any of the other acts enumerated in Article III, shall be submitted to the International Court of Justice at the request of any of the parties to the dispute." Serbia and Montenegro (D), however, challenged jurisdiction, arguing the Convention did not impose upon States the responsibility to refrain from genocide, but merely required States to prevent and punish genocide committed by individuals.

ISSUE: Are the contracting parties to the Convention on the Prevention and Punishment of the Crime of Genocide ("the Convention") bound by the obligation under the Convention not to commit, through their organs or persons or groups whose conduct is attributable to them, genocide and the other acts enumerated in Article III?

HOLDING AND DECISION: [Judge not stated in casebook excerpt.] Yes. The contracting parties to the Convention on the Prevention and Punishment of the Crime of Genocide ("the Convention") are bound by the obligation under the Convention not to commit, through their organs or persons or groups whose conduct is attributable to them, genocide and the other acts enumerated in Article III. Bosnia and Herzegovina (P) contend the Convention created a universal, treaty-based concept of State responsibility, and a State's obligation to prevent genocide under the Convention is eclipsed by the State's responsibility for genocide that occurs, since a State that commits genocide has not met its obligation to prevent it. Serbia and Montenegro (D), on the other hand, contend under the Convention they are only responsible for their failure to prevent genocide, so the sole remedy would be a declaratory judgment. What obligations the Convention imposes on the parties depends on the ordinary meaning of the terms of the Convention, read in context and in light of the Convention's object and purpose. Confusion as to terms, context, or purpose can be resolved by resorting to supplementary means of interpretation, including the Convention's preparatory work and the circumstances of its conclusion.

Article I contains two propositions. The first states genocide is a crime under international law, a statement that recognizes existing requirements of customary international law on the subject. The second is the undertaking by the parties to prevent and punish the crime of genocide. The ordinary meaning of the word "undertake" is to give a formal promise, to bind or engage oneself, and to give a pledge or promise. Thus, Article I, particularly its undertaking to prevent, creates obligations distinct from those that appear in the subsequent Articles. This conclusion is supported by the humanitarian and civilizing purpose of the Convention. Preparatory work of the Convention supports this conclusion as well, because the U.N. General Assembly has said genocide is an international crime entailing national and international responsibility on the part of individuals and States. In addition, during drafting, several States proposed to move from the preamble to Article I of the Convention the language with the undertaking to pre-

Continued on next page.

vent and punish, in order to make it more effective. The parties are also under an obligation under the Convention not to commit genocide themselves. The Convention does not expressly impose the obligation, but the effect of Article II is to prohibit States from themselves committing genocide. The prohibition follows from the fact the Article categorizes genocide as an international law crime, and by agreeing to such a categorization, the parties must logically undertake not to commit the act described. It also follows from the expressly stated obligation to prevent the commission of acts of genocide. Serbia and Montenegro (D) violated their responsibility under the Convention to prevent and punish genocide.

ANALYSIS

The I.C.J. concluded that although Serbia and Montenegro (D) did not directly commit genocide, or incite it, they violated the Convention's obligations to prevent it. Serbia and Montenegro's (D) violations of its obligations derived not only from the Convention, but also from two protective measures issued by the I.C.J. in April and September 1993, under which the then-Federal Republic of Yugoslavia was ordered explicitly to prevent the crimes of genocide and to make sure such crimes were not committed by military or paramilitary formations operating under its control or with its support. Despite the order, Serbia and Montenegro (D) did nothing to prevent the July 1995 Srebrenica massacre, although, according to the I.C.J., it should have "been aware of the serious danger that acts of genocide would be committed." The I.C.J. also concluded Serbia and Montenegro (D) violated their obligation to punish genocide when they failed to transfer Ratko Mladic, an indictee, to the International Criminal Tribunal for the former Yugoslavia.

Quicknotes

GENOCIDE The systematic killing of a particular group.

INTERNATIONAL LAW The body of law applicable to dealings between nations.

Application of the Interim Accord of 13 September 1995 (The Former Yugoslav Republic of Macedonia v. Greece)

State (P) v. State (D)

2011 I.C.J. 644

NATURE OF CASE: Proceedings in the International Court of Justice to determine whether a bilateral treaty had been breached.

FACT SUMMARY: The former Yugoslav Republic of Macedonia ("Applicant") (P) brought proceedings in the International Court of Justice against Greece (also known as the "Hellenic Republic") ("Respondent") (D), asserting that Respondent (D) had breached various provisions of an Interim Accord the parties had entered into on September 13, 1995.

RULE OF LAW

(1) A party to a bilateral treaty does not breach a treaty provision where the provision's plain terms do not impose an obligation on the party.

(2) A party to a bilateral treaty does not breach its duty to negotiate in good faith merely because negotiations between the parties to the treaty do not result in resolution of the parties' differences, or where the party conducts itself in a way that negotiations may be meaningful.

(3) A party to a bilateral treaty does not materially breach the treaty where it violates a provision of the treaty, but when such violation is brought to its attention by the other party, it ceases such violation.

FACTS: When the former Yugoslav Republic of Macedonia ("Applicant") (P) sought admission into the United Nations (U.N.) in 1992, Greece (also known as the "Hellenic Republic") ("Respondent") (D) opposed the admission, primarily on the grounds of the Applicant's (P) adoption of the name "Republic of Macedonia," since Respondent (D) believed that the name "Macedonia" referred to a geographical region in southeast Europe that included an important part of the territory and population of the Respondent (D) and of certain third States. The Respondent (D) further indicated that once a settlement had been reached on these issues, it would no longer oppose the Applicant's (P) admission to the United Nations. The Respondent (D) had also expressed opposition on similar grounds to the Applicant's (P) recognition by the member States of the European Community. Applicant (P) was admitted to the U.N. in 1993 under a "provisional reference" to its name, i.e., "the former Yugoslav Republic of Macedonia." In part as the result of urging from the U.N. Security Council, the parties, on September 13, 1995, entered an Interim Accord in an effort to resolve their dispute over Applicant's (P) name. The Interim Accord referred to the Applicant (P) as "Party of the Second Part" and to the Respondent (D) as "Party of the First Part," so as to avoid using any contentious name. Under the Interim Accord's Article 5, the parties agreed to "continue negotiations . . . with a view to reaching agreement on the difference" they had regarding the Applicant's (P) name. The Respondent (D), in Article 11, also agreed not to object to the application by or the membership of the Applicant (P) in international, multilateral, and regional organizations and institutions of which the Respondent (D) was a member, provided that the Applicant (P) would be referred to in those organizations as "the former Yugoslav Republic of Macedonia," rather than the "Republic of Macedonia." Thereafter, the Applicant (P) was admitted into various organizations of which Respondent (D) was a member. However, the Applicant (P) was denied membership in the North Atlantic Treaty Organization (NATO), which rejected such membership in a meeting of NATO member States in Bucharest (the "Bucharest Summit") in April 2008. The Respondent (D) made clear before, during, and after the Bucharest Summit the resolution of the difference over the name was the "decisive criterion" for the Respondent (D) to accept the Applicant's (P) admission to NATO, as that issue remained unresolved. The Applicant (P) then brought proceedings in the International Court of Justice (I.C.J.), asserting the Respondent (D) had breached various provisions of the Interim Accord. The Respondent (D) maintained any disregard of its obligations under the Interim Accord could be justified as a response to a material breach of the treaty by the Applicant (P), and a partial suspension of the Interim Accord was "justified" under Article 60 of the 1969 Vienna Convention because the Applicant's (P) breaches were material. The Respondent (D) further argued it had not been required to give notice to the Applicant (P) of any alleged material breach of the Interim Accord. The Applicant (P) countered that the Respondent (D) never alerted the Applicant (P) to any alleged material breach of the Interim Accord; never sought to invoke a right of suspension under Article 60 of the 1969 Vienna Convention; and failed to comply with the procedural requirements of Article 65 of the 1969 Vienna Convention. The Respondent (D) asserted the Applicant (P) had breached Article 11 of the Interim Accord by being referred to in some organizations by a name other than "the former Yugoslav Republic of Macedonia." The

Continued on next page.

Respondent (D) also contended the Applicant (P) had failed to negotiate in good faith. The Respondent (D) maintained the parties understood the negotiations under the Interim Accord had always been meant to reach agreement on a single name that would be used for all purposes. The Respondent (D) contended the Applicant (P) departed from this understanding by pressing for a "dual formula" whereby the negotiations were limited solely to finding a name for use in the bilateral relations of the parties, and thus attempted unilaterally to redefine the object and purpose of the negotiations. The Respondent (D) further contended the Applicant's (P) continuous use of its constitutional name to refer to itself and its policy of securing third-State recognition under that name deprived the negotiations of their object and purpose. The Respondent also (D) alleged the Applicant (P) had adopted an intransigent and inflexible stance during the negotiations over the name. For its part, the Applicant (P) asserted it did not give an undertaking to call itself by the provisional reference and maintained its efforts to build third-State support for its constitutional name did not violate its obligation to negotiate in good faith. The Applicant (P) contended the Interim Accord did not prejudge the outcome of the negotiations required by Article 5, by prescribing that those negotiations result in a single name to be used for all purposes. In addition, the Applicant (P) argued it showed openness to compromises, and it was the Respondent (D) that was intransigent. Another contention Respondent (D) made was that Applicant (P) had violated Article 7, paragraph 2 of the Interim Accord, which provided: "Upon entry into force of this Interim Accord, the Party of the Second Part shall cease to use in any way the symbol in all its forms displayed on its national flag prior to such entry into force." The Respondent (D) claimed the Applicant (P) had used the symbol in various ways since the Interim Accord entered into force but acknowledged the Applicant (P) had changed its flag as required. One instance was a use of the symbol by one of the Applicant's (P) army regiments. The Respondent (D), in 2004, raised its concerns about such use, and the regiment was disbanded that year, with no similar use of the symbol thereafter. The Respondent (D) also introduced evidence with respect to fewer than ten additional instances in which the symbol had been used in the Applicant's (P) territory in various ways, mainly in connection with either publications or public displays, but these uses were made primarily by private persons or were not communicated to the Applicant (P) until after the Bucharest Summit.

ISSUE:

(1) Does a party to a bilateral treaty breach a treaty provision where the provision's plain terms do not impose an obligation on the party?

(2) Does a party to a bilateral treaty breach its duty to negotiate in good faith merely because negotiations between the parties to the treaty do not result in resolution of the parties' differences, or where the party conducts itself in a way that negotiations may be meaningful?

(3) Does a party to a bilateral treaty materially breach the treaty where it violates a provision of the treaty, but when such violation is brought to its attention by the other party, it ceases such violation?

HOLDING AND DECISION: [Judge not stated in casebook excerpt.]

(1) No. A party to a bilateral treaty does not breach a treaty provision where the provision's plain terms do not impose an obligation on the party. As a threshold matter, the evidence shows the Respondent (D) objected to the Applicant's (P) admission into NATO, rather than, as the Respondent (D) claims, the Respondent (D) merely made observations to other member States about the Applicant's (P) eligibility to join the organization. Accordingly, the Respondent's (D) actions came within the terms of Article 11 of the Interim Accord, since the Respondent (D) "objected" to the Applicant's (P) admission. As to the Respondent's (D) contention the Applicant (P) breached Article 11, which provides the Respondent (D) may object to the Applicant's (P) admission into an organization if the Applicant (P) is referred to by a name other than "the former Yugoslav Republic of Macedonia," that provision on its face does not impose an obligation on the Applicant (P), but instead specifies the single circumstance under which the Respondent (D) may object to admission. The provision imposes an obligation on the Respondent (D) not to object to admission of the Applicant (P), and it provides for an important exception (if the specified name is not used), but that exception does not impose any kind of obligation on the Applicant (P). Therefore, the Applicant (P) did not breach this provision.

(2) No. A party to a bilateral treaty does not breach its duty to negotiate in good faith merely because negotiations between the parties to the treaty do not result in resolution of the parties' differences, or where the party conducts itself in a way the negotiations may be meaningful. As to the Respondent's (D) claim the Applicant (P) breached its duty to negotiate in good faith, the parties' failure to reach agreement, 16 years after the conclusion of the Interim Accord, does not itself establish either party has breached its obligation to negotiate in good faith. Whether the obligation has been undertaken in good faith cannot be measured by the result obtained. Rather, it must be determined whether the parties conducted themselves in such a way that negotiations may be meaningful. Although there was evidence both parties at times took inflexible positions regarding the use of Applicant's (P) constitutional name, there was also evidence the parties negotiated

Continued on next page.

in earnest, and considered mediators' suggestions for resolution of their differences. Taken as a whole, the evidence indicates the Applicant (P) showed a degree of openness to proposals that differed from either the sole use of its constitutional name or the "dual formula," whereas the Respondent (D apparently changed its initial position and in September 2007 declared it would agree to the word "Macedonia" being included in the Applicant's (P) name as part of a compound formulation. Accordingly, the Respondent (D) has not met its burden of demonstrating the Applicant (P) breached its obligation to negotiate in good faith.

(3) No. A party to a bilateral treaty does not materially breach the treaty where it violates a provision of the treaty, but when such violation is brought to its attention by the other party, it ceases such violation. Article 60, paragraph 3 (b), of the 1969 Vienna Convention provides that a material breach consists in "the violation of a provision essential to the accomplishment of the object or purpose of the treaty," The only breach that has been established is the display of a symbol in breach of Article 7, paragraph 2, of the Interim Accord, a situation that ended in 2004. This incident cannot be regarded as a material breach within the meaning of Article 60 of the 1969 Vienna Convention. Moreover, the Respondent (D) failed to establish that the action it took in 2008 in connection with the Applicant's (P) application to NATO was a response to the breach of Article 7, paragraph 2, approximately four years earlier. Accordingly, the Respondent's (D) action did not fall within Article 60 of the 1969 Vienna Convention as a response to material breaches of the Interim Accord allegedly committed by the Applicant (P).

ANALYSIS

The I.C.J. ultimately held Respondent-Greece (D), by objecting to the admission of the former Yugoslav Republic of Macedonia to NATO, had breached its obligation under Article 11, paragraph 1, of the Interim Accord. The Court, however, did not grant Applicant-Macedonia's (P) request it instruct Greece (D) to refrain from similar actions in the future.

Quicknotes

BREACH The violation of an obligation imposed pursuant to contract or law, by acting or failing to act.

GOOD FAITH An honest intention to abstain from taking advantage of another.

MATERIAL BREACH Breach of a contract's terms by one party that is so substantial as to relieve the other party from its obligations pursuant thereto.

Gabčíkovo-Nagymaros Project (Hungary/Slovakia)

Treaty partners jointly presenting questions to the International Court of Justice

1997 I.C.J. 7

NATURE OF CASE: Proceeding before the International Court of Justice to determine whether impossibility of performance and changed circumstances justified termination of a treaty.

FACT SUMMARY: Hungary claimed impossibility of performance as well as changed circumstances entitled it to terminate a treaty with Slovakia regarding a joint water management project on the Danube River.

RULE OF LAW

(1) Under Article 61 of the Vienna Convention on the Law of Treaties, a party to a treaty may not terminate the treaty on the grounds of impossibility where an object indispensable for the execution of the treaty has not permanently disappeared and has not been destroyed.

(2) Under Article 62 of the Vienna Convention on the Law of Treaties, a party to a treaty may not terminate the treaty on the grounds of changed circumstances where a fundamental change of circumstances was not unforeseen and where the existence of the circumstances at the time of the treaty's conclusion did not constitute an essential basis of the consent of the parties to be bound.

FACTS: Hungary and Czechoslovakia in 1977 entered into a treaty for the construction and operation of a system of locks on the Danube River, which project was started but not completed. The Danube forms the border of these countries for a part of their entire borders. With the passing of time, there was also increased awareness of potentially negative ecological impacts of the project. In 1989, Hungary first suspended, then abandoned, its part of the project, in response to criticism of the project from its citizens. The parties tried, but failed, to negotiate a mutually satisfactory solution. Czechoslovakia began work in 1991 on an alternative project, known as Variant C, but this alternative was unacceptable to Hungary and in 1992, Hungary gave notice of termination of the treaty. The two countries also underwent major transformations in government, with Czechoslovakia dividing into two separate States in 1993, one of which was Slovakia. Hungary and Slovakia later petitioned to the International Court of Justice (I.C.J.) to decide whether Hungary was entitled to suspend and abandon its operations on the basis of changed circumstances and impossibility. The principle of impossibility is contained in Article 61 of the Vienna Convention on the Law of Treaties, while the principle relating to changed circumstances is contained in Article 62.

ISSUE:

(1) Under Article 61 of the Vienna Convention on the Law of Treaties, may a party to a treaty terminate the treaty on the grounds of impossibility where an object indispensable for the execution of the treaty has not permanently disappeared and has not been destroyed?

(2) Under Article 62 of the Vienna Convention on the Law of Treaties, may a party to a treaty terminate the treaty on the grounds of changed circumstances where a fundamental change of circumstances was not unforeseen and where the existence of the circumstances at the time of the treaty's conclusion did not constitute an essential basis of the consent of the parties to be bound?

HOLDING AND DECISION: [Judge not stated in casebook excerpt.]

(1) No. Under Article 61 of the Vienna Convention on the Law of Treaties, a party to a treaty may not terminate the treaty on the grounds of impossibility where an object indispensable for the execution of the treaty has not permanently disappeared and has not been destroyed. Hungary contended the essential object of the treaty was an economic joint investment that was consistent with environmental protection and that was to be operated jointly by the parties to the treaty, and it contended this object had permanently disappeared. Even if "object" in Article 61 embraces a legal regime, here that regime had not ceased to exist. The treaty made available to the parties the necessary means to proceed at any time, by negotiation, to the required adjustments between economic imperatives and ecological imperatives. Further, if the realization of economic benefits envisioned by the project was no longer possible, the cause of this impossibility was originally because Hungary failed to carry out the work for which it was responsible under the treaty. Article 61 of the Vienna Convention provides that impossibility of performance may not be invoked to terminate a treaty by a party to the treaty when such impossibility results from that party's own breach of an obligation it has under the treaty. [Judgment for Slovakia as to this issue.]

(2) No. Under Article 62 of the Vienna Convention on the Law of Treaties, a party to a treaty may not terminate the treaty on the grounds of changed circumstances

Continued on next page.

where a fundamental change of circumstances was not unforeseen and where the existence of the circumstances at the time of the treaty's conclusion did not constitute an essential basis of the consent of the parties to be bound. Hungary argued that profound political changes, the project's diminishing economic viability, the progress of environmental knowledge, and the development of new norms and prescriptions of international environmental law cumulatively constituted a fundamental change of circumstances. First, although the prevailing political and economic conditions were relevant to the conclusion of the 1977 treaty, those conditions were not so closely linked to the object and purpose of the treaty as to constitute an essential basis of the parties' consent. Thus, when those conditions changed, they did not radically alter the extent of the obligations still to be performed. Similarly, the diminishing profitability of the project was not so great as to radically transform the parties' obligations. Second, the new developments in environmental knowledge and law were not completely unforeseen. Moreover, the treaty provisions were designed to accommodate change, and made it possible for the parties to take such changes into account and to respond thereto. Finally, Article 62 makes it clear that the stability of treaty relations requires that the plea of fundamental change of circumstances may only be applied in exceptional cases. For all these reasons, Hungary's plea of changed circumstances fails. [Judgment for Slovakia as to this issue.]

ANALYSIS

This opinion, along with others issued by the I.C.J., makes clear that the "non-foreseeability" element, as well as the "essential basis" and "radical transformation" elements, are fundamental factors of Article 62's changed circumstances rule, and must be met before a plea of changed circumstances will be granted to terminate a treaty.

Quicknotes

DOCTRINE OF IMPOSSIBILITY A doctrine relieving the parties to a contract from liability for nonperformance of their duties thereunder, if the subject matter of the contract ceases to exist, a person essential to the performance of the contract is deceased, or the service or goods contracted for has become illegal.

TREATY An agreement between two or more nations for the benefit of the general public.

Partial Award on Economic Loss Throughout Ethiopia

Bilateral treaty partner (P) v. Bilateral treaty partner (D)

Eritrea Ethiopia Claims Commission (Dec. 19, 2005)

NATURE OF CASE: Claims for economic losses brought before the Eritrea Ethiopia Claims Commission.

FACT SUMMARY: The Federal Democratic Republic of Ethiopia (Ethiopia) (P) claimed it suffered economic losses that resulted from the violation of a series of bilateral treaties it had with the State of Eritrea (Eritrea) (D), which violation Ethiopia (P) contended was the result of armed conflict between the two nations.

RULE OF LAW

Bilateral treaties regulating trade and commerce are not in force during a period of war between the parties.

FACTS: The Federal Democratic Republic of Ethiopia (Ethiopia) (P) and the State of Eritrea (Eritrea) (D) were engaged in armed conflict between 1998 and 2000. At the conclusion of the hostilities, the nations entered into a peace agreement that provided for an international arbitral commission, called the Eritrea Ethiopia Claims Commission, before which the nations could bring claims for loss, damage, or injury during the war that resulted from violations of international law. Ethiopia (P) made claims, inter alia, for economic losses (such as injury to its national airline, loss of tourism, and loss of tax revenues) it contended resulted from the violation of a series of bilateral treaties regulating trade and commerce between the two nations. Eritrea (D) countered the treaties were ineffective, either through suspension or termination, for the duration of the war.

ISSUE: Are bilateral treaties regulating trade and commerce in force during a period of war between the parties?

HOLDING AND DECISION: [Judge not stated in casebook excerpt.] No. Bilateral treaties regulating trade and commerce are not in force during a period of war between the parties. Ethiopia (P) argues the outbreak of war did not automatically terminate the treaties, and under the principle of changed circumstances (*rebus sic stantibus*), Eritrea (D) was responsible for its termination of the treaties as a result of its unlawful aggression against Ethiopia (P). However, this claim must fail if the treaties were not in effect during the war. Although there is not consensus as to whether the outbreak of conflict automatically terminates bilateral treaties, there is broad consensus that, at the very least, treaties of an economic or political nature are suspended for the duration of the war. Thus, here, the treaties at issue became inoperative during the war, either through suspension or termination, so Ethiopia (P) cannot seek compensation for economic losses resulting from a violation of the treaties. Accordingly, Ethiopia's (P) claims are dismissed on the merits. Judgment for Eritrea (D).

ANALYSIS

Draft articles on the effects of armed conflicts on treaties were adopted by the International Law Commission in 2011 (U.N. Doc. A/66/10). These provide, inter alia, that the existence of armed conflict does not automatically terminate or suspend the operation of treaties between States that are parties to the conflict, or between a State that is a party to the conflict and a State that is not (Article 3). The draft also provides that where a treaty itself contains provisions on its operations in situations of armed conflict, those provisions govern (Article 4).

Quicknotes

REBUS SIC STANTIBUS If circumstances are effectively the same as they were when a treaty was signed, a treaty is binding.

CHAPTER 4

Other Sources of Law

Quick Reference Rules of Law

Prosecutor v. Erdemović

Prosecutor (P) v. Convicted war criminal (D)

App. Chamber, Intl. Crim. Trib. for the former Yugoslavia, Case No. IT-96-22 (Judgment Oct. 7, 1997)

NATURE OF CASE: Appeal of sentence before the International Criminal Tribunal for the Former Yugoslavia (ICTY) for crimes against humanity.

FACT SUMMARY: [Drazen Erdemović (D) was sentenced to ten years in prison for crimes against humanity. He appealed on the ground of duress.]

RULE OF LAW

In international law, duress is not a complete defense to the killing of innocents.

FACTS: [Drazen Erdemović (D) was sentenced to ten years in prison for crimes against humanity for his role as a Bosnian Serb in the massacre of thousands of innocents. He appealed on the ground of duress, claiming that he would have been killed along with his victims had he not killed them.]

ISSUE: In international law, is duress a complete defense to the killing of innocents?

HOLDING AND DECISION: [Judge not stated in casebook excerpt.] No. In international law, duress is not a complete defense to the killing of innocents. Under the law of some States, duress may be a complete defense to the killing of innocent people. This law, although constituting State practice, is not entitled to the status of customary international law, because this practice is not consistent, especially with many States that apply common law. Moreover, this practice is not supported by *opinio juris*, i.e., those States that do apply this defense do not do so because they believe they are conforming to an international legal obligation. Because there is no consistent State practice or customary law in this area, normative policy considerations, such as social and political policy, are appropriate. The defense relies on cases that have accepted the duress defense where the accused faced death for not killing a victim who inevitably was going to be killed regardless of whether the accused participated. This utilitarian approach is based on the idea that if the victim is going to die anyway, there is no reason the accused should die as it would be unjust for the law to expect the accused to die for nothing. This balancing-of-harms approach is rejected in favor of a clear rule that duress is not a complete defense to those who kill innocent persons. Instead, a mitigation of punishment is the preferred alternative to duress as a complete defense. Mitigation is a more sophisticated and flexible tool for doing justice in individual cases—in some cases where the accused's life is threatened, mitigation can lead to no punishment at all.

DISSENT: (Cassese, J.) Legal constructs and terms of art, such as duress, that originate in national law, cannot be transferred into international criminal proceedings because those proceedings are substantially different from national criminal proceedings and do not reflect the legal paradigms of any one legal system. The Prosecution's contention that customary international law has excluded the common law defense of duress finds minimal support in various national cases, whereas there is copious support for applying the defense. This inconsistency in State practice leads to the conclusion that there is no special rule in customary law as to whether to allow the defense or not. The absence of such a special rule leads to the conclusion—a conclusion the majority does not make—that one should apply, on a case-by-case basis, the general rule of duress to all crimes. One of the elements of this general rule, a requirement that the crime committed was not disproportionate to the evil threatened, will be extremely hard to fulfill where the underlying crime is the killing of innocents, and may never be satisfied where the accused is saving his own life at the expense of his victims. Where the accused may not be able to save the lives of his potential victims regardless of what he does, then duress may succeed as a defense. This is a relevant factor that should be considered in whether to allow the defense. The law in this area must be based on what society can reasonably expect of its members. In certain situations, it may be unreasonable to expect persons under duress not to perpetrate certain offenses. To say, like the majority does, that duress can be used in mitigation, is to ignore that criminal law must determine criminal culpability in the first place. It is also misplaced to resort to policy considerations when international criminal law is ambiguous since this risks running afoul of the customary principle of *nullum crimen sine lege;* a court must apply law, not policy.

ANALYSIS

Erdemović (D) was ultimately sentenced to five years in prison. This result may have been more favorable than if the court had applied the duress defense as a complete bar, because defense requires, as the Dissent points out, a proportionality requirement that is extremely difficult to satisfy in a case such as this, and also requires that the accused did not voluntarily bring about the situation leading to the duress. Ostensibly, this requirement would bar the defense in Erdemović's (D) case on the ground he voluntarily joined the Serbian army and knew of its methods and practices. Thus, a rule of mitigation may have served Erdemović (D) better than an all-or-nothing duress defense.

Continued on next page.

Quicknotes

DURESS Unlawful threats or other coercive behavior by one person that causes another to commit acts he would not otherwise do.

MITIGATION Reduction in penalty.

OPINIO JURIS An "opinion of law," or belief certain conduct must occur due to legal obligation.

Legal Status of Eastern Greenland (Norway v. Denmark)

Occupier (D) v. Sovereign (P)

1933 P.C.I.J. (ser. A/B) No. 53 at 71

NATURE OF CASE: Proceeding before the Permanent Court of International Justice.

FACT SUMMARY: Denmark (P) claimed that a statement made by a Norwegian Minister was binding on Norway (D).

RULE OF LAW

A reply given by the Minister of Foreign Affairs on behalf of his or her government is binding upon the country to which the Minister belongs.

FACTS: Denmark (P) wanted to obtain from Norway (D) its agreement not to obstruct Danish (P) plans with regard to Greenland. The Norwegian Minister for Foreign Affairs made a declaration on behalf of the Norwegian government (D) that the Norwegian government (D) would not make any difficulty in the settlement of the question.

ISSUE: Is a reply given by the Minister of Foreign Affairs on behalf of his or her government binding upon the country to which the Minister belongs?

HOLDING AND DECISION: [Judge not stated in casebook excerpt.] Yes. A reply given by the Minister of Foreign Affairs on behalf of his or her government is binding upon the country to which the Minister belongs. It is beyond dispute that a reply of the nature given here in response to a request by the diplomatic representative of a foreign power is binding upon the country the Minister represents.

ANALYSIS

The Vienna Convention on the Law of Treaties is the main source of international law on treaties. The Convention was ratified by 35 countries but not by the United States. Unilateral statements may also be binding on states.

Quicknotes

TREATY An agreement between two or more nations for the benefit of the general public.

UNILATERAL One-sided; involving only one person.

Nuclear Tests Case (Australia v. France)

Neighboring countries (P) v. Nuclear testing country (D)

1974 I.C.J. 253

NATURE OF CASE: Proceeding before the International Court of Justice.

FACT SUMMARY: Australia and New Zealand (P) demanded that France (D) cease atmospheric nuclear tests in the South Pacific.

RULE OF LAW

Declarations made by way of unilateral acts may have the effect of creating legal obligations.

FACTS: France (D) completed a series of nuclear tests in the South Pacific. Australia and New Zealand (P) applied to the International Court of Justice demanding that France (D) cease testing immediately. While the case was pending, France (D) announced the series of tests was complete and that it did not plan any further such tests. France (D) moved to dismiss the applications.

ISSUE: May declarations made by way of unilateral acts have the effect of creating legal obligations?

HOLDING AND DECISION: [Judge not stated in casebook excerpt.] Yes. Declarations made by way of unilateral acts may have the effect of creating legal obligations. The sole relevant question is whether the language employed in any given declaration reveals a clear intention. One of the basic principles governing the creation and performance of legal obligations is the principle of good faith. The statements made by the President of the French Republic must be held to constitute an engagement of the State in regard to the circumstances and intention with which they were made. The statements made by the French authorities are therefore relevant and legally binding. Applications dismissed.

ANALYSIS

The unilateral statements made by French authorities were first communicated to the government of Australia. To have legal effect there was no need for the statements to be directed to any particular State. The general nature and characteristics of the statements alone were relevant for evaluation of their legal implications.

Quicknotes

RELEVANCE The admissibility of evidence based on whether it has any tendency to prove or disprove a matter at issue to the case.

UNILATERAL One-sided; involving only one person.

Frontier Dispute Case (Burkina Faso/Mali)

[Parties not identified.]

1986 I.C.J. 554

NATURE OF CASE: Interpretation of a statement made by the head of state.

FACT SUMMARY: The Mali head of state made a declaration that was interpreted to be a unilateral act.

RULE OF LAW

Unilateral declarations made by heads of state bind the State to its terms only when the intention confers on the declaration the character of a legal undertaking.

FACTS: [Facts not stated in casebook excerpt.]

ISSUE: Do unilateral declarations made by heads of state bind the State to its terms only when the intention confers on the declaration the character of a legal undertaking?

HOLDING AND DECISION: [Judge not stated in casebook excerpt.] Yes. Unilateral declarations made by heads of state bind the State to its terms only when the intention confers on the declaration the character of a legal undertaking. It is for the court to "form its own view of the meaning and scope intended by the author of a unilateral declaration which might create a legal obligation." In order to assess the intentions of the author of a unilateral act, account must be taken of all the factual circumstances in which the act occurred. Here, there was nothing to hinder the parties from entering a formal agreement. Since no such agreement was entered, there are no grounds to interpret the Mali Head of State's declaration as a unilateral act with legal implications.

ANALYSIS

In the *Nuclear Tests* case, the Court interpreted the French government's unilateral declarations as effectively communicating the intent to terminate atmospheric testing. In that case, the French government had no alternative but to express its intentions by unilateral declarations. This case is distinguished since the parties had the normal method of formal agreement available.

Quicknotes

LEGAL OBLIGATION A duty to act that is imposed by law.

UNILATERAL ACT One-sided; involving only one person.

CHAPTER 5

States

Quick Reference Rules of Law

Reference re Secession of Quebec

Can. Sup. Ct., 2 S.C.R. 217, 37 I.L.M. 1340 (1998)

NATURE OF CASE: Advisory opinion regarding self-determination in relation to separatist movements.

FACT SUMMARY: Quebec attempted to secede from Canada.

RULE OF LAW

A people's right to self-determination cannot be said to ground a right to unilateral secession.

FACTS: [Facts not stated in casebook excerpt.]

ISSUE: Is there a right to self-determination under international law that would give the National Assembly, legislature, or government of Quebec the right to effect Quebec's unilateral secession from Canada?

HOLDING AND DECISION: [Judge not stated in casebook excerpt.] No. The international law principle of self-determination has evolved within a framework of respect for the territorial integrity of existing states. The right to external self-determination has only been granted to peoples under colonial rule or foreign occupation, based on the assumption that both are entities inherently distinct from the colonialist power and the occupant power. External self-determination has also been bestowed upon peoples totally frustrated in their efforts to exercise internally their rights to self-determinism. In this case, Quebec is neither a colony nor a foreign-occupied land. Further, the people of Quebec have not been victims of attacks on their physical existence or integrity or of massive human rights violations. Quebecers are equitably represented in legislative, executive, and judicial institutions; occupy prominent positions within the government of Canada; and enjoy the freedom to pursue their political, economic, social, and cultural development.

ANALYSIS

The *Reference re Secession of Quebec* leaves open the possibility that the international law right of self-determination could entail secession as a "last resort" in cases of especially severe oppression in which other channels for exercising internal self-determination had been "totally frustrated."

Quicknotes

ADVISORY OPINION A decision rendered at the request of an interested party of how the court would rule should the particular issue arise.

INTERNATIONAL LAW The body of law applicable to dealings between nations.

Tinoco Claims Arbitration (Great Britain v. Costa Rica)

Contracting party (P) v. Restored regime (D)

1 U.N. Rep. Intl. Arb. Awards 369 (1923)

NATURE OF CASE: Arbitration of contract repudiation.

FACT SUMMARY: Great Britain (P) claimed that the former government of Costa Rica (D), the Tinoco regime, had granted oil concessions to a British company that had to be honored by the present regime.

RULE OF LAW

A government that establishes itself and maintains a peaceful de facto administration need not conform to a previous constitution and nonrecognition of the government by other governments does not destroy the de facto status of the government.

FACTS: The Tinoco regime had seized power in Costa Rica by coup. Great Britain (P) and the United States never recognized the Tinoco regime. When the Tinoco regime fell, the restored government nullified all Tinoco contracts, including an oil concession to a British company. Great Britain (P) claimed the Tinoco government was the only government in existence at the time the contract was signed and its acts could not be repudiated. Costa Rica (D) claimed that Great Britain (P) was estopped from enforcing the contract by its nonrecognition of the Tinoco regime. The matter was sent for arbitration.

ISSUE: Does nonrecognition of a new government by other governments destroy the de facto status of the government?

HOLDING AND DECISION: (Taft, C.J., Arb.) No. A government that establishes itself and maintains a peaceful de facto administration need not conform to a previous constitution and nonrecognition of the government by other governments does not destroy the de facto status of the government. Great Britain's (P) nonrecognition of the Tinoco regime did not dispute the de facto existence of that regime. There was no estoppel since the successor government had not been led by British nonrecognition to change its position.

ANALYSIS

The arbitrator found there was no estoppel. The evidence of nonrecognition did not outweigh the evidence of the de facto status of the Tinoco regime. Unrecognized governments thus may have the power to form valid contracts.

Quicknotes

DE FACTO STATUS In fact; something that is recognized by virtue of its existence in reality but is illegal for failure to comply with statutory requirements.

ESTOPPEL An equitable doctrine precluding a party from asserting a right to the detriment of another who justifiably relied on the conduct.

Salimoff & Co. v. Standard Oil

Former owner (P) v. Purchaser (D)

N.Y. Ct. App., 262 N.Y. 220, 186 N.E. 679 (1933)

NATURE OF CASE: Appeal from dismissal of action for an accounting.

FACT SUMMARY: Salimoff (P) claimed that the Soviet government did not have good title to pass when it sold oil property confiscated from Russian nationals.

RULE OF LAW

When no right of action is created at the place of the wrong, no recovery in tort can be had in any other State.

FACTS: Salimoff (P) was the equitable owner of oil property that had been seized by a nationalization decree and confiscated by the Soviet government in Russia. When the Soviet government sold oil extracted from that property to Standard Oil (D), Salimoff (P) sought an accounting, alleging that the confiscatory decrees by the unrecognized Soviet government had no legal effect. The complaint was dismissed and Salimoff (P) appealed.

ISSUE: When no right of action is created at the place of the wrong, can recovery in tort be had in another State?

HOLDING AND DECISION: (Pound, C.J.) No. When no right of action is created at the place of the wrong, no recovery in tort can be had in any other State. The United States government recognizes that the Soviet government has functioned as a de facto government since 1917, ruling within its borders. The courts cannot refuse to recognize a de facto government merely because the State Department has not recognized the Soviet government as a de jure government. Affirmed.

ANALYSIS

Salimoff (P) claimed the Soviet government was nothing more than a band of robbers and had no legitimacy. The court asked the rhetorical question whether Soviet Russia was a band of robbers or a government. Everyone knows it is a government, according to this court.

Quicknotes

CONFISCATORY DECREE A court order to condemn private property for public use.

DE FACTO GOVERNMENT A government that sustains its power against the lawful government by force.

DE JURE GOVERNMENT Government legally vested with the authority to govern.

NATIONALIZATION Government acquisition of a private enterprise.

National Petrochemical Co. of Iran v. M/T Stolt Sheaf

Iranian corporation (P) v. Unidentified party (D)

860 F.2d 551 (2d Cir. 1988)

NATURE OF CASE: Appeal of federal district court dismissal.

FACT SUMMARY: [An Iranian corporation (P) brought suit as a plaintiff in a U.S. federal court. The district court dismissed the claim because the United States had never extended recognition to the government of the Islamic Republic of Iran.]

RULE OF LAW

A foreign government is not necessarily barred from access to U.S. courts if it has not been formally recognized by the United States.

FACTS: [An Iranian corporation (P) brought suit as a plaintiff in a U.S. federal court. The district court dismissed the claim because the United States had never extended recognition to the government of the Islamic Republic of Iran. The U.S. government entered the case as amicus curiae and argued that the Iranian corporation (P) ought to be granted access.]

ISSUE: Is a foreign government necessarily barred from access to U.S. courts if it has not been formally recognized by the United States?

HOLDING AND DECISION: [Judge not stated in casebook excerpt.] No. A foreign government is not necessarily barred from access to U.S. courts if it has not been formally recognized by the United States. Recognition can occur even where the U.S. government has withheld formal recognition, which it sometimes does where recognition can be misinterpreted as approval. In addition, the Executive Branch has the power to deal with foreign nations outside formal recognition. In this case, relations between the United States and Iran have been tumultuous. The Executive Branch must therefore have broad discretion involving matters of foreign relations. Reversed.

ANALYSIS

The case as excerpted does not illustrate the point as clearly as one might hope. But the thrust is that the intervention of the United States as amicus and its arguments in favor of allowing the case to proceed in the U.S. court system were exercises of the power of the Executive Branch over matters of foreign relations, to which the court deferred.

Quicknotes

AMICUS CURIAE A third party, not implicated in the suit, that seeks to file a brief containing information for the court's consideration in conformity with its position.

Island of Palmas Case (United States v. The Netherlands)

Discovering country (P) v. Occupier (D)

Perm. Ct. of Arbitration, 2 U.N. Rep. Intl. Arb. Awards 829 (1928)

NATURE OF CASE: Arbitration of territorial dispute.

FACT SUMMARY: The United States (P) claimed that the Island of Palmas was part of the Philippines but the Netherlands (D) claimed title as well.

RULE OF LAW

An inchoate title cannot prevail over a definite title founded on continuous and peaceful display of sovereignty.

FACTS: The United States (P) claimed the Island of Palmas was part of the Philippines and had been ceded by Spain by the Treaty of Paris in 1898. The United States (P), as successor to the rights of Spain over the Philippines, based its claim of title in the first place on discovery. The Netherlands (D) claimed that it had possessed and exercised rights of sovereignty over the island from 1677 or earlier to the present.

ISSUE: Can an inchoate title prevail over a definite title founded on continuous and peaceful display of sovereignty?

HOLDING AND DECISION: (Huber, Arb.) No. An inchoate title cannot prevail over a definite title founded on continuous and peaceful display of sovereignty. The continuous and peaceful display of territorial sovereignty is as good as title. Discovery alone, without any subsequent act, cannot suffice to prove sovereignty over the island. There is no positive rule of international law that islands situated outside territorial waters should belong to a State whose territory forms the nearest continent or large island. No one contested the exercise of territorial rights by the Netherlands (D) from 1700 to 1906. The title of discovery, at best an inchoate title, does not prevail over the Netherlands, (D) claim of sovereignty.

ANALYSIS

The arbitrator examined evidence of contracts made by the East India Company and the Netherlands (D). The Netherlands (D) also based its claims on conventions it had with the princes and native chieftains of the islands. Spain was found not to have had dominion over the island at the time of the Treaty of Paris in 1898.

Quicknotes

INCHOATE Impartial or incomplete.

SOVEREIGNTY The absolute power conferred to the State to govern and regulate all persons located and activities conducted therein.

Frontier Dispute Case (Burkina Faso v. Mali)

[Parties not identified.]

1986 I.C.J. 554

NATURE OF CASE: Petition to resolve a border dispute.

FACT SUMMARY: Burkina Faso and Mali submitted a question to the International Court of Justice regarding a border dispute.

RULE OF LAW

There exists an obligation to respect pre-existing international frontiers in the event of a State succession.

FACTS: [Facts not stated in casebook excerpt.]

ISSUE: Does there exist an obligation to respect pre-existing international frontiers in the event of a State succession?

HOLDING AND DECISION: (Judges Lachs, Ruda, Bedjaoui, Luchaire, and Abi-Saab) Yes. There exists an obligation to respect pre-existing international frontiers in the event of a State succession, whether or not the rule is expressed in the form of *uti possidetis*. Thus, the numerous declarations of the intangibility of the frontiers at the time of the declaration of independence of the African States are declaratory. The fact that the principle did not exist when the States declared such independence in 1960 does not foreclose its present application.

ANALYSIS

The principle of *uti possidetis* developed with respect to the Spanish American colonies. In a similar dispute between El Salvador and Honduras, the Court described the principle as follows: "The general principle offered the advantage of establishing an absolute rule that there was not in law in the old Spanish America any *terra nullius;* while there might exist many regions that had never been occupied by the Spaniards . . . the regions were reputed to belonging in law to whichever of the republics succeeded to the Spanish province to which these territories attached by virtue of the old Royal ordinances of the Spanish mother country."

Quicknotes

TERRA NULLIUS Land belonging to nobody.

UTI POSSIDETIS In civil law, the granting of a right of possession to one who was already in possession of a thing in order that he or she may be declared the legal possessor.

CHAPTER 6

International and Non-Governmental Organizations

Quick Reference Rules of Law

Reparation for Injuries Suffered in the Service of the United Nations

[Parties not identified.]

I.C.J., Advisory Opinion, 1949 I.C.J. 174

NATURE OF CASE: Advisory opinion.

FACT SUMMARY: [Facts not stated in casebook excerpt.]

RULE OF LAW

The United Nations, as an Organization, has the capacity to bring an international claim against a country that causes an agent of the United Nations to suffer an injury in the performance of his duties with a view to obtaining the reparation due in respect of the damage caused to the United Nations or to the victim or persons entitled through him.

FACTS: [Facts not stated in casebook excerpt.]

ISSUE: Does the United Nations, as an Organization, have the capacity to bring an international claim against a country that causes an agent of the United Nations to suffer an injury in the performance of his duties with a view to obtaining the reparation due in respect of the damage caused to the United Nations or to the victim or persons entitled through him?

HOLDING AND DECISION: [Judge not stated in casebook excerpt.] Yes. The United Nations, as an Organization, has the capacity to bring an international claim against a country that causes an agent of the United Nations to suffer an injury in the performance of his duties with a view to obtaining the reparation due in respect of the damage caused to the United Nations or to the victim or persons entitled through him. The damage means exclusively damage caused to the interests of the organization itself, to its administrative machine, to its property and assets, and to the interests of which it is guardian. With respect to damages caused the victim or persons entitled through him, the Charter does not expressly confer the capacity to include such claim for reparation. However, in order that its agents may perform their duties satisfactorily, they must feel that their protection is assured by the Organization. For this purpose it is necessary when an infringement occurs that the Organization should be able to call upon the responsible State to remedy its default and to obtain reparation for the damage that it might have caused the agent.

ANALYSIS

The Court states that the same conclusion applies whether or not the defendant State is a member of the United Nations. If competing interests arise between the defendant's national State and the United Nations, there is no rule assigning priority to one over the other, so the Court states that goodwill and common sense must apply.

Quicknotes

ADVISORY OPINION A decision rendered at the request of an interested party of how the court would rule should the particular issue arise.

AGENT An individual who has the authority to act on behalf of another.

Prosecutor v. Tadić

International prosecutor (P) v. Alleged war criminal (D)

App. Chamber, Intl. Crim. Trib. for the former Yugoslavia, 1995 Case No. IT-94-1-AR72, 35 I.L.M. 32 (1996)

NATURE OF CASE: Appeal in war crimes case before the International Criminal Tribunal for the former Yugoslavia (I.C.T.Y.), challenging the validity of the I.C.T.Y. and, therefore, its jurisdiction.

FACT SUMMARY: Tadić (D), who had been accused of war crimes and brought before the International Criminal Tribunal for the former Yugoslavia (I.C.T.Y. or "the Tribunal"), challenged, on appeal to the Appeal Chamber, the jurisdiction of the I.C.T.Y. by asserting the United Nations (U.N.) Security Council had exceeded its power to establish the I.C.T.Y.

RULE OF LAW
Chapter VII of the United Nations Charter authorizes the United Nations Security Council to establish an international criminal tribunal as a response to a threat to the peace.

FACTS: The United Nations (U.N.) Security Council established the International Criminal Tribunal for the former Yugoslavia (I.C.T.Y. or "the Tribunal"). Tadić (D), who was the first alleged war criminal brought before the I.C.T.Y., challenged the Tribunal's jurisdiction on the basis, inter alia, that the Security Council had exceeded its authority under Chapter VII of the U.N. Charter by establishing a criminal tribunal. On appeal to the Tribunal's Appeals Chamber, that Chamber determined it had the power to resolve the jurisdictional issue, noting every tribunal has an inherent power to resolve challenges to its own jurisdiction, as a matter of its inherent judicial powers and functions. The Appeals Chamber framed the jurisdictional question as raising constitutional issues that turned on the limits of the power of the Security Council under Chapter VII and whether the Security Council had the power under the Chapter to establish an international criminal tribunal. Article 39 of the Charter, which is the first article in Chapter VII, provides: "The Security Council shall determine the existence of any threat to the peace, breach of the peace, or act of aggression and shall make recommendations, or decide what measures shall be taken in accordance with Articles 41 and 42, to maintain or restore international peace and security." The Appeals Chamber framed the sub-issues as: (1) whether there was threat to the peace justifying the invocation of Chapter VII as a legal basis for the establishment of the Tribunal; (2) assuming such a threat existed, was the Security Council authorized, with a view to restoring or maintaining peace, to take any measures at its own discretion, or was it bound to choose among those expressly provided for in Articles 41 and 42 (and possibly Article 40 as well); and (3) if the Security Council was bound to follow the mandates found in these Articles, how could the establishment of an international criminal tribunal be justified, as it did not figure among the ones mentioned in those Articles, and was of a different nature?

ISSUE: Does Chapter VII of the United Nations Charter authorize the United Nations Security Council to establish an international criminal tribunal as a response to a threat to the peace?

HOLDING AND DECISION: [Judge not stated in casebook excerpt.] Yes. Chapter VII of the United Nations Charter authorizes the United Nations Security Council to establish an international criminal tribunal as a response to a threat to the peace. Under Article 39, it is clear the Security Council has very wide discretion, although its powers are not unfettered, and cannot go beyond those granted to the United Nations. Nor can its powers exceed any express limitations on them, or limitations derived from the division of power within the U.N. In this regard, the Charter, in Article 24, provides that the Security Council must act in accordance with the purposes and principles of the U.N., and that it has specific powers. Under Article 39, the Security Council makes the determination that there exists one of the situations justifying the use of the "exceptional powers" of Chapter VII, and it also chooses the reaction to such a situation: it either makes recommendations (i.e., opts not to use the exceptional powers but to continue to operate under Chapter VI) or decides to use the exceptional powers by ordering measures to be taken in accordance with Articles 41 and 42 with a view to maintaining or restoring international peace and security. The situations justifying resort to the powers provided for in Chapter VII are a "threat to the peace," a "breach of the peace," or an "act of aggression." Here, at the very least, a threat to peace was involved. First, an armed conflict (or a series of armed conflicts) has been taking place in the territory of the former Yugoslavia since long before the decision of the Security Council to establish the I.C.T.Y. If it is considered an international armed conflict, it falls within the literal sense of the words "breach of the peace," but even if it is considered an internal armed conflict, it would still constitute a "threat to the peace" according to the settled practice of the Security Council and the common understanding of the U.N. membership in general. Upon determining the existence of a threat to the peace (or other situation warranting the exercise of its

Continued on next page.

powers under Chapter VII), the Security Council has broad discretion in determining the appropriate response. If it chooses to exercise its exceptional powers under Chapter VII, it then must decide what measures to take under Articles 41 and 42 to maintain or restore international peace and security. The question then becomes whether the Security Council is limited to the measures listed in those Articles, or whether it has even greater discretion in the form of general powers to accomplish Chapter VII's goals. In either event, it is clear the Security Council has very broad discretion in deciding on the course of action and evaluating the appropriateness of the measures to be taken. The language of Article 39 is clear, however, that the very broad and exceptional powers of the Security Council under Chapter VII must be channeled through Articles 41 and 42. Because these two Articles leave to the Security Council such wide latitude, there is no need to seek, on functional or other grounds, for even wider and more general powers than those already expressly provided for in the Charter. Thus, although the establishment of an international criminal tribunal is not expressly mentioned in the Articles, the measures listed in those Articles are merely illustrative examples that do not exclude other measures. Accordingly, the I.C.T.Y. was lawfully established, and has jurisdiction to hear the case against Tadić (D). Judgment for the Prosecutor (P).

ANALYSIS

As the Appeals Chamber in this case notes, the situations justifying resort to the powers provided for in Chapter VII are a "threat to the peace," a "breach of the peace," or an "act of aggression." While the "act of aggression" is more amenable to a legal determination, the "threat to the peace" is more of a political concept. However, the Security Council's discretion to determine that there exists such a threat is not a totally unfettered discretion, as it must remain, at the very least, within the limits of the Purposes and Principles of the U.N. Charter. Nevertheless, as this opinion makes clear, the Security Council's discretion in this regard is extremely broad, and it may craft responses to situations triggering exceptional responses under Chapter VII that are not enumerated in the Charter. Moreover, in crafting such responses, the Security Council is not even obligated to specify a particular Article as a basis for its action.

Quicknotes

JURISDICTION The authority of a court to hear and declare judgment in respect to a particular matter.

Legality of Use of Force (Serbia & Montenegro v. United Kingdom)

Non-U.N. member (P) v. U.N. member (D)

2004 I.C.J. 1307, 1332-38, 1352

NATURE OF CASE: Claim of illegal use of force against various NATO States.

FACT SUMMARY: [The Federal Republic of Yugoslavia (Serbia and Montenegro) (P) brought a claim in the International Court of Justice (I.C.J.) against various North Atlantic Treaty Organization States (D), including the United Kingdom (D), in 1999. The I.C.J. first considered the issue of jurisdiction.]

RULE OF LAW

The legal position of a State within the United Nations must be determined and clearly defined by the competent organs of the United Nations.

FACTS: [The Federal Republic of Yugoslavia (Serbia and Montenegro) ("the F.R.Y.") (P) brought a claim in the International Court of Justice (I.C.J.) against various North Atlantic Treaty Organization (NATO) States (D), including the United Kingdom (D) in 1999. Before considering the claim, the I.C.J. had to determine if it had jurisdiction to hear the case, which would only be the case if the F.R.Y. (P) was at the time of the claim a U.N. member State. Its predecessor State, the Socialist Federal Republic of Yugoslavia ("the S.F.R.Y."), was a member State at the time.]

ISSUE: Must the legal position of a State within the United Nations be determined and clearly defined by the competent organs of the United Nations?

HOLDING AND DECISION: [Judge not stated in casebook excerpt.] Yes. The legal position of a State within the United Nations must be determined and clearly defined by the competent organs of the United Nations. The legal position of the F.R.Y. (P) remained ambiguous between 1992 and 2000, the period during which its claim against certain NATO States (D), including the United Kingdom (D), was filed. The U.N. Security Council and General Assembly both decided that the F.R.Y. (P) could not automatically continue the membership of the Socialist Federal Republic of Yugoslavia in the United Nations, and that the F.R.Y. (P) should reapply for membership. These resolutions were approved by a majority of member voters, but they cannot be construed as conveying an authoritative determination of the F.R.Y.'s (P) legal status in the United Nations, because certain events made the F.R.Y.'s (P) status seem ambiguous—the General Assembly assessed annual contributions to the United Nations, the F.R.Y. (P) maintained that it continued the legal personality of the S.F.R.Y., and the Secretariat of the United Nations kept up the practice of the status quo ante that was in place up to the dissolution of the S.F.R.Y. But the situation cleared when the elected president of the F.R.Y. (P) in 2000 requested admission to the United Nations from the Secretary-General, which then recommended the State's admission. F.R.Y. (P) was admitted in late 2000. In hindsight, then, the F.R.Y. (P) was not a member of the United Nations when it began this action in 1999. Therefore, there was no jurisdiction to hear its claim.

ANALYSIS

The I.C.J.'s opinion focused on the F.R.Y.'s (P) status within the United Nations. But note that non-U.N. members may also become parties to the I.C.J.'s statute under Article 93(2). Remember also that while a State that is a party to the I.C.J.'s statute is entitled to participate in cases before the I.C.J., being a party to the statute does not automatically give the I.C.J. jurisdiction over disputes involving those parties.

Quicknotes

CLAIM The demand for a right to payment or equitable relief; the fact or facts giving rise to such demand.

JURISDICTION The authority of a court to hear and declare judgment in respect to a particular matter.

CHAPTER 7

Individuals and Corporations

Quick Reference Rules of Law

LaGrand Case (Germany v. United States)

State (P) v. State (D)

2001 I.C.J. 466

NATURE OF CASE: Multiple plaintiff action against a State for violation of the Vienna Convention on Consular Relations.

FACT SUMMARY: Germany (P) filed suit in the International Court of Justice against the United States (D), claiming that U.S. law enforcement personnel failed to advise aliens upon their arrests of their rights under the Vienna Convention on Consular Relations.

RULE OF LAW

Under the Vienna Convention on Consular Relations, a State that breaches its obligations to another by failing to inform an arrested alien of the right to consular notification and to provide judicial review of the alien's conviction and sentence also violates individual rights held by the alien under international law.

FACTS: Article 36(1)(b) of the Vienna Convention on Consular Relations [of 24 April 1963] ("the Convention") provides that a State trying an alien in a death sentence case must inform the alien of his rights to have his consular authorities informed of the arrest. Paraguay (P), Germany (P), and Mexico (P) filed suit in the International Court of Justice (I.C.J.) against the United States (D), claiming that U.S. law enforcement personnel failed to advise aliens upon their arrest of their rights, and that as a remedy for violation of the Vienna Convention, States' courts should review and reconsider the death sentences to determine if the lack of consular access prejudiced the aliens. Germany's (P) case involved LaGrand and his brother, who was executed before the matter came to the I.C.J. The I.C.J. found that the United States (D) breached its obligations to Germany (P) under the Convention by not immediately informing LaGrand and his brother of the right of consular notification, and by failing to provide judicial review of the conviction and sentence.

ISSUE: Under the Vienna Convention on Consular Relations, does a State that breaches its obligations to another by failing to inform an arrested alien of the right to consular notification and to provide judicial review of the alien's conviction and sentence also violate individual rights held by the alien under international law?

HOLDING AND DECISION: [Judge not stated in casebook excerpt.] Yes. Under the Vienna Convention on Consular Relations, a State that breaches its obligations to another by failing to inform an arrested alien of the right to consular notification and to provide judicial review of the alien's conviction and sentence also violates individual rights held by the alien under international law. The ordinary meaning of the clause "said authorities shall inform the person concerned without delay of his rights under this subparagraph" of Article 36 suggests that the right to be informed of the rights under the Convention is an individual right of every national of a State that is party to the Convention. LaGrands's rights were violated in the instant case.

ANALYSIS

Diplomatic efforts by the German ambassador and German Members of Parliament and the recommendation of Arizona's clemency board, failed to change the mind of Arizona Governor Jane Dee Hull, who insisted that the executions of the LaGrand brothers be carried out. Karl LaGrand was executed on February 24, 1999, by lethal injection, and Walter LaGrand was executed March 3, 1999, by gas chamber. Compare this case to a ruling by the I.C.J. involving Mexican nationals, *Avena and other Mexican Nationals (Mexico v. United States),* 2004 I.C.J. 12, and the U.S. Supreme Court's refusal to give effect to the I.C.J.'s *Avena* decision in *Medellin v. Texas,* 128 S. Ct. 1346 (2008).

Quicknotes

BREACH The violation of an obligation imposed pursuant to contract or law, by acting or failing to act.

INTERNATIONAL LAW The body of law applicable to dealings between nations.

JUDICIAL REVIEW The authority of the courts to review decisions, actions, or omissions committed by another agency or branch of government.

Nottebohm Case (Liechtenstein v. Guatemala)

Country of citizenship (P) v. Country of residence (D)

1995 I.C.J. 4

NATURE OF CASE: Appeal by a State from the refusal of another State to admit one of its nationals.

FACT SUMMARY: Nottebohm (P), a German citizen, lived in Guatemala (D) for 34 years and applied for Liechtenstein (P) citizenship one month after the start of World War II.

RULE OF LAW

While nationality conferred on a party is normally only the concern of that nation, such nationality may be disregarded by other States where it is clear it was a mere device/subterfuge.

FACTS: Nottebohm (P) was a German by birth. Nottebohm (P) lived in Guatemala (D) for 34 years, retaining his German citizenship and family and business ties with it. One month after the outbreak of World War II, Nottebohm (P) applied for citizenship with Liechtenstein (P), a neutral country. Nottebohm (P) had no ties with Liechtenstein (P) and intended to remain in Guatemala (D). Liechtenstein (P) approved the naturalization application and impliedly waived its three-year residency requirement. Nottebohm (P) briefly visited Liechtenstein (P) and, on his return to Guatemala (D), was refused admittance, being deemed a German national. Nottebohm's (P) Liechtenstein (P) citizenship was not honored. Liechtenstein (P) brought an action before the International Court to compel Guatemala (D) to recognize Nottebohm (P) as one of its nationals. Guatemala (D) challenged the validity of Nottebohm's (P) citizenship and the right of Liechtenstein (P) to bring the action, and alleged its belief that Nottebohm (P) remained a German national.

ISSUE: Must a nation automatically recognize the citizenship conferred on a party by another nation?

HOLDING AND DECISION: [Judge not stated in casebook excerpt.] No. As a general rule, matters concerning citizenship are solely the concern of the granting nation. It alone will normally bear the burdens or attain the benefits from the conferral of citizenship on a party. However, the conferring State may not require other States to automatically accept its designation unless it has acted in conformity with the general aim of forging a genuine bond between it and its national. Here, no relationship exists between Liechtenstein (P) and Nottebohm (P). There was never an intent to reside in Liechtenstein (P), no business or family connections, no acceptance of traditions and the severing of old ties, etc. The change in nationality was a mere convenience/subterfuge mandated by the war. Under such circumstances, Guatemala (D) was not forced to recognize it. Dismissed.

ANALYSIS

A State putting forth a claim must establish a *locus standi* for that purpose. This is almost exclusively a showing of nationality of the claimant. The real claimant must have continuously and without interruption from the time of the injury to the making of an award been a national of the State making the claim and must not have been a national of the State against whom the claim has been filed. L. Oppenheim and H. Lauterpacht, *International Law* 347 (8th Ed. 1955) Vol. 1.

Quicknotes

LOCUS STANDI Standing to bring suit in court.

NATIONALITY The country in which a person is born or naturalized.

Iran-United States Claims Tribunal, Case No. A/18

Dual citizens (P) v. Iran (D)

Dec. No. 32-A/18-FT, 5 Iran-U.S. Cl. Trib. Rep. 251 (1984-I)

NATURE OF CASE: Jurisdictional consideration by arbitral tribunal.

FACT SUMMARY: People with dual Iranian-U.S. citizenship (P) filed claims against Iran (D) in an arbitral tribunal in The Hague under a Claims Settlement Declaration, which was part of the Algiers Accords reached in the aftermath of the 1979 Iranian seizure of U.S. diplomatic and consular personnel in Iran (D) as hostages. Iran (D) challenged the jurisdiction of the tribunal.

RULE OF LAW

The Claims Settlement Declaration arbitral tribunal has jurisdiction over claims against Iran by dual Iran-United States nationals if the dominant and effective nationality of the claimant is that of the United States.

FACTS: Iranian militants seized U.S. diplomatic and consular personnel in Iran (D) as hostages after the 1979 Iranian revolution. The United States seized Iranian assets in the United States, and people and companies with claims against Iran (D) filed suit in U.S. courts, levying attachments against blocked Iranian assets. Algeria mediated a solution in January 1981, and the Algiers Accords was adopted by both States. The Algiers Accords included a Claims Settlement Declaration and created an arbitral tribunal in The Hague to hear claims by the nationals of either State against the government of the other State. Certain people with dual Iranian-U.S. citizenship (P) filed claims against Iran (D) in the tribunal, and Iran (D) challenged its jurisdiction.

ISSUE: Does the Claims Settlement Declaration arbitral tribunal have jurisdiction over claims against Iran (D) by dual Iran-United States nationals (P) if the dominant and effective nationality of the claimant is that of the United States?

HOLDING AND DECISION: [Judge not stated in casebook excerpt.] Yes. The Claims Settlement Declaration arbitral tribunal has jurisdiction over claims against Iran (D) by dual Iran-United States nationals (P) if the dominant and effective nationality of the claimant is that of the United States. The text of the Claims Settlement Declaration is not completely unambiguous on the issue, but the 1930 Hague Convention as modified by recent developments in international law, precedent, and legal literature suggest a person's dominant and effective nationality is determined by the stronger factual ties between the person concerned and one of the States whose nationality is involved. Factors to consider when determining the stronger factual ties include residence, center of interests, family ties, and participation in public life. Use of the word "national" or "nationals" in the Algiers Accords must be understood in a way that is consistent with this rule of international law, and jurisdiction under the Claims Settlement Agreement in these cases involving persons with dual citizenship against Iran (D) when the dominant and effective nationality of the person during the relevant period was that of the United States.

ANALYSIS

In 1982, the tribunal closed to new claims by private individuals. In total, it received approximately 4,700 private U.S. claims, ordered payments by Iran (D) to U.S. nationals totaling over $2.5 billion.

Quicknotes

ACCORD An agreement between two parties, one of whom has a valid claim against the other, to settle the controversy.

ARBITRAL Relating to arbitration or arbiters

ARBITRATION An alternative resolution process where a dispute is heard and decided by a neutral third party, rather than through legal proceedings.

Eritrea Ethiopia Claims Commission, Partial Award, Civilian Claims, Eritrea's Claims 15, 16, 23 & 27-32

Eritrea (P) v. Ethiopia (D)

Decided Dec. 17, 2004, 44 I.L.M. 601 (2005)

NATURE OF CASE: Review of denationalization procedures.

FACT SUMMARY: Ethiopia (D) denationalized nationals that voted for the creation of an independent State of Eritrea (P). Eritrea (P) challenged the action.

RULE OF LAW

In time of war, a State may denationalize persons whose second nationality is that of an enemy State, provided denationalization is not arbitrary.

FACTS: A new State of Eritrea (P) was admitted to the United Nations in May 1993 after persons of Eritrean origin voted overwhelmingly in favor of establishing the new State from a portion of Ethiopia (D). Persons who obtained an Eritrean "national identity card" were allowed to vote. After the 1998–2000 border war between Eritrea (P) and Ethiopia (D), approximately 66,000 people who voted were still living in Ethiopia (D). Ethiopia (D) claimed that because they voted, they were Eritrean nationals, and could therefore be expelled to Eritrea (P) under international law as enemy nationals. Eritrea (P) argued that they never relinquished their Ethiopian nationality and were being unlawfully denationalized and expelled. A bilateral claims commission that was established by Eritrea (P) and Ethiopia (D) concluded that persons still living in Ethiopia (D), who also voted to create Eritrea (P), were dual nationals—they acquired Eritrean nationality by voting in the referendum, and retained Ethiopian nationality by continuing to live in Ethiopia (D) and receive the benefits of Ethiopian nationality.

ISSUE: In time of war, may a State denationalize persons whose second nationality is that of an enemy State, provided denationalization is not arbitrary?

HOLDING AND DECISION: [Judge not stated in casebook excerpt.] Yes. In time of war, a State may denationalize persons whose second nationality is that of an enemy State, provided denationalization is not arbitrary. International law does not prohibit States from permitting nationals to possess another nationality, but also does not prohibit States from prohibiting the possession of another nationality. Ethiopia (D) allowed Ethiopians who had also acquired Eritrean nationality to continue to exercise their Ethiopian nationality, while agreeing with Eritrea (P) that these people would have to choose one nationality or the other at some future time.

The war then came, and Ethiopia (D) denationalized dual nationals falling in six groups: (1) those who Ethiopia (D) believed posed a security risk; (2) those who chose to leave Ethiopia (D) during the war and go to Eritrea (P); (3) those who remained in Ethiopia (D); (4) those who were in third countries or who left Ethiopia (D) to go to third countries; (5) those who were in Eritrea (P); and (6) those who were expelled for other reasons. International law limits States' power to deprive persons of their nationality through the Universal Declaration of Human Rights, Article 15 of which states that "no one shall be arbitrarily deprived of his nationality." Because deprivation of nationality is serious, with lasting consequences to those affected, those affected must be given adequate notice of the proceedings, the opportunity to present a case against denationalization before an objective decision maker, and the opportunity for outside review. With respect to the first group, Ethiopia's (D) complex process of identifying and denationalizing security risks fell short of this standard. But given the wartime circumstances, the loss of Ethiopian nationality after being identified through the security process was not arbitrary or contrary to international law. As to the second group, their decision to leave one country for another while the two are at war is a serious act that could not be without consequences. The termination of the Ethiopian nationality of these persons was not arbitrary and not in violation of international law. There was no evidence that members of the third group threatened Ethiopian security, and there was no process for identifying individuals warranting special consideration, and no possibility of review or appeal. Such a wide-scale deprivation of Ethiopian nationality of persons remaining in Ethiopia (D) is arbitrary and contrary to international law. The same is true for members of the fourth group: There is no evidence that they, by their "mere presence" in third countries could be presumed to be security threats, or that Ethiopia (D) employed an individualized assessment process to determine their potential threat. They were allowed to contest their treatment only through Ethiopian diplomatic or consular establishments abroad. Members of this group were arbitrarily deprived of their Ethiopian citizenship in violation of international law. Ethiopia's (D) denationalization of members of the fifth group was not arbitrary or otherwise unlawful, even though their mere presence in Eritrea (P) was not proof of security risk, because there are evident risks and wartime impediments to communication to provide notice of denationalization. Finally, the termination of the Ethiopian nationality of all persons in the sixth group was arbitrary and unlawful, since in many cases, most or all

Continued on next page.

dual nationals were sometimes rounded up by local authorities and forced into Eritrea (P) for reasons that cannot be established.

ANALYSIS

As the commission stated, the consequences of denationalization are high to the persons affected, and yet the standard applied to determine its legality under international law seems low: The Universal Declaration of Human Rights only requires that denationalization not be "arbitrary." The commission's focus was therefore on the procedures followed by Ethiopia (D) in the denationalization process, the circumstances in which it occurred, and the actions of, and consequences to, the persons affected. Its decision may have been different had the process not taken place during and in the aftermath of war.

Quicknotes

INTERNATIONAL LAW The body of law applicable to dealings between nations.

NATIONALITY The country in which a person is born or naturalized.

REFERENDUM Right constitutionally reserved to people of state, or local subdivision thereof, to have submitted for their approval or rejection, under prescribed conditions, any law or part of law passed by a lawmaking body.

Jesner v. Arab Bank, PLC

Foreign victim of terrorist acts that occurred abroad (P) v. Foreign bank corporation (D)

138 S. Ct. 1386 (2018)

NATURE OF CASE: Appeal from affirmance of dismissal of action brought under the Alien Tort Statute (ATS) against a foreign corporation.

FACT SUMMARY: Foreign nationals (P), on behalf of themselves or their family members who had been injured or killed by terrorist acts abroad, brought suit under the Alien Tort Statute (ATS), 28 U.S.C.A. § 1350, against Arab Bank, PLC (D), a Jordanian bank corporation with a New York branch, claiming Arab Bank (D) in part caused or facilitated those terrorist acts, and thus could be held liable under the ATS.

RULE OF LAW
Foreign corporations may not be defendants in suits brought under the Alien Tort Statute (ATS).

FACTS: Foreign nationals (P), on behalf of themselves or their family members who had been injured or killed by terrorist acts abroad, brought suit under the Alien Tort Statute (ATS), 28 U.S.C.A. § 1350, against Arab Bank, PLC (D), a Jordanian bank corporation with a branch in New York, claiming Arab Bank (D) in part caused or facilitated those terrorist acts, and could be held liable under the ATS for the ensuing damages. They (P) claimed that Arab Bank (D) used its New York branch to clear dollar-denominated transactions that benefited terrorists and to launder money for a Texas-based charity allegedly affiliated with a terrorist organization, and that those actions constituted torts "in violation of the law of nations" under the ATS. The district court dismissed the suit, holding that foreign corporations could not be sued as defendants under the ATS. The court of appeals affirmed, and the United States Supreme Court granted certiorari.

ISSUE: May foreign corporations be defendants in suits brought under the Alien Tort Statute (ATS)?

HOLDING AND DECISION: (Kennedy, J.) No. Foreign corporations may not be defendants in suits brought under the Alien Tort Statute (ATS). The Court's precedents cast doubt on courts' authority to extend or create private causes of action, even in the realm of domestic law, rather than leaving such decisions to the legislature, which is better positioned to consider if the public interest would be served by imposing a new substantive legal liability. Such caution extends to the question of whether the courts should exercise the judicial authority to mandate a rule imposing liability upon artificial entities like corporations. Neither the language of the ATS nor precedent supports an exception to these general principles in this context. Separation-of-powers concerns that counsel against courts creating private rights of action apply with particular force in the context of the ATS, which implicates foreign-policy concerns that are the province of the political branches. In sum, it would be inappropriate for courts to extend ATS liability to foreign corporations absent further action from Congress. The ATS was intended to promote harmony in international relations by ensuring foreign plaintiffs a remedy for international-law violations when the absence of such a remedy might provoke foreign nations to hold the United States accountable. However, here, and in other similar cases, the opposite is happening insofar as suits such as the one at bar are creating diplomatic difficulties for the United States. At a minimum, the relatively minor connection between the terrorist attacks and the alleged conduct in the United States illustrates the perils of extending the scope of ATS liability to foreign multinational corporations like Arab Bank (D). Because foreign corporate defendants create unique problems, and because courts are not well suited to make the required policy judgments that are implicated by corporate liability in cases like this one, foreign corporations may not be defendants in suits brought under the ATS. Affirmed.

DISSENT: (Sotomayor, J.) The history of the Alien Tort Statute's (ATS's) enactment does not rebut the presumption that the statute incorporated the accepted principle of corporate liability for tortious conduct, and there is nothing about the corporate form that by itself justifies categorically foreclosing corporate liability in all ATS actions. By imposing such an absolute bar on ATS suits against foreign corporations, the Court ensures that foreign corporations will be immune from liability for human rights abuses, regardless of how egregious such abuses might be. That some corporations might engage in such abuses is borne out by history. Immunizing corporations that violate human rights from liability under the ATS undermines the system of accountability for law-of-nations violations that the ATS sought to create.

ANALYSIS

According to Justice Alito, given that the Alien Tort Statute (ATS) was enacted to help the United States avoid diplomatic friction, and that federal courts, exercising their authority in limited circumstances to make federal common law, are limited in creating new causes of action under the ATS, federal courts should decline to create federal common-law causes of action whenever doing so

Continued on next page.

would not materially advance the ATS's objective of avoiding diplomatic strife. Applying that principle here, Justice Alito concludes that courts should not create causes of action under the ATS against foreign corporate defendants, since customary international law does not generally require corporate liability, so declining to create it under the ATS cannot give other nations just cause for complaint against the United States. To the contrary, in Justice Alito's estimation, creating causes of action against foreign corporations under the ATS may instead provoke exactly the sort of diplomatic strife inimical to the statute's fundamental purpose.

Quicknotes

CAUSE OF ACTION A fact or set of facts the occurrence of which entitles a party to seek judicial relief.

Barcelona Traction, Light and Power Company, Ltd. (Belgium v. Spain)

State of shareholders (P) v. Expropriating state (D)

1970 I.C.J. 3

NATURE OF CASE: Action for damages for the expropriation of a corporation.

FACT SUMMARY: Belgium (P) brought an action for damages against Spain (D) on the ground that its nationals as shareholders of the Barcelona Traction, Light and Power Co., Ltd. incorporated and registered in Canada, had been seriously harmed by actions of Spain (D) resulting in expropriation.

RULE OF LAW

The State of the shareholders of a corporation has a right of diplomatic protection only when the State whose responsibility is invoked is the national State of the company.

FACTS: The Barcelona Traction, Light and Power Co., Ltd. (Barcelona Traction) was incorporated and registered in Canada for the purpose of developing and operating electrical power in Spain (D). After the Spanish Civil War, Barcelona Traction was declared bankrupt by a Spanish court and its assets were seized. After the Canadian interposition ceased, Belgium (P) brought an action for damages against Spain (D) for what it termed expropriation of the assets of Barcelona Traction on the ground that a large majority of the stock of the company was owned by Belgian (P) nationals. Spain (D) raised the preliminary objection that Belgium (P) lacked standing to bring suit for damages to a Canadian company.

ISSUE: Does the State of the shareholders of a company have a right of diplomatic protection if the State whose responsibility is invoked is not the national State of the company?

HOLDING AND DECISION: [Judge not stated in casebook excerpt.] No. In order for a State to bring a claim in respect of the breach of an obligation owed to it, it must first establish its right to do so. This right is predicated on a showing that the defendant State has broken an obligation toward the national State in respect of its nationals. In the present case it is therefore essential to establish whether the losses allegedly suffered by Belgian (P) shareholders in Barcelona Traction were the consequence of the violation of obligations of which they are beneficiaries. In the present state of the law, the protection of shareholders requires that recourse be had to treaty stipulations or special agreements directly concluded between the private investor and the State in which the investment is placed. Barring such agreements, the obligation owed is to the corporation, and only the State of incorporation has standing to bring an action for violations of such an obligation. Nonetheless, for reasons of equity a theory has been developed to the effect that the State of the shareholders has a right of diplomatic protection when the State whose responsibility is invoked is the national State of the company. This theory, however, is not applicable to the present case, since Spain (D) is not the national State of Barcelona Traction. Barcelona Traction could have approached its national State, Canada, to ask for its diplomatic protection. For the above reasons, the Court is of the opinion that Belgium (P) lacks standing to bring this action.

ANALYSIS

The Restatement of the Foreign Relations Law of the United States, § 185, states that failure of a State to pay just compensation for the taking of the property of an alien is wrongful under international law, regardless of whether the taking itself is conceived as wrongful. Such a wrongful taking is characterized either as tortious conduct or as unjust enrichment.

Quicknotes

DIPLOMATIC PROTECTION The act by which a State, on behalf of one of its citizens who is an injured party, intervenes when a rule of international law has been violated.

EQUITY Fairness; justice; the determination of a matter consistent with principles of fairness and not in strict compliance with rules of law.

EXPROPRIATION The government's taking of property pursuant to its eminent domain powers.

NATIONALITY The country in which a person is born or naturalized.

SHAREHOLDER An individual who owns shares of stock in a corporation.

STATE OF INCORPORATION Where a corporation's articles of incorporation are filed.

CHAPTER **8**

Rules on State Responsibility

Quick Reference Rules of Law

Application of the Convention on the Prevention and Punishment of the Crime of Genocide (Bosnia and Herzegovina v. Serbia and Montenegro)

State (P) v. State (D)

2007 I.C.J. 191

NATURE OF CASE: Proceedings in the International Court of Justice to determine whether a State, through the attribution to the State of the conduct of its organs or individuals or entities, had committed genocide.

FACT SUMMARY: Bosnia and Herzegovina (P) contended that Serbia and Montenegro (D), which later became known as the Federal Republic of Yugoslavia ("the F.R.Y.") (D), was responsible for acts of genocide on the theory such acts could be attributed to the F.R.Y. (D), either because the acts were committed by a F.R.Y. (D) organ, or because they were committed by individuals or entities acting under the direction or control of the F.R.Y. (D).

RULE OF LAW

(1) Conduct may not be attributed to a State as having been committed by an organ of the State where the conduct has been committed by persons, groups, or entities that are neither de jure nor de facto organs of the State or are not wholly dependent on the State.

(2) Conduct may not be attributed to a State where the conduct has been committed by persons, groups, or entities that have not in fact been acting on the instructions of, or under the direction or control of, the State.

FACTS: The Socialist Federal Republic of Yugoslavia ("the S.F.R.Y.") began to break up in the early 1990s, and the republics of Bosnia and Herzegovina (P), Croatia, Macedonia, and Slovenia declared independence. Serbia and Montenegro (D) eventually declared themselves the Federal Republic of Yugoslavia ("the F.R.Y.") (D). Bosnian Serbs attempted to create their own republic, Republika Srpska, with their own army, the Vojska Reublike Srpske ("the V.R.S.") that was headed by Ratko Mladic. During armed conflicts that arose in 1992–1995 within Bosnia and Herzegovina (P), a massacre was perpetrated by Serbian forces on 8000 Bosnian Muslim men of fighting age in a small village called Srebrenica in July 1995. In 1993, Bosnia and Herzegovina (P) brought suit against the F.R.Y. (Serbia and Montenegro) (D) in the International Court of Justice (I.C.J.), claiming violations of the Convention on the Prevention and Punishment of the Crime of Genocide, on the theory the F.R.Y. (D) was responsible for the actions of the Serbian forces. The Court framed the key issue as whether the massacres committed at Srebrenica were attributable, in whole or in part, to the F.R.Y. The Court broke this question into two parts. The first was whether the acts committed at Srebrenica were perpetrated by F.R.Y. (D) organs, i.e., by persons or entities whose conduct was necessarily attributable to it, because they were in fact the instruments of its action. If this question was answered in the negative, the Court believed it had to ascertain whether the acts in question were committed by persons who, while not F.R.Y. (D) organs, did nevertheless act on the instructions of, or under the direction or control of, the F.R.Y. (D).

ISSUE:

(1) May conduct be attributed to a State as having been committed by an organ of the State where the conduct has been committed by persons, groups, or entities that are neither de jure nor de facto organs of the State or are not wholly dependent on the State?

(2) May conduct be attributed to a State where the conduct has been committed by persons, groups, or entities that have not in fact been acting on the instructions of, or under the direction or control of, the State?

HOLDING AND DECISION: [Judge not Stated in casebook excerpt.]

(1) No. Conduct may not be attributed to a State as having been committed by an organ of the State where the conduct has been committed by persons, groups, or entities that are neither de jure nor de facto organs of the State or are not wholly dependent on the State. This issue relates to the well-established rule of State responsibility that the conduct of any State organ is to be considered an act of the State under international law, therefore giving rise to the responsibility of the State if the conduct constitutes a breach of an international obligation of the State. This is a rule of customary international law that was codified in Article 4 of the International Law Commission (ILC) Articles on State Responsibility. Here, there is no evidence the Serbian forces were de jure organs of the F.R.Y. (D). The army of the F.R.Y. (D) did not take part in the massacres, and there is no evidence the political leaders of the State had any part in it. Further, there is no evidence V.R.S. officers or Mladic were, according to the internal law of the F.R.Y. (D), officers in the F.R.Y. (D) army. There is no doubt F.R.Y (D) was providing substantial financial support, in addition to other support, to the Serbian

Continued on next page.

forces that carried out the genocide, but that does not automatically make them organs of the F.R.Y. (D). Instead, the V.R.S. officers were appointed by the president of the Republika Srpska and took their orders therefrom. Bosnia and Herzegovina (P), however, also argue those who committed the acts of genocide at Srebrenica were de facto organs of the F.R.Y. (D). It is possible to attribute to a State the conduct of persons, groups, or entities who, while they do not have the legal status of State organs under the State's internal law, are de facto organs of the State, on the theory they act under strict control by the State. This is so in cases where the persons, groups or entities act in "complete dependence" on the State, of which they are ultimately merely the instrument. Here, however, the evidence fails to show that the Republika Srpska or the V.R.S. were mere instruments through which the F.R.Y. (D) was acting, or as lacking any real autonomy. The acts of genocide at Srebrenica cannot therefore be attributed to the F.R.Y. (D) under the "complete dependence" theory.

(2) No. Conduct may not be attributed to a State where the conduct has been committed by persons, groups, or entities that have not in fact been acting on the instructions of, or under the direction or control of, the State. As a matter of customary law, conduct that has been committed on the instructions of a State, or under its direction or control, may be attributed to the State. This rule is laid down in Article 8 ILC Articles on State Responsibility. However, here, there is no evidence that supports finding those who committed acts of genocide at Srebrenica were acting pursuant to the F.R.Y.'s (D) instructions, or under its direction or control. For the purpose of determining this issue, it is not necessary to show the persons, groups or entities who performed the acts were in a relationship of "complete dependence" on the State, but it has to be proved either they acted in accordance with that State's instructions, or were under its "effective control," or (at least in some instances) were under its "overall control." "Effective control" is demonstrated by showing the State controlled all aspects of the operation in question. The "overall control" test, unlike the "effective control" test, does not require a showing every operation by the group was under supervision of the State, but that the State was in general control. The Appeals Chamber used the overall control test in the *Tadic´* case (IT-94-1-A, Judgment, 15 July 1999) to determine that acts committed by Bosnian Serbs rose to international responsibility of the F.R.Y. (D), on the basis of the overall control exercised by the F.R.Y. (D) over the Republika Srpska and the V.R.S., without there being any need to prove each operation during which acts were committed in breach of international law was carried out on the F.R.Y.'s instructions, or under its effective control. The use of the overall control test, while it may have been appropriate in the *Tadic´* case, where the Appeals Chamber used the test solely to determine whether the armed conflict at issue was international, is not suitable for answering the question presented here of State responsibility for acts committed by paramilitary units or armed forces that are not among its official organs The two issues are distinct, and logic does not require the same test be used to resolve the two separate issues—which are very different in nature. Further, the "overall control" test has the major drawback of broadening the scope of State responsibility beyond the fundamental international law principle that a State is responsible only for its own conduct, and for this reason, the test is unsuitable here. That leaves the "effective control" test. Under that test, the evidence fails to demonstrate that the F.R.Y. (D) was involved in the planning of the acts committed at Srebrenica, or that it incited them. Accordingly, it cannot be said the F.R.Y. (D) effectively controlled those who committed those acts, and, therefore, the F.R.Y. (D) is not responsible under international law for the massacres.

ANALYSIS

In rejecting the use of the "overall control" test, and distinguishing the use of that test in the *Tadić* case, the Court observed the Intl. Crim. Trib. for the former Yugoslavia (ICTY) was not called upon in *Tadić*, nor is it in general called upon, to rule on questions of State responsibility, since that tribunal's jurisdiction is criminal and extends over persons only. Thus, in the Court's view, in the *Tadić* judgment, the tribunal addressed an issue that was not indispensable for the exercise of its jurisdiction. Thus, the Court did not perceive *Tadić* as persuasive precedent on the issues of general international law relating to State responsibility presented in this case, notwithstanding the ICTY expressed its belief the "overall control" test was appropriate for determining State responsibility for acts by paramilitary units or armed forces that are not among a State's official organs.

Quicknotes

BREACH The violation of an obligation imposed pursuant to contract or law, by acting or failing to act.

GENOCIDE The systematic killing of a particular group.

INTERNATIONAL LAW The body of law applicable to dealings between nations.

Barcelona Traction, Light and Power Company, Ltd. (Belgium v. Spain)

Shareholders (P) v. Corporation (D)

1970 I.C.J. 3

NATURE OF CASE: Proceeding before the International Court of Justice.

FACT SUMMARY: Belgium (P) claimed that Spain (D) should be held responsible for injury to a Canadian corporation operating in Spain.

RULE OF LAW

When a State admits into its territory foreign investments or foreign nationals, it assumes an obligation concerning their treatment based on general international law.

FACTS: Belgium (P) sued Spain (D) on behalf of Belgian nationals (P) who had invested in a Canadian corporation (Barcelona Traction, Light and Power Co., Ltd.). Belgium (P) alleged that Spain (D) was responsible for acts in violation of international law that had caused injury to the Canadian corporation and its Belgian shareholders (P).

ISSUE: When a State admits into its territory foreign investments or foreign nationals, does it assume an obligation concerning their treatment based on general international law?

HOLDING AND DECISION: [Judge not stated in casebook excerpt.] Yes. When a State admits into its territory foreign investments or foreign nationals, it assumes an obligation concerning their treatment based on general international law. An essential distinction should be drawn between those obligations of a State toward the international community as a whole and those arising from the field of diplomatic protection. If a breach of an obligation that is the subject of diplomatic protection occurs, only the party to whom an international obligation is due can bring a claim.

ANALYSIS

The Court mentioned the basic rights of all human persons to be protected against slavery and racial discrimination as deriving from basic general international law. Such rights may derive from international instruments of a universal or quasi-universal character. Such obligations are obligations *erga omnes,* that is, all States have a legal interest in their protection.

Quicknotes

DIPLOMATIC PROTECTION The act by which a State, on behalf of one of its citizens who is an injured party, intervenes when a rule of international law has been violated.

ERGA OMNES Toward all.

Rainbow Warrior (New Zealand v. France)

[Parties not identified.]

France-New Zealand Arbitration Tribunal, 82 I.L.R. 500, 551-64 (1990)

NATURE OF CASE: Arbitration regarding removal of prisoners.

FACT SUMMARY: France removed two agents convicted of destroying a ship docked in New Zealand on the basis that they required emergency medical treatment.

RULE OF LAW

The wrongfulness of an act of a State not in conformity with an international obligation is precluded by the "distress" of the author State if there exists a situation of extreme peril in which the organ of the State has, at that particular moment, no means of saving himself or persons entrusted to his care other than to act in a manner inconsistent with the requirements of the obligation at issue.

FACTS: A team of French agents destroyed a civilian vessel docked in New Zealand. Agents Mafart and Prieur were extradited and New Zealand sought reparations from the incident. Following the transfer of the two agents to a French military facility, they were later transported to Paris on the basis that they each needed medical treatment. The dispute was submitted to an arbitral tribunal. New Zealand demanded a declaration that France had breached its obligations and ordered that it return the agents to the facility for the remainder of their sentences.

ISSUE: Is the wrongfulness of an act of a State not in conformity with an international obligation precluded by the "distress" of the author State if there exists a situation of extreme peril in which the organ of the State has, at that particular moment, no means of saving himself or persons entrusted to his care other than to act in a manner inconsistent with the requirements of the obligation at issue?

HOLDING AND DECISION: [Judge not stated in casebook excerpt.] Yes. The wrongfulness of an act of a State not in conformity with an international obligation is precluded by the "distress" of the author State if there exists a situation of extreme peril in which the organ of the State has, at that particular moment, no means of saving himself or persons entrusted to his care other than to act in a manner inconsistent with the requirements of the obligation at issue. Three conditions here would be required to justify France's conduct: (1) very exceptional circumstances of extreme urgency involving medical or other considerations, provided prompt recognition of such circumstances is provided by New Zealand; (2) the reestablishment of the original situation of compliance; and (3) a good faith effort to try to obtain the consent of New Zealand. The unilateral removal of Mafart without obtaining New Zealand's consent was justified; however, the removal of Prieur was a material breach of France's obligations.

ANALYSIS

The court rejects France's contention that the circumstances here constituted a force majeure. "Force majeure" is usually invoked to justify unintentional acts and refers to "unforeseen external events" that render it "materially impossible" to act in conformity with the obligation.

Quicknotes

FORCE MAJEURE CLAUSE Included in contracts to protect against nonperformance due to causes outside control of the parties; unforeseen external event that results in impossibility.

MATERIAL BREACH Breach of a contract's terms by one party that is so substantial as to relieve the other party from its obligations pursuant thereto.

UNILATERAL One-sided; involving only one person.

Gabčíkovo-Nagymaros Project (Hungary/Slovakia)

Treaty partners jointly presenting questions to the International Court of Justice

1997 I.C.J. 7

NATURE OF CASE: Proceeding before the International Court of Justice to determine, inter alia, whether a "state of necessity" justified the suspension and abandonment of obligations under a bilateral treaty.

FACT SUMMARY: Hungary claimed it was no longer bound to a bilateral treaty entered into with Czechoslovakia regarding a joint water management project on the Danube River, contending it was justified in abandoning and suspending works due to a "state of necessity" arising from grave ecological threats posed by the project.

RULE OF LAW

A party to a bilateral treaty is not entitled to suspend or abandon its treaty obligations on the basis of a "state of necessity" where a peril arising from the performance of the treaty that is claimed to be threatening an essential interest of the party is uncertain and not imminent.

FACTS: Hungary and Czechoslovakia in 1977 entered into a treaty for the construction and operation of a system of locks on the Danube River, which project was started but not completed. The Danube forms the border of these countries for a part of their entire borders. With the passing of time, there was also increased awareness of potentially negative ecological impacts of the project. In 1989, Hungary first suspended, then abandoned, its part of the project, in response to criticism of the project from its citizens. The parties tried, but failed, to negotiate a mutually satisfactory solution. Czechoslovakia began work in 1991 on an alternative project, known as Variant C, but this alternative was unacceptable to Hungary and in 1992, Hungary gave notice of termination of the treaty. The two countries also underwent major transformations in government, with Czechoslovakia dividing into two separate States in 1993, one of which was Slovakia. Hungary and Slovakia later petitioned to the International Court of Justice to decide whether Hungary was entitled to suspend and abandon its operations on the basis, inter alia, of a "state of necessity" arising from what Hungary claimed were grave ecological threats posed by the project.

ISSUE: Is a party to a bilateral treaty entitled to suspend or abandon its treaty obligations on the basis of a "state of necessity" where a peril arising from the performance of the treaty that is claimed to be threatening an essential interest of the party is uncertain and not imminent?

HOLDING AND DECISION: [Judge not stated in casebook excerpt.] No. A party to a bilateral treaty is not entitled to suspend or abandon its treaty obligations on the basis of a "state of necessity" where a peril arising from the performance of the treaty that is claimed to be threatening an essential interest of the party is uncertain and not imminent. The existence of a state of necessity must be evaluated in light of the criteria set forth in Article 33 of the Draft Articles on the International Responsibility of States, which reflect customary international law. These criteria are: the state of necessity must be occasioned by an "essential interest" of the State authoring the act conflicting with its international obligations; interest must be threatened by a grave and imminent peril; the act being challenged is the only means of safeguarding that interest; the act challenged must not have seriously impaired an essential interest of the State toward which the obligation existed; and the State that authored the act must not have contributed to the State of necessity. Here, Hungary's concern for its natural environment constitutes an "essential interest," as a State's safeguarding of ecological balance has come to be considered an "essential interest" of all States. However, the evidence shows even Hungary was uncertain about the project's ecological impacts and sought scientific studies to determine the extent of those impacts. As serious as those uncertainties might have been, they alone cannot objectively establish a "peril" sufficient to support a claim of state of necessity. Such a peril must be established at the relevant point in time; a mere apprehension of a possible "peril" is insufficient, since a peril must be grave and imminent. Nevertheless, it is possible a peril appearing in the long term might be "imminent" as soon as it is established, at the relevant point in time, the realization of that peril, however far off it might be, is not any less certain or inevitable. Here, any ecological dangers were long-term and uncertain, so at the time Hungary suspended, and then abandoned, its obligations, it could not be said the peril was "imminent," especially given there was evidence the waters of the Danube had been steadily improving. Additionally, Hungary could have resorted to means other than suspension and abandonment to respond to potential dangers, as it had some control over the river's water flows. For all these reasons, the perils invoked by Hungary, without determining their gravity, were insufficiently established and were not imminent, so Hungary failed to establish a State of necessity. [Judgment for Slovakia as to this issue.]

ANALYSIS

The ground of State of necessity, when used to preclude the wrongfulness of an act not in conformity with an

Continued on next page.

international obligation, is accepted only in exceptional circumstances and under very strictly defined conditions that must be cumulatively satisfied. Here, the Court effectively determined such conditions were not met, since Hungary had a degree of control over potential environmental impacts of the project, and the perils it pointed to as justifying its breach were neither sufficiently certain nor imminent. Based on its conclusions, the Court did not need to reach the issue of whether the perils invoked by Hungary were "grave."

Quicknotes

NECESSITY A defense to liability for unlawful activity where the conduct is unavoidable and is justified by preventing an injury to life or health.

REPUDIATION The actions or statements of a party to a contract that evidence the party's intent not to perform, or to continue performance of, the party's duties or obligations thereunder.

TREATY An agreement between two or more nations for the benefit of the general public.

Gabčíkovo-Nagymaros Project (Hungary/Slovakia)

Treaty partners jointly presenting questions to the International Court of Justice

1997 I.C.J. 7

NATURE OF CASE: Proceeding before the International Court of Justice to determine, inter alia, whether countermeasures taken by a party to a bilateral treaty in response to the other party's alleged breach were justifiable.

FACT SUMMARY: Hungary and Czechoslovakia (which later became Slovakia, in part) in 1977 entered into a bilateral treaty for the construction and operation of a system of locks on the Danube River. Slovakia contended its diversion of waters on the Danube River, pursuant to a plan known as Variant C, was justified as a countermeasure to Hungary's failure to comply with its obligations under the treaty.

RULE OF LAW

A State's countermeasure to another State's failure to meet its obligations under a bilateral treaty is not justifiable where the countermeasure is not a proportionate response to the injury suffered by the State taking the countermeasure.

FACTS: Hungary and Czechoslovakia in 1977 entered into a treaty for the construction and operation of a system of locks on the Danube River, which project was started but not completed. The Danube forms the border of these countries for a part of their entire borders. With the passing of time, there was also increased awareness of potentially negative ecological impacts of the project. In 1989, Hungary first suspended, then abandoned, its part of the project, in response to criticism of the project from its citizens. The parties tried, but failed, to negotiate a mutually satisfactory solution. Czechoslovakia began work in 1991 on an alternative project, known as Variant C, but this alternative was unacceptable to Hungary and, in 1992, Hungary gave notice of termination of the treaty. The two countries also underwent major transformations in government, with Czechoslovakia dividing into two separate States in 1993, one of which was Slovakia. Hungary and Slovakia later petitioned to the International Court of Justice (I.C.J.) to decide whether Hungary was entitled to suspend and abandon its operations. One of the issues before the I.C.J. was whether Czechoslovakia's adoption of Variant C—which the Court ruled was on its own an internationally wrongful act—was a justifiable countermeasure to Hungary's failure to comply with its obligations under the treaty.

ISSUE: Is a State's countermeasure to another State's failure to meet its obligations under a bilateral treaty justifiable where the countermeasure is not a proportionate response to the injury suffered by the State taking the countermeasure?

HOLDING AND DECISION: [Judge not stated in casebook excerpt.] No. A State's countermeasure to another State's failure to meet its obligations under a bilateral treaty is not justifiable where the countermeasure is not a proportionate response to the injury suffered by the State taking the countermeasure. An important consideration in determining whether a countermeasure is justified is that the effects of a countermeasure must be commensurate with the injury suffered, considering the rights involved. It is established that the States have a common legal right in a navigable river and have equal riparian rights therein. This principle is increasingly being applied to non-navigational uses of international watercourses, as well. Thus, Czechoslovakia's unilateral assumption of control of a shared resource, thereby depriving Hungary of its rights to an equitable and reasonable share of the Danube waters, with continuing adverse ecological impacts on certain riparian areas, failed to respect the proportionality that is required under international law. Accordingly, Variant C, with its diversion of Danube waters, was not a lawful countermeasure. [Judgment for Hungary as to this issue.]

ANALYSIS

In addition to being proportionate, a legal countermeasure must meet other conditions. First, the countermeasure must be taken in response to another State's unlawful act and must be directed at the wrongdoing State. Here, the Court determined this condition was satisfied, since Variant C was taken in response to Hungary's wrongful acts. Second, the injured State must demand the wrongdoing State cease its wrongful conduct or make reparations therefor. Here, Czechoslovakia repeatedly requested Hungary resume its treaty obligations, and, on this basis, the Court determined this condition had been satisfied. Another condition for the lawfulness of a countermeasure is that its purpose must be to induce the wrongdoing State to comply with its obligations, and the measure must therefore be reversible. Here, having determined Variant C was not a lawful countermeasure on proportionality grounds, the Court concluded it did not need to assess whether this final condition had been met.

Quicknotes

RIPARIAN RIGHT The right of an owner of real property to the use of water naturally flowing through his or her land.

TREATY An agreement between two or more nations for the benefit of the general public.

UNILATERAL One-sided; involving only one person.

CHAPTER 9

Dispute Settlement

Quick Reference Rules of Law

PAGE

Armed Activities on the Territory of the Congo (New Application: 2002) (Democratic Republic of the Congo v. Rwanda)

State (P) v. State (D)

2006 I.C.J. 6

NATURE OF CASE: Proceeding in the International Court of Justice.

FACT SUMMARY: The Democratic Republic of the Congo (P) brought an application against Rwanda (D), and Rwanda (D) challenged the jurisdiction of the International Court of Justice.

RULE OF LAW

Where one party to a treaty excludes dispute settlement obligations under the treaty before becoming a party and fails to take formal acts to bring about withdrawal of the reservation, the International Court of Justice lacks jurisdiction based on that treaty.

FACTS: The Democratic Republic of the Congo (DRC) (P) brought an application against Rwanda (D). The DRC (P) tried to base the jurisdiction of the International Court of Justice (I.C.J.) on nine treaties with dispute settlement clauses that provided for such jurisdiction. Rwanda (D) was not party to two of the treaties, and with respect to the other seven, Rwanda (D) excluded dispute settlement obligations. Rwanda (D) challenged the jurisdiction of the I.C.J. on the nature of its obligations. [The excerpt omits discussion of some of the treaties. The treaties involved were: Convention on the Prevention and Punishment of the Crime of Genocide, Article IX; Convention on Racial Discrimination, Article 22; Convention on Discrimination against Women, Article 29; World Health Organization Constitution, Article 75; Unesco Convention, Article XIV; Montreal Convention for the Suppression of Unlawful Acts against the Safety of Civil Aviation, Article 14; Vienna Convention on the Law of Treaties, Article 66; Convention Against Torture and Other Cruel, Inhuman or Degrading Treatment or Punishment; and Convention on Privileges and Immunities of the Specialized Agencies. Rwanda (D) was not party to the last two.]

ISSUE: Where one party to a treaty excludes dispute settlement obligations under the treaty before becoming a party and fails to take formal acts to bring about withdrawal of the reservation, does the International Court of Justice lack jurisdiction based on that treaty?

HOLDING AND DECISION: [Judge not Stated in casebook excerpt.] Yes. Where one party to a treaty excludes dispute settlement obligations under the treaty before becoming a party and fails to take formal acts to bring about withdrawal of the reservation, the International Court of Justice lacks jurisdiction based on that treaty. First, Rwanda (D) may have committed itself at the time of a 1993 peace agreement to withdrawing all reservations to human rights treaties, and the Rwanda (D) Minister of Justice effectuated the withdrawal, but Rwanda (D) never took formal acts to bring about withdrawal of the reservation. A decision to withdraw a reservation within a State's domestic legal order is not the same as implementation of that decision by the national authorities within the international legal order, which can only occur by notification to the other State parties to the treaty in question through the Secretary-General of the United Nations. Second, the existence of a dispute that implicates peremptory norms of general international law is not an exception to the principle that jurisdiction always depends on the consent of parties. The DRC (P) may have made numerous protests against Rwanda's (D) actions at the bilateral and multilateral levels, and therefore satisfied preconditions to the seisin of the I.C.J. in the compromissory clauses within some of the treaties, including the Convention on Discrimination against Women, but whatever the dispute, there was no evidence that the DRC (P) sought negotiations with respect to interpretation or application of the Convention. The DRC (P) also failed to show that it initiated arbitration proceedings with Rwanda (D) under the Convention on Discrimination against Women. The treaty cannot therefore form the basis of jurisdiction.

ANALYSIS

The I.C.J.'s analysis of all treaties involved was similar to that included in the casebook excerpt. The main principle here is that where a State has apparently not granted consent to the jurisdiction of the I.C.J., the I.C.J. will not advance the case past the preliminary matter of jurisdiction, whatever atrocities have in fact been committed by the non-consenting State. Additionally, where, as here, there is evidence of non-consent, reversal of the position requires an overt act by the State, in order to convince the Court that, after all, consent to the I.C.J.'s jurisdiction was granted.

Quicknotes

ERGA OMNES Toward.

DÉCRET-LOI Statutory law.

Military and Paramilitary Activities in and Against Nicaragua (Nicaragua v. United States)

State (P) v. Militarily intervening state (D)

1984 I.C.J. 392

NATURE OF CASE: Determination of court's jurisdiction in proceedings before the International Court of Justice alleging unlawful military and paramilitary acts.

FACT SUMMARY: Nicaragua (P) filed suit in 1984 in the International Court of Justice (I.C.J. or "the Court") against the United States (or "the U.S.") (D), claiming the U.S. (D) was responsible for illegal military and paramilitary activities in and against Nicaragua (P). The U.S. (D) challenged the I.C.J.'s jurisdiction to hear the case

RULE OF LAW

Under Article 36 of the International Court of Justice's Statute of the Court, a party's attempt to modify its declaration accepting the Court's jurisdiction does not deprive the Court of jurisdiction to hear a case involving the party where the party has failed to abide by its own notice terms made in the declaration.

FACTS: Nicaragua (P) filed suit on April 9, 1984 in the International Court of Justice (I.C.J.) against the United States (or "the U.S.") (D), claiming it was responsible for illegal military and paramilitary activities in and against Nicaragua (P). The United States (D) challenged I.C.J.'s jurisdiction to hear the case. Though the United States (D) had deposited a declaration accepting the compulsory jurisdiction of the Court in 1946, it attempted to qualify that declaration in an April 6, 1984, notification (the "1984 notification") referring to the declaration of 1946 and stating in part that the declaration "shall not apply to disputes with any Central American State. . . ." To be able to rely on the U.S. Declaration of 1946, Nicaragua (P) had to show it was a State "accepting the same obligation." Although Nicaragua (P) had in 1929 made a declaration accepting the jurisdiction of the Permanent Court of International Justice (P.C.I.J.), the I.C.J.'s predecessor, it had never filed an instrument ratifying the P.C.I.J.'s Statute. Nicaragua (P) did, however, ratify the United Nations (U.N.) Charter. Accordingly, the I.C.J. held that Nicaragua's (P) 1929 acceptance was still in effect, and that once it ratified the U.N. Charter, it became subject to the I.C.J.'s compulsory jurisdiction. Thus, Nicaragua (P) had accepted "the same obligation." In this regard, the Court pointed out that numerous official international publications had placed Nicaragua (P) on the list of those States that had accepted the I.C.J.'s compulsory jurisdiction.

ISSUE: Under Article 36 of the International Court of Justice's Statute of the Court, does a party's attempt to modify its declaration accepting the Court's jurisdiction deprive the Court of jurisdiction to hear a case involving the party where the party has failed to abide by its own notice terms made in the declaration?

HOLDING AND DECISION: [Judge not stated in casebook excerpt.] No. Under Article 36 of the International Court of Justice's Statute of the Court, a party's attempt to modify its declaration accepting the Court's jurisdiction does not deprive the Court of jurisdiction to hear a case involving the party where the party has failed to abide by its own notice terms made in the declaration. Nicaragua (P) concedes that if the 1984 notification is a valid modification or termination of the 1946 Declaration as to Nicaragua (P), the I.C.J. lacks jurisdiction under Article 36 of its Statute. However, Nicaragua (P) contends the 1984 notification was ineffective as an invalid attempt to unilaterally modify the 1946 Declaration, unless the U.S. (D) had expressly reserved to make such a modification—which it had not. The U.S. (D) maintained the notification was a valid modification of the Declaration and was valid against Nicaragua (P) regardless of whether it was characterized as a modification or termination. Declarations of acceptance of the compulsory jurisdiction of the Court are facultative, unilateral engagements, which States are absolutely free to make or not to make. In making the declaration, a State is equally free either to do so unconditionally and without limit of time for its duration, or to qualify it with conditions or reservations. In particular, it may limit its effect to disputes arising after a certain date, or it may specify how long the declaration itself shall remain in force, or what notice (if any) will be required to terminate it. However, the unilateral nature of declarations does not signify the State making the declaration is free to amend the scope and the contents of its solemn commitments as it pleases. Thus, here the most important question becomes whether the U.S. (D) was free to ignore the clause of six months' notice it had appended to the 1946 Declaration. Under this clause, the U.S. (D) had obligated itself to other States to not have any modification become effective until six months after the U.S. (D) had given notice of the modification. The U.S. (D) argues because Nicaragua's (P) 1929 Declaration was of undefined duration and, therefore, could be terminated immediately absent any notice, Nicaragua (P) had not accepted the same obligation as had the U.S. (D). This argument is rejected, since the notion of reciprocity is concerned with the scope and substance of the commitments entered,

Continued on next page.

including reservations, and not with the formal conditions of their creation, duration or extinction. In other words, reciprocity cannot be invoked in order to excuse departure from the terms of a State's own declaration, whatever its scope, limitations or conditions. Thus, while the U.S. (D) cannot invoke reciprocity to justify its action in making the 1984 notification without adequate notice, Nicaragua (P) can invoke the six months' notice provision against the U.S. (D) on the basis the notice was an undertaking that was integral to the instrument that contained it, i.e., the Declaration of 1946. In addition, the U.S. (D) acted on April 6, 1984, in effort to bar Nicaragua's (P) Application, which was filed three days later. To be able to rely on reciprocity, the Nicaraguan Declaration would have to be terminable immediately, but it is far from clear under international law that declarations with indefinite durations are, in fact, immediately terminable. Requirements of good faith require that they be treated under the law of treaties, which requires a reasonable time for withdrawal from or termination of treaties that contain no provision regarding the duration of their validity. Since Nicaragua (P) has, in fact, not manifested any intention to withdraw its own declaration, the question of what reasonable period of notice would legally be required does not need to be reached, but, in any event, three days is not "reasonable time." The Court has jurisdiction to entertain Nicaragua's (P) Application. [Judgment for Nicaragua (P) as to this issue.]

ANALYSIS

Seemingly in response to this decision, the U.S. (D), on October 7, 1985, terminated the U.S. (D) acceptance of compulsory jurisdiction, with effect six months from that date (thus, this time around, complying with its own notice provision). However, the U.S. (D) is not the only country that has either terminated acceptance of the Court's jurisdiction, or never accepted it in the first place. In fact, of the five members of the Security Council, only the United Kingdom currently accepts the Court's compulsory jurisdiction (but with significant limitations). This state of the I.C.J.'s compulsory jurisdiction illustrates the principle the I.C.J. has only as much power as that agreed to by the States.

Quicknotes

JURISDICTION The authority of a court to hear and declare judgment in respect to a particular matter.

RECIPROCITY The courtesy of the same rights and benefits of its own citizens that a state provides the citizens of another state in exchange for the similar treatment of its own citizens.

Military and Paramilitary Activities in and Against Nicaragua (Nicaragua v. United States)

State (P) v. Militarily intervening state (D)

1984 I.C.J. 392

NATURE OF CASE: Determination of the admissibility of an application in proceedings before the International Court of Justice alleging unlawful military and paramilitary acts.

FACT SUMMARY: Nicaragua (P) filed suit in 1984 in the International Court of Justice (I.C.J.) against the United States (U.S.) (D), claiming the U.S. (D) was responsible for illegal military and paramilitary activities in and against Nicaragua (P). The U.S. (D) challenged the admissibility of Nicaragua's (P) application.

RULE OF LAW

The application by a State to the International Court of Justice is admissible where no grounds exist to exclude it.

FACTS: Nicaragua (P) filed suit in 1984 in the International Court of Justice (I.C.J. or "the Court") against the United States (U.S.) (D), claiming it was responsible for illegal military and paramilitary activities in and against Nicaragua (P). The U.S. (D) challenged the I.C.J.'s jurisdiction to hear the case, and it also challenged the admissibility of Nicaragua's (P) application on five separate grounds. The first ground was that Nicaragua (P) failed to bring before the Court parties whose presence and participation was necessary for the rights of those parties to be protected and for the adjudication of the issues raised in the application. The second ground was that Nicaragua's (P) allegations constituted a single fundamental claim—the U.S. (D) was engaged in an unlawful use of armed force, a breach of the peace, or acts of aggression against Nicaragua (P)—that was committed to the U.N. Security Council. The third ground was that a draft resolution made by Nicaragua (P) a few days before it submitted its application, corresponding to the claims submitted in the application, failed to achieve a majority in the Security Council, so its application in effect amounted to an appeal to the Court from an adverse consideration in the Security Council. The fourth was that the I.C.J. is unable to deal with situations involving ongoing armed conflict, and the fifth was that Nicaragua (P) failed to exhaust established processes for the resolution of the conflicts that were the subject of its application.

ISSUE: Is the application by a State to the International Court of Justice admissible where no grounds exist to exclude it?

HOLDING AND DECISION: [Judge not stated in casebook excerpt.] Yes. The application by a State to the International Court of Justice is admissible where no grounds exist to exclude it. The first ground—Nicaragua (P) failed to bring forth necessary parties—fails because there is no "indispensable parties" rule. Other States that believe they are affected may institute separate proceedings or intervene as a third party. The second and third—Nicaragua (P) is asking the Court to consider the existence of a threat to peace, or unlawful use of armed force, or acts of aggression, which is the exclusive province of the Security Council, and the Security Council voted down a resolution paralleling the claims in the application, so the application is effectively an appeal from an adverse Security Council decision—fails because the I.C.J. can exercise jurisdiction concurrent with that of the Security Council. Both proceedings can be pursued *pari passu.* Moreover, the subject of the application, which does not relate to ongoing armed conflict, but rather disputes between two States, requires the peaceful settlement of those disputes through the Court. Additionally, Article 24 of the U.N. Charter endows the Security Council with primary responsibility for maintaining international peace and security, so it cannot be said that such responsibility is exclusive. The Council has functions of a political nature assigned to it, whereas the Court exercises purely judicial functions. Both organs can therefore perform their separate but complementary functions with respect to the same events. Finally, in this regard, as to the inherent right to self-defense, which Nicaragua (P) raised before the Security Council, a determination, if any, relating to this "right" will be a legal one, and the Court cannot be precluded from adjudicating this right merely because there is a procedure for the States concerned to report to the Security Council in connection with this issue. The fourth ground—the I.C.J. is unable to deal with situations involving ongoing armed conflict—is not a show-stopper because any judgment on the merits is limited to the evidence submitted and proven by the litigants. The fifth ground—Nicaragua (P) failed to exhaust established processes, and the case is incompatible with the Contadora process, to which Nicaragua (P) is a party—fails because there is nothing compelling the I.C.J. to decline to consider one aspect of a dispute just because the dispute has other aspects. The fact negotiations are being conducted subject to the Contadora process does not pose any legal obstacle to the exercise by the Court of its judicial function. In addition, there is no requirement of prior exhaustion of regional negotiation processes as a precondition for submitting claims to the Court. For all these

Continued on next page.

reasons, the application is admissible. [Judgment for Nicaragua (P) as to this issue.]

ANALYSIS

A ground for inadmissibility, as this decision shows, can be considered as a legal bar to adjudication or as a matter requiring the exercise of prudential discretion in the interest of the integrity of the judicial function. Some of the grounds of inadmissibility presented by the United States (D), in fact, were presented in terms suggesting that they were matters of competence or jurisdiction rather than admissibility. The Court, however, determined that it was not of critical importance how they were classified in this respect.

Quicknotes

ADMISSIBILITY OF EVIDENCE Refers to whether particular evidence may be received by the court to aid the jury in determining the resolution of a controversy.

PARI PASSU Proportionally; at an equal pace.

Application of the International Convention on the Elimination of All Forms of Racial Discrimination (Georgia v. Russian Federation)

State (P) v. State (D)

2008 I.C.J. 353

NATURE OF CASE: Order on request for the indication of provisional measures.

FACT SUMMARY: Georgia (P) filed proceedings against the Russian Federation (D), claiming that Russia (D) engaged in ethnic cleansing in Georgia (P), in violation of the Convention on Elimination of Racial Discrimination (CERD).

RULE OF LAW

Under certain circumstances, the International Court of Justice may assess facts and order provisional measures to protect rights under international treaties without deciding the merits of a dispute.

FACTS: Georgia (P) filed proceedings against the Russian Federation (D), claiming violation of the Convention on Elimination of Racial Discrimination (CERD). Georgia (P) alleged that Russia (D) was engaging in ethnic cleansing in the South Ossetia and Abkhazia regions of Georgia (P). Georgia (P) asked the International Court of Justice to decide whether the circumstances required provision measures to protect rights under CERD, not to decide the merits of Georgia's (P) argument that Russia (D) breached CERD.

ISSUE: Under certain circumstances, may the International Court of Justice assess facts and order provisional measures to protect rights under international treaties without deciding the merits of a dispute?

HOLDING AND DECISION: [Judge not Stated in casebook excerpt.] Yes. Under certain circumstances, the International Court of Justice (I.C.J.) may assess facts and order provisional measures to protect rights under international treaties without deciding the merits of a dispute. The evidence shows that the Georgian population in the affected areas remains vulnerable, and there is an imminent risk that the rights of the population and of Georgia (P) under CERD may suffer irreparable prejudice without intervention. In addition, the I.C.J. has the power, under its Statute, to indicate measures to protect those rights, even if they are not exactly as requested, without prejudging the question of the jurisdiction of the I.C.J. to deal with the merits of the case. Therefore, both parties shall refrain from any act of racial discrimination against persons, groups of persons, or institutions, abstain from supporting racial discrimination, and do all in their power to prevent such discrimination.

ANALYSIS

The ruling of the I.C.J. went beyond what Georgia (P) asked for, which was to stop Russia (D) from engaging in racial discrimination and ethnic cleansing, by applying it to both parties. That is the way in which the I.C.J. used its statutory authority to indicate measures that were not exactly as requested. The protective measures are similar to common law preliminary injunction.

Quicknotes

BREACH The violation of an obligation imposed pursuant to contract or law, by acting or failing to act.

INJUNCTION A court order requiring a person to do, or prohibiting that person from doing, a specific act.

Request for Interpretation of the Judgment of 15 June 1962 in the Case Concerning *The Temple of Preah Vihear (Cambodia v. Thailand)* (Cambodia v. Thailand)

State (P) v. State (D)

2013 I.C.J. 281

NATURE OF CASE: Proceeding before the International Court of Justice to resolve a dispute over the interpretation and scope of a prior judgment.

FACT SUMMARY: In 1962, the International Court of Justice rendered a judgment Cambodia (P) was sovereign over the Temple of Preah Vihear. In 2011, Cambodia (P) sought the Court's interpretation of the 1962 judgment for a determination as to whether Cambodia (P) had sovereignty over the entire territory of the Temple's promontory.

RULE OF LAW

Under Article 60 of the Statute of the International Court of Justice, the Court may interpret a prior judgment where the States bound by the judgment have a difference of opinion as to whether the judgment decided a particular issue.

FACTS: In 1962, the International Court of Justice (I.C.J. or "the Court") rendered a judgment Cambodia (P) was sovereign over the Temple of Preah Vihear. In 2011, Cambodia (P) sought the Court's interpretation of the 1962 judgment for a determination as to whether Cambodia (P) had sovereignty over the entire territory of the Temple's promontory, so Thailand (D) would have to withdraw its forces stationed there. The Court, as a matter of interpretation, decided for Cambodia (P). In reaching its decision, the Court explicated the standard to be applied when a State seeks an interpretation of a prior judgment.

ISSUE: Under Article 60 of the Statute of the International Court of Justice, may the Court interpret a prior judgment where the States bound by the judgment have a difference of opinion as to whether the judgment decided a particular issue?

HOLDING AND DECISION: [Judge not stated in casebook excerpt.] Yes. Under Article 60 of the Statute of the International Court of Justice, the Court may interpret a prior judgment where the States bound by the judgment have a difference of opinion as to whether the judgment decided a particular issue. Under Article 60 of the Court's Statute, the Court's jurisdiction is not preconditioned on any other basis of jurisdiction as between the parties to the original case, and, the Court may entertain a request for interpretation where there is a "dispute" as to the meaning or scope of the prior judgment. The meaning of "dispute" in this context differs from the meaning of "dispute" in Article 36. Under Article 60, "dispute" means a difference of opinion as to the meaning or scope of the prior judgment, and such difference of opinion need not be manifested in any formal way; it is sufficient if the parties have in fact demonstrated that they hold opposite views regarding such meaning or scope. Further, such a dispute must relate to the operative clause of the prior judgment, rather than to any reasons for the judgment, except as such reasons are inseparable from the operative clause. Accordingly, a difference of opinion as to whether a point of law has or has not been decided also comes within the meaning of Article 60.

ANALYSIS

Under Article 98 of the Rules of the Court of the I.C.J., in the event of a dispute as to the meaning or scope of a judgment, any party bound by the judgment may make a request for its interpretation. In doing so, the party must indicate in its request the precise point or points in dispute.

Quicknotes

JURISDICTION The authority of a court to hear and declare judgment in respect to a particular matter.

Accordance with International Law of the Unilateral Declaration of Independence in Respect of Kosovo

[Parties not identified.]

I.C.J., Advisory Opinion, 2010 I.C.J. 403

NATURE OF CASE: Advisory opinion of the International Court of Justice as to whether a political body's unilateral declaration of independence was in accordance with international law.

FACT SUMMARY: The Provisional Institutions of Self-Government of Kosovo (Kosovo) unilaterally declared independence from Serbia in 2008, and the United Nations General Assembly asked the International Court of Justice to opine as to whether such declaration was in accordance with international law.

RULE OF LAW

The International Court of Justice will exercise jurisdiction in a case where it is called upon to render an advisory opinion absent compelling reasons for it to refuse to exercise such jurisdiction.

FACTS: The Provisional Institutions of Self-Government of Kosovo (Kosovo) unilaterally declared independence from Serbia in 2008, and the United Nations (U.N.) General Assembly asked the International Court of Justice (I.C.J. or "the Court") to render an advisory opinion as to whether such declaration was in accordance with international law. After determining it had jurisdiction, the Court analyzed whether there were any considerations that would prevent it from exercising that jurisdiction.

ISSUE: Will the International Court of Justice exercise jurisdiction in a case where it is called upon to render an advisory opinion absent compelling reasons for it to refuse to exercise such jurisdiction?

HOLDING AND DECISION: [Judge not stated in casebook excerpt.] Yes. The International Court of Justice will exercise jurisdiction in a case where it is called upon to render an advisory opinion absent compelling reasons for it to refuse to exercise such jurisdiction. Under Article 65 of the Court's Statute, the Court has discretion to decline to give an advisory opinion notwithstanding that jurisdictional requirements are met. However, the Court should not lightly refuse such a request, and should do so only if there are compelling reasons for its refusal. The argument has been advanced that the resolution requesting the advisory opinion here was made not to aid the General Assembly, but to serve the interests of the sole State that sponsored the resolution. The Court's advisory opinions are not given to States, however, and are given to the organs that have requested them. For this reason, the motives of States that sponsor or vote for resolutions seeking advisory opinions are irrelevant to the Court's determination of whether it will exercise its jurisdiction. Also unpersuasive is the argument the General Assembly failed to give a purpose for its request. The Court has consistently held that it is up to the organ requesting the advisory opinion to determine whether it needs the opinion for the proper performance of its functions. Additionally, considerations of adverse political consequences of an advisory opinion are not sufficiently compelling to cause the Court to refuse to render the opinion. That is because the Court cannot substitute its own view as to whether its opinion will likely have an adverse effect. An important consideration, though, is whether the Court should decline to render the requested advisory opinion on the ground the request came from the General Assembly, rather than the Security Council, which has taken measures for over ten years in Kosovo to ensure international peace and security. However, the General Assembly has also adopted resolutions relating to the situation in Kosovo. Although the request put to the Court concerns one aspect of a situation the Security Council has characterized as a threat to international peace and security, and continues to feature on the agenda of the Council in that capacity, that does not mean the General Assembly has no legitimate interest in the question. Given the General Assembly's broad powers to engage in discussions of international situations, and the fact Article 12 limits the General Assembly in making recommendations so as to protect the role of the Security Council, but does not limit its powers to engage in discussion, and does not completely limit its ability to take certain actions to promote international peace and security, the fact the request for the advisory opinion came from the General Assembly rather than the Security Council, in this case is not a compelling reason for the Court to decline to exercise its jurisdiction. The Court cannot determine what steps the General Assembly may wish to take after receiving the Court's opinion or what effect that opinion may have in relation to those steps. The General Assembly is entitled to discuss the declaration of independence and to make certain recommendations in respect of that or other aspects of the situation in Kosovo without trespassing on the powers of the Security Council. That being the case, the fact that, hitherto, the declaration of independence has been discussed only in the Security Council and the Council has been the organ that has taken action with regard to the situation in Kosovo does not constitute a compelling

Continued on next page.

reason for the Court to refuse to respond to the request from the General Assembly. Further, the fact that it will necessarily have to interpret and apply the provisions of Security Council resolution 1244 (1999) in the course of answering the question put by the General Assembly does not constitute a compelling reason not to respond to that question. While the interpretation and application of a decision of one of the political organs of the U.N. is, in the first place, the responsibility of the organ that took that decision, the Court, as the principal judicial organ of the U. N., has also frequently been required to consider the interpretation and legal effects of such decisions. Thus, where, as here, the General Assembly has a legitimate interest in the answer to a question, the fact that answer may turn, in part, on a decision of the Security Council is not sufficient to justify the Court in declining to give its opinion to the General Assembly. For all these reasons, the Court finds there are no compelling reasons for it to decline to exercise its jurisdiction in respect of the present request.

ANALYSIS

The discretion whether to respond to a request for an advisory opinion exists so as to protect the integrity of the Court's judicial function and its nature as the principal judicial organ of the United Nations. The Court is, nevertheless, mindful of the fact its answer to a request for an advisory opinion represents its participation in the activities of the United Nations, and, in principle, should not be refused, which is why the "compelling reason" standard for refusing to exercise jurisdiction has consistently been applied by the Court when considering whether to render an advisory opinion or not.

Quicknotes

ADVISORY OPINION A decision rendered at the request of an interested party as to how the court would rule should the particular issue arise.

UNILATERAL One-sided; involving only one person.

United States—Final Anti-Dumping Measures on Stainless Steel from Mexico

State (D) v. State (P)

WTO, App. Body, 47 I.L.M. 475 (2008)

NATURE OF CASE: Appeal to Appellate Body of the World Trade Organization.

FACT SUMMARY: Mexico (P) complained that the United States (D) violated Article VI of GATT 1994 and the Anti-Dumping Agreement by using incorrect methodology for calculation of margins of dumping. The panel that convened for the complaint did not follow the Appellate Body's prior holdings, and instead relied on panel reports that the Appellate Body had reversed.

RULE OF LAW

In ruling on a dispute brought before a World Trade Organization (WTO) panel, the panel must follow previously adopted Appellate Body reports addressing the same issues.

FACTS: Mexico (P) complained that the United States (D) violated Article VI of GATT 1994 and the Anti-Dumping Agreement by using incorrect methodology for calculation of margins of dumping. The Appellate Body of the World Trade Organization (WTO) had addressed similar complaints filed against the United States (D) by the European Community and Japan, but the panel that convened for Mexico's (P) complaint did not follow the Appellate Body's prior holdings, and instead relied on panel reports that the Appellate Body had reversed.

ISSUE: In ruling on a dispute brought before a World Trade Organization (WTO) panel, must the panel follow previously adopted Appellate Body reports addressing the same issues?

HOLDING AND DECISION: [Judge not identified.] Yes. In ruling on a dispute brought before a World Trade Organization (WTO) panel, the panel must follow previously adopted Appellate Body reports addressing the same issues. While Appellate Body reports are not binding, except with respect to resolving the particular dispute between the parties, subsequent panels are not free to disregard the legal interpretations and reasoning contained in previous Appellate Body reports that have been adopted. The Appellate Body functions to provide consistency and stability in interpretation of rights and obligations under covered agreements, and the panel's failure to follow previously adopted Appellate Body reports undermines the development of a coherent and predictable body of jurisprudence. The panel's erroneous legal interpretation is corrected, and its findings and conclusions that have been appealed are reversed. Whether the panel failed to discharge its duties under Article 11 of the Dispute Settlement Understanding is not ruled upon.

ANALYSIS

"Dumping" is the act of a manufacturer in one country exporting a product to another country at a price that is either below the price it charges in its home market or is below its cost of production. "Free market" advocates view "dumping" as beneficial for consumers and believe that actions to prevent it would have negative consequences. The use of "zeroing" in the context of calculating anti-dumping duties in domestic trade remedy proceedings has been one of the most contentious issues in World Trade Organization dispute settlement, and that in part explains the panel's deviation from prior rulings by the Appellate Body in this case.

Quicknotes

INTERPRETATION The determination of the meaning of a statute.

REMEDY Compensation for violation of a right or for injuries sustained.

CHAPTER 10

International Law in National Law

Quick Reference Rules of Law

CHAPTER 10

15. *Kadi and Al Barakaat Intl. Foundation v. Council and Commission.* The courts of the member States of the European Union have jurisdiction to review measures adopted by the European Community that give effect to resolutions of the U.N. Security Council. *98*

Trial of Gideon Henfield

[Parties not identified.]

C.C.D. Pa., 1793, reprinted in *Wharton, State Trials* 49, 52-53 (1849)

NATURE OF CASE: Prosecution of a U.S. national for violation of a presidential proclamation.

FACT SUMMARY: Henfield was prosecuted in federal court for violating President Washington's Proclamation of Neutrality. As there was no statute forbidding Henfield's conduct, the court instructed the jury on other sources of law under which Henfield might be found liable for his actions.

RULE OF LAW

Sources of U.S. law include treaties made under the authority of the United States, and the law of nations, as well as the U.S Constitution and statutes.

FACTS: George Washington, the President of the United States, issued a Proclamation of Neutrality that declared U.S. neutrality in the Napoleonic wars, as well as declaring legal action would be taken against any American whose conduct breached that neutrality. Henfield, a U.S. national, was charged with seizing a French ship in violation of the Proclamation, and he was prosecuted in federal court. However, because there was no statute prohibiting Henfield's conduct, the court instructed the jury on other areas of law under which Henfield might be found liable for his actions. Henfield was ultimately acquitted by the jury on the facts.

ISSUE: Do sources of U.S. law include treaties made under the authority of the United States, and the law of nations, as well as the U.S. Constitution and statutes?

HOLDING AND DECISION: (Jay, C.J.) Yes. Sources of U.S. law include treaties made under the authority of the United States, and the law of nations, as well as the U.S. Constitution and statutes. Treaties, which are binding contracts, cannot be unilaterally changed, and, therefore, are the supreme law of the land. Any disputes over treaties must be settled according to the laws of nations, and principles thereunder. The nation's peace, prosperity, and reputation depend on adherence to our treaty obligations, regardless of the other nations that are parties to the treaties that give rise to those obligations. The U.S. is a nation subject to the laws of nations, and it has duties and rights under those laws. Thus, it exercises common rights in the earth's seas with all other nations and must use that common highway in the manner required by the laws of nations and treaties. Given the political climate, it is particularly important U.S. nationals observe the obligations imposed by the laws of nations and treaties, as those form a very important part of the nation's laws.

ANALYSIS

This is one of the earliest cases to recognize that infractions of the law of nations form a part of the common law code of criminal jurisprudence. This case also was the first significant federal criminal prosecution in U.S. history.

Quicknotes

INTERNATIONAL LAW The body of law applicable to dealings between nations.

TREATY An agreement between two or more nations for the benefit of the general public.

Ware v. Hylton

British creditor (P) v. U.S. debtor (D)

3 U.S. (3 Dall.) 199, 28 1 (1796)

NATURE OF CASE: [The procedural posture of the case is not stated in casebook extract.]

FACT SUMMARY: Ware (P), a British creditor of Hylton (D), a citizen of Virginia, contended the 1783 Treaty of Paris, which formally ended the U.S. Revolutionary War, and which provided British creditors could collect debts owed to them from U.S. citizens, overrode a valid Virginia law that would have prevented Ware (P) from collecting on the debt.

RULE OF LAW
The law of nations regarding the confiscation of debts applies to the United States.

FACTS: The 1783 Treaty of Paris formally ended the U.S. Revolutionary War. In the treaty, the United States agreed British creditors could collect debts owed to them by U.S. citizens. Ware (P), a British creditor of Hylton (D), a citizen of Virginia, sought to collect on a debt owed by Hylton (D), but Hylton (D), citing Virginia law, refused to pay. Ware (P) brought suit, contending the Treaty of Paris overrode Virginia law. The case made its way to the United States Supreme Court, which agreed with Ware (P). In a concurring opinion, Justice Wilson articulated his view of the role of the law of nations in U.S. law.

ISSUE: Does the law of nations regarding the confiscation of debts apply to the United States?

HOLDING AND DECISION: (Wilson, J.) Yes. The law of nations regarding the confiscation of debts applies to the United States. When the United States became independent, it became a nation bound by the laws of nations. Under that law, the confiscation of debts is in disrepute, and no nation involved in the Revolutionary War had laws permitting confiscation of debts. Additionally, Congress did not authorize the confiscation of debts. Thus, in no instance can the act of confiscation of debts be considered as a valid act of the United States

ANALYSIS

Justice Wilson added even if Virginia had the power to confiscate British debts, notwithstanding the laws of nations, the Treaty of Paris effectively annulled the confiscation.

Quicknotes

INTERNATIONAL LAW The body of law applicable to dealings between nations.

TREATY An agreement between two or more nations for the benefit of the general public.

The Paquete Habana

Country at war (P) v. Fishermen (D)

175 U.S. 677 (1900)

NATURE OF CASE: Appeal from judgment condemning two fishing vessels and their cargoes as prizes of war.

FACT SUMMARY: The owners (D) of fishing vessels seized by officials of the United States (P) argued that international law exempted coastal fishermen from capture as prizes of war.

RULE OF LAW
Coastal fishing vessels, with their cargoes and crews, are exempt from capture as prizes of war.

FACTS: The owners (D) of two separate fishing vessels brought this appeal of a district court decree condemning two fishing vessels and their cargoes as prizes of war. Each vessel was a fishing smack, running in and out of Havana, sailing under the Spanish flag, and regularly engaged in fishing on the coast of Cuba. The cargoes of both vessels consisted of fresh fish, which had been caught by their respective crews. Until stopped by the blockading United States (P) squadron, the owners (D) had no knowledge of the existence of a war or of any blockage. The owners (D) had no arms or ammunition on board the vessels and had made no attempt to run the blockade after learning of its existence. The owners (D) did not offer any resistance at the time of capture. On appeal, the owners (D) argued that both customary international law and the writings of leading international scholars recognized an exemption from seizure at wartime of coastal fishing vessels.

ISSUE: Are coastal fishing vessels, with their cargoes and crews, exempt from capture as prizes of war?

HOLDING AND DECISION: (Gray, J.) Yes. Coastal fishing vessels, pursuing their vocation of catching and bringing in fresh fish, have been recognized as exempt, with their cargoes and crews, from capture as prizes of war. The doctrine that exempts coastal fishermen, with their vessels and cargoes, from capture as prizes of war, has been familiar to the United States (P) from the time of the War of Independence, and has been recognized explicitly by the French and British governments. Where there are no treaties and no controlling executive or legislative acts or judicial decisions, as is the case here, resort must be had to the customs and usages of civilized nations, and, as evidence of these, to the works of jurists and commentators, who are well acquainted with the field. Such works are resorted to by judicial tribunals, not for the speculations of their authors concerning what the law ought to be, but for trustworthy evidence of what the law really is. At the present time, by the general consent of the civilized nations of the world, and independently of any express treaty or other public act, it is an established rule of international law that coastal fishing vessels, with their implements and supplies, cargoes, and crews, unarmed and honestly pursuing their peaceful calling of catching and bringing in fresh fish, are exempt from capture as prizes of war. Reversed.

ANALYSIS

In a dissenting opinion in the case, Chief Justice Fuller argued that the captured vessels were of such a size and range as to not fall within the exemption. The Chief Justice also contended that the exemption in any case had not become a customary rule of international law, but it was only an act of grace that had not been authorized by the President.

Quicknotes

BLOCKADE When one country prevents materials or persons from entering or leaving another.

CUSTOM Generally any habitual practice or course of action that is repeated under like circumstances.

INTERNATIONAL LAW The body of law applicable to dealings between nations.

Sosa v. Alvarez-Machain

[Parties not identified.]

542 U.S. 692 (2004)

NATURE OF CASE: [The procedural posture of the case is not stated in the casebook extract.]

FACT SUMMARY: [The facts of the case are not stated in the casebook extract.]

RULE OF LAW

International law, including international norms intended to protect individuals, is part of United States (U.S.) law.

FACTS: [The facts of the case are not stated in the casebook extract.]

ISSUE: Is international law, including international norms intended to protect individuals, part of U.S. law?

HOLDING AND DECISION: (Souter, J.) Yes. International law, including international norms intended to protect individuals, is part of U.S. law. The law of nations comprises two principal elements. The fist covers the general norms regarding the relationship of nation States, which is the purview of the Executive and Legislative Branches of government. The second aspect, which falls within the judicial sphere, is a body of judge-made law regulating the conduct of individuals situated outside domestic boundaries. Finally, there is a sphere in which the rules binding individuals for the benefit of other individuals, overlaps with the norms of State relationships, including violation of safe conducts, infringement of the rights of ambassadors, and piracy. In *Erie R. Co. v. Tompkins*, 304 U.S. 64 (1938), this Court denied the existence of any federal "general" common law, which largely withdrew to havens of specialty, with the general practice being to look for legislative guidance before exercising innovative authority over substantive law, including law relating to foreign affairs. Because *Erie* did not bar judicial recognition of new substantive rules, and because it has been understood for over two centuries that the law of nations is a part of U.S. law, federal courts may recognize relatively new international norms intended to protect individuals.

ANALYSIS

The extract presented here affirms federal judges are authorized to make law in certain circumstances, including in the development of customary international law, and it also recognizes customary international human rights law is evolving, and the federal courts may take notice of these evolving norms.

Quicknotes

COMMON LAW A body of law developed through the judicial decisions of the courts as opposed to the legislative process.

INTERNATIONAL LAW The body of law applicable to dealings between nations.

SUBSTANTIVE LAW Law that pertains to the rights and interests of the parties and upon which a cause of action may be based.

United States v. Dire

Federal government (P) v. Somali citizen convicted of piracy (D)

680 F.3d 446 (4th Cir. 2012)

NATURE OF CASE: Appeal from conviction and sentence for piracy under 18 U.S.C. § 1651.

FACT SUMMARY: A group of Somalis (D), who attacked a U.S. Navy frigate, and who were convicted of piracy under 18 U.S.C. § 1651 and sentenced to life in prison, challenged their conviction and sentence on the grounds piracy, under both U.S. and international law, requires actual robbery, which they had not committed.

RULE OF LAW

An attack on a vessel at high seas may constitute piracy under 18 U.S.C. § 1651 and international customary law notwithstanding that such attack does not result in robbery.

FACTS: A group of Somalis (D) attacked the *USS Nicholas*, a U.S. Navy frigate, on the high seas. The Somalis (D) were brought to the United States (P) and convicted, under 18 U.S.C. § 1651, of piracy, among myriad other criminal offenses. The Somalis (D) received life-plus-80-years sentences. On appeal, they challenged their convictions and sentences, arguing, inter alia, their fleeting and fruitless attack on the *Nicholas* did not, as a matter of law, constitute piracy, which, they contended, required actual robbery under both U.S. and international customary law. The court of appeals granted review.

ISSUE: May an attack on a vessel at high seas constitute piracy under 18 U.S.C. § 1651 and international customary law notwithstanding that such attack does not result in robbery?

HOLDING AND DECISION: [Judge not stated in casebook excerpt.] Yes. An attack on a vessel at high seas may constitute piracy under 18 U.S.C. § 1651 and international customary law notwithstanding that such attack does not result in robbery. The Somalis (D) claim the crime of piracy has been narrowly defined as robbery at sea. Here, they boarded the *Nicholas* as captives, and took no property. Congress has the power under Article I of the Constitution to define and punish piracies committed on the high seas. Also, the language of 18 U.S.C. § 1651 can be traced to an 1819 act of Congress, which defined piracy under the law of nations. Cases interpreting this act held that under the law of nations, piracy was robbery upon the sea. However, the law of nations has evolved as to whether robbery is an essential element of piracy. More recently, it has been held by courts of other nations, including England's Privy Council, that a frustrated attempt to commit a piratical robbery is equally piracy *jure gentium.* Courts from other nations have also concluded that piracy encompasses more than just robbery at sea. A more recent view of piracy is that it consists of sailing the seas for private ends without authorization from the government of any state with the object of committing depredations upon property or acts of violence against persons. Treaties, including the Geneva Convention on the High Seas (High Seas Convention), and the United Nations Convention on the Law of the Sea (UNCLOS), contain this broader formulation of piracy. The United States (P) has ratified the former, but not the latter. The Somalis (D) also argue the definition of piracy was fixed by Congress in 1819, and it is immutable. This argument is rejected, since precedent provides a concept of the law of nations as evolving. Moreover, if the Congress of 1819 had believed either the law of nations generally or its piracy definition specifically to be inflexible, the Act of 1819 could easily have been drafted to specify that piracy consisted of "piracy as defined [on the date of enactment], by the law of nations," or solely of "robbery upon the sea." As with § 1651, numerous criminal statutes incorporate a definition of an offense supplied by some other body of law that may change or develop over time. Also rejected is the Somalis' (D) argument that giving "piracy" an evolving definition would violate the principle that there are no federal common-law crimes. The § 1651 piracy offense cannot be considered a common-law crime because Congress properly made an act a crime, affixed a punishment to it, and declared the court would have jurisdiction to hear claims involving the offense. If the Somalis' (P) position were accepted, U.S. law would not be in uniformity with the laws of nations, and, therefore, it would be prevented from exercising universal jurisdiction in piracy cases. Thus, this position is irreconcilable with the noncontroversial notion that Congress intended in § 1651 to define piracy as a universal jurisdiction crime. For these reasons, § 1651 incorporates a definition of piracy that changes with advancements in the law of nations. Accordingly, the Somalis' (D) conduct came within the modern definitions of piracy, as expressed in the UNCLOS, as well as the High Seas Convention. This definition continues to be espoused by the international community as it battles the escalating scourge of piracy, especially emanating from Somalia. Because the district court correctly applied the UNCLOS definition of piracy as customary international law, the defendants' challenge to their piracy convictions, as well as their mandatory life sentences, is rejected.

ANALYSIS

By including "Piracies" in the Define and Punish Clause of Article I of the U.S. Constitution, the Framers distinguished

Continued on next page.

that crime from "Felonies committed on the high Seas" and "Offences against the Law of Nations." This distinction makes sense, since at the time the Constitution was written, piracy on the high seas was a unique offense because it permitted nations to invoke universal jurisdiction, such that any country could arrest and prosecute pirates in its domestic courts, irrespective of the existence of a jurisdictional nexus. Thus, the Define and Punish Clause accords to Congress the special power of criminalizing piracy in a manner consistent with exercise of universal jurisdiction.

Quicknotes

INTERNATIONAL LAW The body of law applicable to dealings between nations.

JURE GENTIUM By the law of nations.

TREATY An agreement between two or more nations for the benefit of the general public.

Missouri v. Holland

State (P) v. Game warden (D)

252 U.S. 416 (1920)

NATURE OF CASE: Action seeking a declaratory judgment.

FACT SUMMARY: The state of Missouri (P) brought this suit to prevent Holland (D), a game warden of the United States, from attempting to enforce the Migratory Bird Treaty Act on the ground that the statute was an unconstitutional interference with the rights reserved to the states by the Tenth Amendment.

RULE OF LAW

Acts of Congress are the supreme law of the land only when made in pursuance of the Constitution, while treaties are declared to be so when made under the authority of the United States.

FACTS: This is a bill in equity brought by the state of Missouri (P) to prevent Holland (D), a game warden of the United States, from attempting to enforce the Migratory Bird Treaty Act, the enactment statute of a treaty between the United States and Great Britain proclaimed by the President. The ground of the bill is that the statute is an unconstitutional interference with the rights reserved to the states by the Tenth Amendment, and that the acts of Holland (D) done and threatened under that authority invade the sovereign right of the state of Missouri (P) and contravene its will manifested in statutes. A motion to dismiss was sustained by the district court on the ground that the act of Congress is constitutional.

ISSUE: Are treaties the supreme law of the land when made under the authority of the United States?

HOLDING AND DECISION: (Holmes, J.) Yes. It is contended that a treaty cannot be valid if it infringes the Constitution, that there are limits, therefore, to the treaty-making power, and that one such limit is that what an act of Congress could not do unaided, in derogation of the powers reserved to the states, a treaty cannot do. Although it is true that acts of Congress are the supreme law of the land only when made in pursuance of the Constitution, treaties are declared to be so when made under the authority of the United States. Furthermore, valid treaties are as binding within the territorial limits of the states as they are elsewhere throughout the dominion of the United States. Since the Migratory Bird Treaty Act was made pursuant to a treaty between the United States and Canada, its provisions are the supreme law of the land and binding on the state of Missouri (P). The treaty and the statute must be upheld. The decree of the lower court is affirmed.

ANALYSIS

Justice Sutherland, in discussing the foreign affairs power in *United States v. Curtiss-Wright Export Corp.,* 299 U. S. 304 (1936), stated that as a result of the separation from Great Britain by the colonies acting as a unit, the powers of external sovereignty passed from the Crown not to the colonies severally but to the colonies in their collective and corporate capacity as the United States. Even before the Declaration, the colonies were a unit in foreign affairs, and the powers to make treaties and maintain diplomatic relations, if they had never been mentioned in the Constitution, would have vested in the federal government as necessary concomitants of nationality.

Quicknotes

DECLARATORY JUDGMENT An adjudication by the courts that grants not relief but is binding over the legal status of the parties involved in the dispute.

EQUITY Fairness; justice; the determination of a matter consistent with principles of fairness and not in strict compliance with rules of law.

JURISDICTION The authority of a court to hear and declare judgment in respect to a particular matter.

TENTH AMENDMENT The Tenth Amendment to the United States Constitution reserving those powers therein, not expressly delegated to the federal government or prohibited to the states, to the states or to the people.

TREATY An agreement between two or more nations for the benefit of the general public.

Whitney v. Robertson

Importer (P) v. Customs (D)

124 U.S. 190 (1888)

NATURE OF CASE: Appeal from judgment for defendant in customs dispute.

FACT SUMMARY: Whitney (P) claimed that a treaty between the United States and the Dominican Republic guaranteed that no higher duty would be assessed on goods from the Dominican Republic than was assessed on goods from any other country and that duties had been wrongfully assessed on his sugar imports.

RULE OF LAW

Where a treaty and an act of legislation conflict, the one last in date will control.

FACTS: Whitney (P) sought to recover the duties he had paid for importing sugar from the Dominican Republic. Whitney (P) alleged that sugar from Hawaii was admitted free of duty and that under the terms of a treaty, the United States could not assess a higher duty on imports from the Dominican Republic.

ISSUE: Where a treaty and an act of legislation conflict, will the one last in date control?

HOLDING AND DECISION: (Field, J.) Yes. Where a treaty and an act of legislation conflict, the one last in date will control. The act of Congress under which the duties were collected was passed after the treaty and therefore is controlling. Affirmed.

ANALYSIS

A treaty is not abrogated or repealed by a later inconsistent statute. The treaty still exists as an international obligation. The terms of the treaty may not be enforceable, however.

Quicknotes

TREATY An agreement between two or more nations for the benefit of the general public.

Breard v. Greene

Convicted murderer (D) v. State (P)

523 U.S. 371 (1998)

NATURE OF CASE: Appeal from denial of habeas corpus.

FACT SUMMARY: Breard (D) claimed that his conviction should be overturned because of alleged violations of the Vienna Convention on Consular Relations.

RULE OF LAW

When a statute that is subsequent in time is inconsistent with a treaty, the statute to the extent of conflict renders the treaty null.

FACTS: Breard (D) was scheduled to be executed following his conviction for murder. Breard (D) filed for habeas relief in federal court, arguing that the arresting authorities had wrongfully failed to inform him that, as a foreign national, he had the right to contact the Paraguayan consulate (P).

ISSUE: When a statute that is subsequent in time is inconsistent with a treaty, does the statute render the treaty null?

HOLDING AND DECISION: (Per curiam) Yes. When a statute that is subsequent in time is inconsistent with a treaty, the statute to the extent of conflict renders the treaty null. Breard's (D) argument that the Vienna Convention was violated must fail because Congress enacted the Antiterrorism and Effective Death Penalty Act after the Vienna Convention. The Executive Branch has authority over foreign relations and may utilize diplomatic channels to request a stay of execution. Petition denied.

ANALYSIS

The Court also held that the Eleventh Amendment barred suits against states. The Consul General of Paraguay (P) tried to raise a § 1983 suit. The Court found that Paraguay (P) was not authorized to do so.

Quicknotes

42 U.S.C. § 1983 Provides that every person, who under color of state law subjects or causes to be subjected any citizen of the United States or person within its jurisdiction to be deprived of rights, privileges, and immunities guaranteed by the federal constitution and laws, is liable to the injured party at law or in equity.

ELEVENTH AMENDMENT The Eleventh Amendment to the United States Constitution prohibiting the extension of the judicial powers of the federal courts to suits brought against a state by citizens of another state, or of a foreign State, without the state's consent.

HABEAS CORPUS A proceeding in which a defendant brings a writ to compel a judicial determination of whether he is lawfully being held in custody.

Foster v. Neilson

Grantees (P) v. Landowner (D)

27 U.S. (2 Pet.) 253 (1829)

NATURE OF CASE: Appeal from decision for defendant in dispute over land.

FACT SUMMARY: Foster (P) and Elam claimed that a tract of land in Louisiana had been granted to them by the Spanish governor.

RULE OF LAW

When the terms of a treaty require a legislative act, the treaty cannot be considered law until such time as the legislature ratifies and confirms the terms.

FACTS: Foster (P) and Elam sued to recover a tract of land in Louisiana that the Spanish governor had granted them. Neilson (D) successfully argued that the grant was void because it was made subsequent to the transfer to France and the United States of the territory on which the land was situated. Foster (P) and Elam relied on a treaty between the United States and Spain that provided that all grants of land made by Spain would be ratified by the United States. The case was taken to the United States Supreme Court on a writ of error.

ISSUE: When the terms of a treaty require a legislative act, can the treaty be considered law before such time as the legislature ratifies and confirms the terms?

HOLDING AND DECISION: (Marshall, C.J.) No. When the terms of a treaty require a legislative act, the treaty cannot be considered law until such time as the legislature ratifies and confirms the terms. The treaty does not operate in itself to ratify or confirm title in land. The legislature must act before the terms of the contract are binding. Affirmed.

ANALYSIS

Some international agreements are self-executing. Others are non-self-executing. The court must decide whether an agreement is to be given effect without further legislation.

Quicknotes

LAND GRANT Donation of public lands for use by another entity.

TITLE The right of possession over property.

TREATY An agreement between two or more nations for the benefit of the general public.

WRIT OF ERROR A writ issued by an appellate court, ordering a lower court to deliver the record of the case so that it may be reviewed for alleged errors.

Medellín v. Texas

Mexican national (D) v. State (P)

552 U.S. 491 (2008)

NATURE OF CASE: Appeal of death sentence.

FACT SUMMARY: After Texas (P) convicted José Medellín (D) of rape and murder, he appealed on the grounds that Texas (P) failed to inform him of his right to have consular personnel notified of his detention by the state, as required under the Vienna Convention on Consular Relations ("the Vienna Convention"). On appeal to the United States Supreme Court, Medellín (D) argued that a case decided by the International Court of Justice suggested that his conviction must be reconsidered to comply with the Vienna Convention.

RULE OF LAW

(1) The U.S. Constitution does not require state courts to honor a treaty obligation of the United States by enforcing a decision of the International Court of Justice.

(2) The U.S. Constitution does not require state courts to provide review and reconsideration of a conviction without regard to state procedural default rules as required by a Memorandum by the President.

FACTS: José Medellín (D), a Mexican national, was convicted and sentenced to death for participating in the gang rape and murder of two teenage girls in Houston. In his appeal, Medellín (D) argued that the state had violated his rights under the Vienna Convention on Consular Relations ("the Vienna Convention"), to which the United States is a party. Article 36 of the Vienna Convention gives any foreign national detained for a crime the right to contact his consulate. The United States Supreme Court dismissed the petition and Medellín's (D) case was remanded to the Texas Court of Criminal Appeals, which also denied him relief. The United States Supreme Court took up his case again, and Medellín's (D) argument rested in part on a holding by the International Court of Justice (I.C.J.) in *Case Concerning Avena and Other Mexican Nationals (Mex. v. U.S.)*, 2004 I.C.J. 12, that the United States had violated the Vienna Convention rights of 51 Mexican nationals (including Medellín (D)) and that their state-court convictions must be reconsidered, regardless of any forfeiture of the right to raise the Vienna Convention claims because of a failure to follow state rules governing criminal convictions. Medellín (D) argued that the Vienna Convention granted him an individual right that state courts must respect. Medellín (D) also cited a memorandum from the U.S. President that instructed state courts to comply with the I.C.J.'s rulings by rehearing the cases. Medellín (D) argued that the Constitution gives the President broad power to ensure that treaties are enforced, and that this power extends to the treatment of treaties in state court proceedings.

ISSUE:

(1) Does the U.S. Constitution require state courts to honor a treaty obligation of the United States by enforcing a decision of the International Court of Justice?

(2) Does the U.S. Constitution require state courts to provide review and reconsideration of a conviction without regard to state procedural default rules as required by a Memorandum by the President?

HOLDING AND DECISION: (Roberts, C.J.)

(1) No. The U.S. Constitution does not require state courts to honor a treaty obligation of the United States by enforcing a decision of the International Court of Justice (I.C.J.). The Vienna Convention provides that if a person detained by a foreign country asks, the authorities of the detaining national must, without delay, inform the consular post of the detainee of the detention. The Optional Protocol of the Convention provides that the I.C.J. is the venue for resolution of issues of interpretation of the Vienna Convention. By ratifying the Optional Protocol to the Vienna Convention, the United States consented to the jurisdiction of the I.C.J. with respect to claims arising out of the Vienna Convention. In 2005, however, after *Avena* was decided, the United States gave notice of withdrawal from the Optional Protocol. While *Avena* constitutes an international law obligation on the part of the United States, it does not help Medellín (D) because not all international law obligations automatically constitute binding federal law. *Avena* does not have automatic domestic legal effect such that the judgment of its own force applies in state and federal courts, because it is not a self-executing treaty, and Congress did not enact legislation implementing binding effect. Thus, the I.C.J. judgment is not automatically enforceable domestic law, immediately and directly binding on state and federal courts under the Supremacy Clause.

(2) No. The U.S. Constitution does not require state courts to provide review and reconsideration of a conviction without regard to state procedural default rules as required by a Memorandum by the President. The presidential memorandum was an attempt by the Executive Branch to enforce a non-self-executing treaty without

Continued on next page.

the necessary congressional action, giving it no binding authority on state courts. Affirmed.

CONCURRENCE: (Stevens, J.) Although the judgment is correct, Texas (P) ought to comply with *Avena*. *Avena* may not be the supreme law of the land, but it constitutes an international law obligation on the part of the United States. Since Texas (P) failed to provide consular notice in accordance with the Vienna Convention, thereby getting the United States into this mess, and since that violation probably didn't prejudice Medellín (D), Texas (P) ought to comply with *Avena*.

DISSENT: (Breyer, J.) the Supremacy Clause requires Texas (P) to enforce the I.C.J.'s judgment in *Avena*. The majority does not point to a single ratified U.S. treaty that contains the self-executing language it says is required in this case. The absence or presence of language in a treaty about a provision's self-execution proves nothing. The relevant treaty provisions should be found to be self-executing, because (1) the language supports direct judicial enforceability, (2) the Optional Protocol applies to disputes about the meaning of a provision that is itself self-executing and judicially enforceable, (3) logic requires a conclusion that the provision is self-executing since it is "final" and "binding," (4) the majority's decision has negative practical implications, (5) the I.C.J. judgment is well suited to direct judicial enforcement, (6) such a holding would not threaten constitutional conflict with other branches, and (7) neither the President nor Congress has expressed concern about direct judicial enforcement of the I.C.J. decision.

ANALYSIS

Medellín (D) was executed on August 5, 2008, after last-minute appeals to the United States Supreme Court were rejected. Governor Rick Perry rejected calls from Mexico and Secretary of State Condoleezza Rice and Attorney General Michael Mukasey to delay the execution, citing the torture, rape, and strangulation of two teenage girls in Houston as just cause for the death penalty. Though a bill was introduced in the House of Representatives to respond to the Court's ruling, Congress took no action.

Quicknotes

INTERNATIONAL LAW The body of law applicable to dealings between nations.

TREATY An agreement between two or more nations for the benefit of the general public.

Hamdan v. Rumsfeld

Detained terrorist (P) v. United States (D)

548 U.S. 557 (2006)

NATURE OF CASE: Appeal from circuit court holding that a military commission violated a detainee's rights under the Geneva Convention.

FACT SUMMARY: A U.S. military commission began proceedings against Hamdan (P), who was captured in Afghanistan. Hamdan (P) challenged the authority of the commission.

RULE OF LAW

(1) The military commission established to try those deemed "enemy combatants" for alleged war crimes in the War on Terror was not authorized by the Congress or the inherent powers of the President.

(2) The rights protected by the Geneva Convention may be enforced in federal court through habeas corpus petitions.

FACTS: Salim Ahmed Hamdan (P) was captured by Afghani forces and imprisoned by the U.S. military in Guantanamo Bay. He filed a petition for a writ of habeas corpus in federal district court to challenge his detention. Before the district court ruled on the petition, a U.S. military commission began proceedings against Hamdan (P), which designated him an enemy combatant. Hamdan (P) challenged the authority of the commission, arguing that the commission trial would violate his rights under Article 102 of the Geneva Convention, which provides that a "prisoner of war can be validly sentenced only if the sentence has been pronounced by the same courts according to the same procedure as in the case of members of the armed forces of the Detaining Power." The district court granted Hamdan's (P) habeas petition, ruling that a hearing to determine whether he was a prisoner of war under the Geneva Convention must have taken place before he could be tried by a military commission. The D.C. Circuit Court of Appeals reversed the decision, finding that the Geneva Convention could not be enforced in federal court and that the establishment of military tribunals had been authorized by Congress and was therefore not unconstitutional.

ISSUE:

(1) Was the military commission established to try those deemed "enemy combatants" for alleged war crimes in the War on Terror authorized by the Congress or the inherent powers of the President?

(2) May the rights protected by the Geneva Convention be enforced in federal court through habeas corpus petitions?

HOLDING AND DECISION: [Judge not stated in casebook excerpt.]

(1) No. The military commission established to try those deemed "enemy combatants" for alleged war crimes in the War on Terror was not authorized by the Congress or the inherent powers of the President. Neither an act of Congress nor the inherent powers of the Executive Branch laid out in the Constitution expressly authorized the sort of military commission at issue in this case. Absent that express authorization, the commission had to comply with the ordinary laws of the United States and the laws of war.

(2) Yes. The rights protected by the Geneva Convention may be enforced in federal court through habeas corpus petitions. The Geneva Convention, as a part of the ordinary laws of war, could be enforced by the United States Supreme Court, along with the statutory Uniform Code of Military Justice (UCMJ), since the military commission was not authorized. Hamdan's (P) exclusion from certain parts of his trial deemed classified by the military commission violated both of these and the trial was therefore illegal. Article 3, or "Common Article 3" as it is sometimes known, does apply to Hamdan (P), despite a holding to the contrary by the court of appeals, and arguments to the contrary by the government. Common Article 3 provides minimal protection to individuals associated with neither a signatory nor a non-signatory "Power" who are involved in a conflict in the territory of a signatory. Common Article 3 is applicable here and requires that Hamdan (P) be tried by a "regularly constituted court affording all the judicial guarantees which are recognized as indispensable by civilized peoples."

ANALYSIS

Many U.S. and international human rights organizations have determined that violations might occur through the non-application of the Geneva Convention to detainees in the U.S. war on terrorism.

Quicknotes

GENEVA CONVENTION International agreement that governs the conduct of warring nations.

HABEAS CORPUS A proceeding in which a defendant brings a writ to compel a judicial determination of whether he is lawfully being held in custody.

United States v. Belmont

Government (P) v. Banker (D)

301 U.S. 324 (1937)

NATURE OF CASE: Appeal from denial of claim for payment of money deposited by Russian corporation.

FACT SUMMARY: The United States (P) claimed that it was due funds deposited in a U.S. bank by a Russian corporation that had been nationalized by the Soviet government.

RULE OF LAW

The national government has complete power in the conduct of international affairs and states cannot curtail or interfere in that power.

FACTS: A Russian corporation had deposited money in Belmont (D), a private bank in New York City, prior to the 1918 nationalization and liquidation by the Soviet government of the corporation. In 1933, the Soviet Union and the United States (P) agreed to a final settlement of claims and counterclaims. The Soviet Union agreed to take no steps to enforce claims against American nationals and assigned and released all such claims to the United States (P). When the United States (P) sought to recover the money, the court held that the *situs* of the bank deposit was within the state of New York and was not an intangible property right within Soviet territory and that it would be contrary to the public policy of the state of New York to recognize or enforce the nationalization decree. The United States (P) appealed and the United States Supreme Court granted certiorari.

ISSUE: Does the national government have complete power in the conduct of international affairs?

HOLDING AND DECISION: (Sutherland, J.) Yes. The national government has complete power in the conduct of international affairs and states cannot curtail or interfere in that power. The United States (P) recognized the Soviet government coincidentally with the assignment of all claims. The President has the power to conduct foreign relations, without the consent of the Senate. In respect of foreign relations generally, state lines disappear. Reversed.

ANALYSIS

The Court noted that recognition of the Soviet Union and the release of all claims were interdependent. Thus, it was purely in the realm of foreign policy to make this agreement. States cannot interfere in the conduct of foreign relations.

Quicknotes

CERTIORARI A discretionary writ issued by a superior court to an inferior court in order to review the lower court's decisions; the Supreme Court's writ ordering such review.

TREATY An agreement between two or more nations for the benefit of the general public.

Banco Nacional de Cuba v. Sabbatino

National financial institution (P) v. Court-appointed receiver (D)

376 U.S. 398 (1964)

NATURE OF CASE: Appeal from an action for conversion.

FACT SUMMARY: Banco Nacional de Cuba (P), which assigned the bills of lading for a shipment of sugar contracted between Farr, Whitlock & Co. (Farr), an American commodities broker and another Cuban bank, instituted this action, alleging conversion of the bills of lading and seeking to recover the proceeds thereof from Farr, and to enjoin Sabbatino (D), a court-appointed receiver, from exercising control over such proceeds.

RULE OF LAW

Pursuant to the Act of State Doctrine, the judiciary will not examine the validity of a taking of property within its own territory by a foreign sovereign government, recognized by this country, in the absence of international agreements to the contrary, even if the taking violates customary international law.

FACTS: Farr, Whitlock & Co. (Farr), an American commodities broker, contracted to purchase Cuban sugar from a wholly owned subsidiary of Compania Azucarera Vertientes–Camaquey de Cuba (CAV), a corporation organized under Cuban law whose stock was owned principally by United States residents. Farr agreed to pay for the sugar in New York upon presentation of the shipping documents. Shortly thereafter, a law was enacted in Cuba giving the government power to nationalize by forced expropriation of property or enterprises in which American nationals had an interest. The sugar contracted for by Farr was expropriated from CAV. In order to obtain consent from the Cuban government before a ship carrying sugar could leave Cuba, Farr entered into contracts, identical to those it had made with CAV, with the Banco Para el Comercio Exterior de Cuba, an instrumentality of the Cuban government. This bank assigned the bills of lading to the Banco Nacional de Cuba (P), also an instrumentality of the Cuban government, which presented the bills and a sight draft as required under the contract to Farr in New York in return for payment. Farr refused the documents after being notified by CAV of its claim to the proceeds as rightful owner of the sugar. Farr was served with a court order that had appointed Sabbatino (D) as receiver of CAV's New York assets and enjoined it from removing the payments from the state. The Banco Nacional (P) then instituted this action, alleging conversion of the bills of lading seeking to recover the proceeds thereof from Farr, and to enjoin Sabbatino (D), the receiver, from exercising dominion over such proceeds. The district court granted summary judgment against Banco Nacional (P), holding that the Act of State Doctrine does not apply when the questioned foreign act is in violation of international law. The court of appeals affirmed the judgment.

ISSUE: Does the judiciary have the authority to examine the validity of a taking of property within its own territory by a foreign sovereign even if the taking violated international law?

HOLDING AND DECISION: (Harlan, J.) No. The Judicial Branch will not examine the validity of a taking of property within its own territory by a foreign sovereign government, extant and recognized by this country at the time of suit, in the absence of a treaty or other agreement, even if the complaint alleges that the taking violates customary international law. The plain implication of past cases is that the Act of State Doctrine is applicable even if international law has been violated. The Act of State Doctrine does not deprive the courts of jurisdiction once acquired over a case. It requires only that when it is made to appear that the foreign government has acted in a given way on the subject matter of the litigation, the details of such action or the merit of the result cannot be questioned but must be accepted by our courts as a rule for their decision. It results that title to the property in this case must be determined by the result of the expropriation action taken by the authorities of the Cuban government. The damages of adjudicating the propriety of such expropriation acts, regardless of whether the State Department has, as it did in this case, asserted that the act violated international law, are too far-reaching for the Judicial Branch to attempt. The judgment of the court of appeals is reversed and the case remanded to the district court.

DISSENT: (White, J.) According to the majority opinion, not only are the courts powerless to question acts of state proscribed by international law, but they are likewise powerless to refuse to adjudicate the claim founded upon a foreign law; they must render judgment and thereby validate the lawless act. The Act of State Doctrine does not require American courts to decide cases in disregard of international law and of the rights of litigants to a full determination on the merits.

ANALYSIS

In the instant case the Court also concluded that the Act of State Doctrine, even in diversity of citizenship cases, must

Continued on next page.

be determined according to federal rather than state law. The Court stated that it is constrained to make it clear that an issue concerned with a basic choice regarding the competence and function of the judiciary and national executive in ordering our relationships with other members of the international community must be treated exclusively as an aspect of federal law.

Quicknotes

ACT OF STATE DOCTRINE Prohibits United States courts from investigating acts of other countries committed within their borders.

ENJOIN The ordering of a party to cease the conduct of a specific activity.

Roper v. Simmons

Convicted murderer (D) v. State (P)

543 U.S. 551 (2005)

NATURE OF CASE: United States Supreme Court review of a state court determination involving a death sentence for a juvenile offender.

FACT SUMMARY: After Christopher Simmons (D) was convicted of a murder he committed when he was 17 years old, the Missouri Supreme Court ruled that the death penalty was unconstitutional as applied to persons under the age of 18. The United States Supreme Court reviewed the decision.

RULE OF LAW

The opinion of the world community is relevant, though not controlling, to consideration of the juvenile death penalty in the United States.

FACTS: The state of Missouri (P) convicted Christopher Simmons (D) of a murder he committed when he was 17 years old. The Missouri Supreme Court ruled that the death penalty was unconstitutional as applied to persons under the age of 18 and set aside the sentence of death imposed on Simmons (D). The United States Supreme Court reviewed the decision, and in the process of reaching its conclusion, considered the opinion on the matter of the international community.

ISSUE: Is the opinion of the world community relevant, though not controlling, to consideration of the juvenile death penalty in the United States?

HOLDING AND DECISION: (Kennedy, J.) Yes. The opinion of the world community is relevant, though not controlling, to consideration of the juvenile death penalty in the United States. Precedent suggests that reference to the laws of other countries and to international authorities for interpretation of the prohibition of "cruel and unusual punishments" is proper. Every country in the world has ratified the United Nations Convention on the Rights of the Child, which contains an express prohibition on capital punishment for crimes committed by juveniles under 18, except Somalia and the United States. Since 1990, only seven countries other than the United States have executed juvenile offenders, and since then each country, except the United States, has either abolished capital punishment for juveniles or made public disavowal of the practice. The United Kingdom's abolishment of the death penalty for juveniles, which is particularly relevant given the ties between the United Kingdom and the United States, occurred before the international conventions on the subject were created. International opinion against the death penalty for minors is based in large part on the understanding that the instability and emotional imbalance of young people may often be a factor in the crime, and that opinion, while not controlling, is relevant. The Eighth and Fourteenth Amendments forbid imposition of the death penalty on offenders under the age of 18 when the crime was committed. Affirmed.

ANALYSIS

Not stated in the casebook excerpt is that the Court applied the "evolving standards of decency" test. Justice Kennedy cited a body of sociological and scientific research that found juveniles have a lack of maturity and sense of responsibility compared to adults. The Court reasoned that in recognition of the comparative immaturity and irresponsibility of juveniles, almost every state prohibited those under age 18 from voting, serving on juries, or marrying without parental consent. Kennedy reasoned that the trend internationally against the death penalty for minors was relevant because of its basis in this evolving notion that the death penalty is inappropriate for juvenile offenders because of their instability and emotional imbalance.

Quicknotes

EIGHTH AMENDMENT The Eighth Amendment to the federal Constitution prohibits the imposition of excessive bail, fines, and cruel and unusual punishment.

FOURTEENTH AMENDMENT Declares that no state shall make or enforce any law that shall abridge the privileges and immunities of citizens of the United States. No state shall deny to any person within its jurisdiction the equal protection of the laws.

Kadi and Al Barakaat Int'l. Foundation v. Council and Commission

Terrorists (D) v. European Union (P)

European Court of Justice, 2008 E.C.R. I 6351 (Sept. 3, 2008)

NATURE OF CASE: Appeal of judgment by a European Community Court of First Instance.

FACT SUMMARY: A regulation of the Council of the European Union (EU) (P) froze the funds of Yassin Abdullah Kadi (D) and Al Barakaat International Foundation (D), following a resolution by the U.N. Security Council. The EU Court of First Instance ruled it did not have jurisdiction to review measures adopted by the European Community giving effect to resolutions of the Security Council adopted against the Al Qaeda and Taliban terrorist networks. Kadi (D) and Al Barakaat (D) appealed.

RULE OF LAW

The courts of the member States of the European Union have jurisdiction to review measures adopted by the European Community that give effect to resolutions of the U.N. Security Council.

FACTS: In its effort to fight terrorism, the U.N. Security Council imposed sanctions under Chapter VII of the U.N. Charter against individuals and entities allegedly associated with Osama bin Laden, the Al-Qaeda network, and the Taliban. The U.N. Sanctions Committee made a list of alleged offenders, and sanctions included freezing such persons' and entities' assets. To give effect to the Security Council resolutions, the Council of the European Union (P) adopted a regulation ordering the freezing of the assets of those on the list, which included Yassin Abdullah Kadi (D), a resident of Saudi Arabia, and Al Barakaat International Foundation (D). Kadi (D) and Al Barakaat (D) began proceedings in the Court of First Instance (CFI) and requested annulment of the Council regulation, arguing the Council lacked jurisdiction to adopt the regulation and that the regulation infringed several of their fundamental rights, including the right to respect for property, the right to be heard before a court of law, and the right to effective judicial review. The CFI rejected all claims and confirmed the validity of the regulation, ruling specifically it had no jurisdiction to review the validity of the contested regulation and, indirectly, the validity of the relevant U.N. Security Council resolution, except in respect of *jus cogens* norms. Kadi (D) and Al Barakaat (D) appealed. The European Court of Justice granted review.

ISSUE: Do the courts of the member States of the European Union have jurisdiction to review measures adopted by the European Community that give effect to resolutions of the U.N. Security Council?

HOLDING AND DECISION: [Judge not stated in casebook excerpt.] Yes. The courts of the member States of the European Union have jurisdiction to review measures adopted by the European Community that give effect to resolutions of the U.N. Security Council. European Community courts have the power to review the legality of all Community acts, including the contested regulation, that aim to give effect to resolutions adopted by the U.N. Security Council under the U.N. Charter. The review of lawfulness applies only to the European Community act purporting to give effect to the international agreement, not to the international agreement itself. Thus, European Community courts do not have competence to review the legality of a resolution adopted by an international body, even if the courts limited their review to examination of the compatibility of that resolution with *jus cogens* norms. A judgment by an EU court that a European Community measure is contrary to a higher rule of law in the European Community legal order would not implicate a challenge to the legitimacy of that resolution in international law. Examining the challenged measure, it cannot be said its sanctions are inappropriate or disproportionate, given the threats to international peace and security posed by acts of terrorism. However, the measure does not conform with fundamental human rights insofar as it does not provide adequate procedures for an affected individual to plead his or her case to the competent authorities. Accordingly, the measure must be annulled, and the European Community authorities have three months to implement a new scheme that remedies the defects of the current measure.

ANALYSIS

This case marks the first time that the European Court of Justice confirmed its jurisdiction to review the lawfulness of a measure giving effect to U.N. Security Council resolutions. It also constitutes the first time the European Court of Justice quashed a European Community measure giving effect to a U.N. Security Council resolution for being unlawful.

Quicknotes

JUDICIAL REVIEW Authority of the courts to review decisions, actions, or omissions committed by another agency or branch of government.

JURISDICTION The authority of a court to hear and declare judgment in respect to a particular matter.

***JUS COGENS* NORMS** Universally understood principles of international law that cannot be set aside because they are based on fundamental human values.

CHAPTER 11

Jurisdiction at the National Level

Quick Reference Rules of Law

United States v. Bowman

Federal government (P) v. Convicted criminal (D)

260 U.S. 94 (1922)

NATURE OF CASE: Appeal from dismissal of indictment, under § 35 of the Criminal Code, of conspiracy to defraud a corporation of which the United States was a shareholder.

FACT SUMMARY: The United States (P) contended that because a conspiracy to defraud a corporation in which it was a shareholder occurred on a ship owned by the United States (P), there was no lack of jurisdiction to prosecute the crime in the United States merely because the crime occurred on the high seas.

RULE OF LAW

A federal criminal statute that criminalizes conduct that injures the government and is capable of being perpetrated without regard to a particular locality, is applicable to citizens of the United States upon the high seas or in a foreign country, notwithstanding that the statute does not expressly indicate it is applicable outside the United States

FACTS: The steamship *Dio* was owned by a corporation in which the United States (P) was the sole shareholder. On a trip to Rio de Janeiro, Brazil, members of the *Dio's* crew, including three U.S. citizens (D), conspired to defraud the corporation in violation of § 35 of the Criminal Code. The indictees demurred to the indictment on the grounds the crime was committed outside of U.S. jurisdiction, either on the high seas or within the jurisdiction of Brazil. The district court sustained the demurrer, observing that although private and public ships that fly the flag of the United States (P) on the high seas are constructively part of U.S. territory, jurisdiction for criminal offenses must be expressly indicated by Congress, and the high seas were not referred to by § 35 of the Criminal Code as being part of the locus of the crime defined by it. The United States Supreme Court granted a writ of error to review the district court's judgment.

ISSUE: Is a federal criminal statute that criminalizes conduct that injures the government and is capable of being perpetrated without regard to a particular locality, applicable to citizens of the United States upon the high seas or in a foreign country, notwithstanding that the statute does not expressly indicate that it is applicable outside the United States?

HOLDING AND DECISION: (Taft, C.J.) Yes. A federal criminal statute that criminalizes conduct that injures the government and is capable of being perpetrated without regard to a particular locality, is applicable to citizens of the United States upon the high seas or in a foreign country, notwithstanding that the statute does not expressly indicate it is applicable outside the United States. The issue here is one of statutory construction, and the locus of a crime must be determined from Congress's purpose. Where certain crimes naturally occur within U.S. territory, e.g., burglary, it is natural for Congress to indicate whether punishment for such crimes will extend to acts committed extraterritorially. For such crimes, Congress's failure to expressly extend jurisdiction extraterritorially may be construed as an indication jurisdiction is not to be extended. However, such an interpretation should not apply to criminal statutes that are not logically dependent on their locality for the government's jurisdiction but are enacted to protect the government from certain crimes wherever they are committed. If Congress fails to expressly extend jurisdiction as to such crimes, that should not be construed as indication jurisdiction is limited and does not encompass acts that occur on the high seas or in foreign countries. Regarding such crimes, it would be going too far to say because Congress did not fix any locus in the statute as being a part of the crimes, it intended to exclude the high seas in respect of such crimes. This conclusion is supported by other sections of the Criminal Code that criminalize "Offenses against the Operation of the Government"—which includes § 35—that contemplate crimes being committed outside of the United States, either on the high seas or in foreign countries. Section 35 was intended to protect the United States (P) from the type of fraud committed by the indictees; and it cannot be supposed that when Congress enacted the statute or amended it, it did not have in mind that a wide field for such frauds upon the government would occur in private and public vessels of the United States (P) on the high seas and in foreign ports and beyond the land jurisdiction of the United States (P). Therefore, it must be concluded Congress did not intend to exclude from the reach of the statute conduct that occurred in such locations.

ANALYSIS

As the Court observes, it was engaged in statutory construction to determine Congress's intent. Here, the Court concluded from the nature of the statute Congress intended it to apply extraterritorially beyond U.S. land. However, it is not always clear from a statute whether Congress intended to regulate conduct beyond the nation's borders. Thus, U.S. courts must still determine when Congress has intended to regulate extraterritorially when faced with an ambiguous criminal statute. As the

Continued on next page.

district court in this case noted, the presumption is that ambiguous statutes do not apply extraterritorially unless Congress indicated an extraterritorial intent. *Bowman* is still used to support the exception to this presumption, and the extraterritorial application of criminal laws.

Quicknotes

JURISDICTION The authority of a court to hear and declare judgment in respect to a particular matter.

STATUTORY CONSTRUCTION The examination and interpretation of statutes.

WRIT OF ERROR A writ issued by an appellate court, ordering a lower court to deliver the record of the case so that it may be reviewed for alleged errors.

Kiobel v. Royal Dutch Petroleum Co.

Nigerian national residing in U.S. (P) v. Foreign corporation (D)

569 U.S. 108 (2013)

NATURE OF CASE: Appeal in action brought under the Alien Tort Statute. [The procedural posture of the case is not stated in the casebook extract.]

FACT SUMMARY: Nigerian nationals residing in the United States (P) brought suit under the Alien Tort Statute (ATS) alleging certain foreign corporations (D) aided and abetted the Nigerian government in committing violations of the law of nations in Nigeria. The issue was whether U.S. courts could recognize a cause of action under the ATS for violations occurring within the territory of a sovereign other than the United States.

RULE OF LAW

The presumption against extraterritoriality applies to claims arising under the Alien Tort Statute (ATS), and nothing in the statute rebuts that presumption.

FACTS: Nigerian nationals residing in the United States (P) filed suit in federal court under the Alien Tort Statute (ATS), alleging certain Dutch, British, and Nigerian corporations aided and abetted the Nigerian government in committing violations of the law of nations in Nigeria, including atrocities and crimes against humanity, such as the beating, killing, raping and arresting of residents. The United States Supreme Court granted certiorari in the case. [The procedural posture of the case is not stated in the casebook extract.]

ISSUE: Does the presumption against extraterritoriality apply to claims arising under the Alien Tort Statute (ATS), and does nothing in the statute rebut that presumption?

HOLDING AND DECISION: [Judge not listed in casebook extract.] Yes. The presumption against extraterritoriality applies to claims arising under the Alien Tort Statute (ATS), and nothing in the statute rebuts that presumption. The ATS provides that "[t]he district courts shall have original jurisdiction of any civil action by an alien for a tort only, committed in violation of the law of nations or a treaty of the United States." Thus, the question is not whether a proper claim has been stated, but, rather, whether a claim may reach conduct occurring in the territory of a foreign sovereign. The foreign corporations (D) claim that the presumption against extraterritorial application precludes the ATS from reaching such claims. That presumption provides that when a statute gives no clear indication of an extraterritorial application, it has none. The presumption serves to protect against unintended clashes between our laws and those of other nations that could result in international discord, and it is applied to discern whether an Act of Congress regulating conduct applies abroad. The presumption's underlying principles similarly constrain courts when considering causes of action that may be brought under the ATS. Indeed, the danger of unwarranted judicial interference in the conduct of foreign policy is magnified in this context, where the question is not what Congress has done but what courts may do. These concerns, which are implicated in any case arising under the ATS, are all the more pressing when the question is whether a cause of action under the ATS reaches conduct within the territory of another sovereign. For these reasons, the presumption applies for causes of action brought under the ATS. Moreover, there is nothing in the ATS's text, history, or purpose that rebuts this presumption. It is true that Congress, even in a purely jurisdictional provision such as the ATS, can indicate it intends federal law to apply to conduct occurring abroad. Nevertheless, to rebut the presumption, the ATS would need to evince a "clear indication of extraterritoriality." Nothing in the ATS's text suggests that Congress intended causes of action recognized under it to have extraterritorial reach. The ATS covers actions by aliens for violations of the law of nations, but that does not imply extraterritorial reach—such violations affecting aliens can occur either within or outside the United States. Nor does the fact that the text reaches "any civil action" suggest application to torts committed abroad; it is well established that generic terms like "any" or "every" do not rebut the presumption against extraterritoriality. Similarly, the historical background against which the ATS was enacted does not overcome the presumption. At the time of the statute's enactment, Congress was concerned with three principal offenses against the law of nations: violation of safe conducts, infringement of the rights of ambassadors, and piracy. The first two offenses have no necessary extraterritorial application. The third, piracy, while typically occurring on the high seas, does not occur with the territorial jurisdiction of another sovereign. Therefore, applying U.S. law to piracy carries less direct foreign policy consequences. Thus, the existence of a cause of action against pirates under the ATS is not a sufficient basis for concluding that other causes of action under the ATS reach conduct that does occur within the territory of another sovereign. Finally, there is no indication the ATS was passed to make the United States a uniquely hospitable forum for the enforcement of international norms. Applying these principles to this case, because all the relevant conduct occurred in Nigeria, the claims may not proceed under the ATS. [The Court

Continued on next page.

affirmed the court of appeals, which had dismissed the claims.]

ANALYSIS

The Court also observed that even where claims "touch and concern" the territory of the United States, they must do so with such force to displace the presumption against extraterritorial application. Here, even though the corporations being sued were multinational corporations, with some U.S. contacts, the Court concluded that mere corporate presence would not suffice to rebut the presumption. Justice Breyer, concurring in the opinion, added that it would be farfetched to believe, based solely upon the corporations' minimal and indirect U.S. presence, that the cause of action at bar would vindicate a distinct American interest, such as in not providing a safe harbor for an "enemy of all mankind."

Quicknotes

CAUSE OF ACTION A fact or set of facts the occurrence of which entitles a party to seek judicial relief.

JURISDICTION The authority of a court to hear and declare judgment in respect to a particular matter.

PRESUMPTION A rule of law requiring the court to presume certain facts to be true based on the existence of other facts, thereby shifting the burden of proof to the party against whom the presumption is asserted to rebut.

Al-Skeini v. Secretary of State for Defence

Families of deceased (P) v. United Kingdom (D)

U.K. House of Lords, [2007] UKHL 26

NATURE OF CASE: Wrongful death proceedings under international convention.

FACT SUMMARY: The families (P) of six Iraqi civilians who were killed in Basra in 2003 where the United Kingdom (D) was an occupying power appealed a decision by U.K. authorities not to conduct an independent investigation into the circumstances of the deaths, arguing that the Human Rights Act 1998 has extraterritorial application where the United Kingdom (D) is an occupying power.

RULE OF LAW

The Human Rights Act 1998 applied to acts a U.K. public authority performed outside its territory only where the victim was within the jurisdiction of the United Kingdom for purposes of the European Convention on Human Rights.

FACTS: Six Iraqi civilians were killed in Basra in 2003 where the United Kingdom (D) was an occupying power. Five of them were shot dead by members of U.K. armed forces in the course of patrol operations, and the sixth was arrested and died in a military base. U.K. authorities refused to conduct an independent investigation into the circumstances of the deaths. The U.K. government argued that the deaths occurred outside the territory of the United Kingdom (D), and consequently the European Convention for Human Rights, which imposes an obligation for independent and thorough investigation, does not apply. The families (P) of the deceased sued.

ISSUE: Did the Human Rights Act 1998 apply to acts a U.K. public authority performed outside its territory only where the victim was within the jurisdiction of the United Kingdom (D) for purposes of the European Convention on Human Rights?

HOLDING AND DECISION: (Lord Rodger of Earlsferry, J. [for the majority]) Yes. The Human Rights Act 1998 (HRA) applied to acts a U.K. public authority performed outside its territory only where the victim was within the jurisdiction of the United Kingdom (D) for purposes of the European Convention on Human Rights. The rule of statutory construction adopted by Lord Bingham must be taken against the background of international law, and jurisdiction under the HRA should be co-extensive with the interpretation given by the European Court to jurisdiction under the Convention. The Convention applies outside the territory of the United Kingdom (D) where the deceased were linked to the United Kingdom (D) when they were killed. The HRA does not have a more restrictive jurisdictional scope than the Convention rights it was meant to implement. With the exception of the claimant who had been mistreated inside a British military detention unit, the claimants were not within U.K. jurisdiction within the meaning of the Convention.

DISSENT: (Lord Bingham of Cornhill, J.) No. The Human Rights Act 1998 has no extraterritorial application. To succeed in this case, the claimants must show that a public authority acted in contravention of the European Convention on Human Rights and the Human Rights Act 1998. Typically, claims relate to conduct within the borders of contracting States, such as the United Kingdom (D), and the only question is whether a claimant's Convention right has been violated, and if so, by whom. Here, however, the alleged violations took place in Iraq, which is not a contracting State. The rule of statutory construction urged by the U.K. government is that unless contrary intention appears, Parliament should be taken to intend an act to extend to each territory of the United Kingdom (D) but not to any territory outside the United Kingdom (D). In passing the HRA, Parliament could not have intended to legislate for foreign lands, because between 1953 and 1997, British forces were almost always involved in hostilities or peacekeeping activities in some part of the world, and such situations must have been on the minds of members of Parliament when they passed the HRA. Had they intended to legislate for activity by British soldiers in foreign lands, they would have expressly stated as much.

ANALYSIS

There were actually four Lords forming the majority (Lord Rodger included), and Lord Bingham was the sole dissenter. Lord Rodger's basic rule is that the presumption against extraterritoriality must be seen against the background of international law, that Parliament had a legitimate interest in regulating the conduct of its citizens, and therefore could intend its legislation to affect their position in other States.

Quicknotes

INTERNATIONAL LAW The body of law applicable to dealings between nations.

JURISDICTION The authority of a court to hear and declare judgment in respect to a particular matter.

STATUTORY CONSTRUCTION The examination and interpretation of statutes.

F. Hoffmann-La Roche Ltd. v. Empagran S.A.

[Parties not identified.]

542 U.S. 155 (2004)

NATURE OF CASE: Appeal in action brought under the Sherman Act for antitrust harms resulting both abroad and, independently, in the United States. [The procedural posture of the case is not presented in the casebook extract.]

FACT SUMMARY: [Foreign purchasers of vitamins, among others, brought suit under U.S. antitrust laws, claiming that a worldwide price-fixing conspiracy for the sale of vitamins was actionable under U.S. antitrust laws for harm caused to the purchasers solely in foreign countries. The foreign plaintiffs' theory was that because the conspiracy also independently harmed U.S. vitamin purchasers, the Foreign Trade Antitrust Improvements Act of 1982 (FTAIA), 15 U.S.C. § 6a, which ordinarily precludes the application of U.S. antitrust laws, such as the Sherman Act, to conduct involving trade or commerce with foreign nations, but excepts conduct that significantly harms imports, domestic commerce, or American exporters, did not preclude their action.]

RULE OF LAW

Where price-fixing conduct significantly and adversely affects both customers outside and within the United States, but the adverse foreign effect is independent of any adverse domestic effect, the Foreign Trade Antitrust Improvements Act of 1982 (FTAIA), 15 U.S.C. § 6a, which ordinarily precludes the application of the Sherman Act to conduct involving trade or commerce with foreign nations, but excepts conduct that significantly harms imports, domestic commerce, or American exporters, precludes a claim under the Sherman Act where the claim is based solely on the foreign effect.

FACTS: [Foreign purchasers of vitamins, among others, brought suit under U.S. antitrust laws, claiming that a worldwide price-fixing conspiracy for the sale of vitamins was actionable under U.S. antitrust laws for harm caused to the purchasers solely in foreign countries. The foreign plaintiffs' theory was that because the conspiracy also independently harmed U.S. vitamin purchasers, the Foreign Trade Antitrust Improvements Act of 1982 (FTAIA), 15 U.S.C. § 6a, which ordinarily precludes the application of U.S. antitrust laws, such as the Sherman Act, to conduct involving trade or commerce with foreign nations, but excepts conduct that significantly harms imports, domestic commerce, or American exporters, did not preclude their action. The district court ruled that the FTAIA exception was inapplicable, but the court of appeals reversed.]

ISSUE: Where price-fixing conduct significantly and adversely affects both customers outside and within the United States, but the adverse foreign effect is independent of any adverse domestic effect, does the Foreign Trade Antitrust Improvements Act of 1982 (FTAIA), 15 U.S.C. § 6a, which ordinarily precludes the application of the Sherman Act to conduct involving trade or commerce with foreign nations, but excepts conduct that significantly harms imports, domestic commerce, or American exporters, preclude a claim under the Sherman Act where the claim is based solely on the foreign effect?

HOLDING AND DECISION: (Breyer, J.) Yes. Where price-fixing conduct significantly and adversely affects both customers outside and within the United States, but the adverse foreign effect is independent of any adverse domestic effect, the Foreign Trade Antitrust Improvements Act of 1982 (FTAIA), 15 U.S.C. § 6a, which ordinarily precludes the application of the Sherman Act to conduct involving trade or commerce with foreign nations, but excepts conduct that significantly harms imports, domestic commerce, or American exporters, precludes a claim under the Sherman Act where the claim is based solely on the foreign effect. The Court ordinarily construes ambiguous statutes to avoid unreasonable interference with other nations' sovereign authority. This rule of construction reflects customary international law principles and cautions courts to assume that U.S. legislators take account of other nations' legitimate sovereign interests when writing American laws. It thereby helps the potentially conflicting laws of different nations work together in harmony. Although applying U.S. antitrust laws to foreign conduct can interfere with a foreign nation's ability to regulate its own commercial affairs, courts have long held such application nonetheless reasonable, and hence consistent with prescriptive comity principles, insofar as the laws reflect a legislative effort to redress domestic antitrust injury caused by foreign anticompetitive conduct. However, it is not reasonable to apply American laws to foreign conduct insofar as that conduct causes independent foreign harm that alone gives rise to a plaintiff's claim. There is insubstantial justification in such cases for interference with another nation's ability to regulate its own commerce. Although some of the anticompetitive conduct alleged here took place in the United States, the higher foreign prices were not the consequence of any domestic anticompetitive conduct sought to be forbidden by Congress, which, instead, sought to release domestic (and foreign) anticompetitive conduct from Sherman Act constraint

Continued on next page.

when that conduct causes foreign harm. Thus, principles of prescriptive comity counsel against interpreting the FTAIA so its exception applies where foreign anticompetitive conduct plays a significant role and where foreign injury is independent of domestic effects, since it must be presumed that Congress did not seek to impose U.S. antitrust principles on foreign sovereigns through an act of legal imperialism, through legislative fiat. [The disposition of the case is not presented in the casebook extract.]

ANALYSIS

Justice Breyer's reliance on principles of prescriptive comity to narrowly construe the Foreign Trade Antitrust Improvements Act of 1982 (FTAIA) is consistent with the principle that statutes should be read in accord with the customary deference to the application of foreign countries' laws within their own territories.

Quicknotes

ANTITRUST ACTS Federal and state statutes to protect trade and commerce from unlawful restraints, price discriminations, price fixing and monopolies.

ANTITRUST LAW Body of federal law prohibiting business conduct that constitutes a restraint on trade.

COMITY A rule pursuant to which courts in one state give deference to the statutes and judicial decisions of the court of another state.

Blackmer v. United States

Citizen (D) v. Federal government (P)

284 U.S. 421 (1932)

NATURE OF CASE: Appeal from contempt conviction.

FACT SUMMARY: Blackmer (D) was found to be in contempt of court for failing to respond to subpoenas served upon him in France requiring his appearance in the United States.

RULE OF LAW

For the exercise of judicial jurisdiction in personam, there must be due process.

FACTS: Blackmer (D) was a U.S. (P) citizen who resided in France. He was served subpoenas to appear in court as a witness in a criminal trial in the United States. When he failed to respond to the subpoenas, contempt proceedings were initiated and Blackmer (D) was found guilty and fined. Blackmer (D) appealed, claiming the federal statute was unconstitutional.

ISSUE: For the exercise of judicial jurisdiction in personam, must there be due process?

HOLDING AND DECISION: (Hughes, C.J.) Yes. For the exercise of judicial jurisdiction in personam, there must be due process. Due process requires appropriate notice of the judicial action and an opportunity to be heard. The statute provides that when the presence of a citizen of the United States who resides abroad is required in court, a subpoena be issued addressed to a consul of the United States. The consul must serve the subpoena on the witness personally with a tender of traveling expenses. Upon proof of such service and of the failure of the witness to appear, a court order may be issued. If the witness fails to comply with the court order, the court may adjudge the witness guilty of contempt. Congress acted pursuant to its authority in enacting the statute and it could prescribe a penalty to enforce it. Affirmed.

ANALYSIS

The Court did not find the statute to be unconstitutional. Blackmer (D) alleged that there was inadequate notice. Since Blackmer (D) retained his U.S. citizenship, he was still subject to U.S. authorities.

Quicknotes

CONTEMPT An act of omission that interferes with a court's proper administration of justice.

DUE PROCESS RIGHTS The constitutional mandate requiring the courts to protect and enforce individuals' rights and liberties consistent with prevailing principles of fairness and justice and prohibiting the federal and state governments from such activities that deprive its citizens of a life, liberty, or property interest.

IN PERSONAM JURISDICTION The jurisdiction of a court over a person as opposed to his interest in property.

SERVICE OF PROCESS The communication of reasonable notice of a court proceeding to a defendant in order to provide him with an opportunity to be heard.

United States v. Neil

Federal government (P) v. Foreign citizen convicted of crime (D)

312 F.3d 419 (9th Cir. 2002)

NATURE OF CASE: Appeal from conviction for sexual contact with a minor in violation of 18 U.S.C. § 2244(a)(3).

FACT SUMMARY: Neil (D), a foreign citizen, contended the United States (P) lacked jurisdiction to bring criminal charges against him for conduct that occurred aboard a foreign vessel in foreign territorial waters, notwithstanding that the victim of that conduct was a United States citizen, and that the vessel departed from, and returned to, a U.S. port.

RULE OF LAW

A United States criminal statute has extraterritorial effect where Congress intended to apply the statute extraterritorially, and where the exercise of extraterritorial jurisdiction comports with principles of international law.

FACTS: A Panamanian-registered ship departed from a port in California on a round-trip cruise to Mexico. Neil (D), a non-U.S. citizen who worked on the cruise ship, felt the breasts and buttocks of a 12-year-old U.S. girl through her clothing while the ship was in Mexican territorial waters. Upon returning to the United States, the girl sought therapy. Neil (D) was indicted under 18 U.S.C. § 2244(a)(3) for three counts of sexual contact with a minor. When the district court denied his motion to dismiss the indictment for lack of jurisdiction, he conditionally pled guilty to two of those counts, while reserving the right to appeal the district court's ruling as to jurisdiction. Neil (D) appealed, and the court of appeals granted review.

ISSUE: Does a United States criminal statute have extraterritorial effect where Congress intended to apply the statute extraterritorially, and where the exercise of extraterritorial jurisdiction comports with principles of international law?

HOLDING AND DECISION: (Fletcher, J.) Yes. A United States criminal statute has extraterritorial effect where Congress intended to apply the statute extraterritorially, and where the exercise of extraterritorial jurisdiction comports with principles of international law. Although the Constitution does not prohibit the extraterritorial application of U.S. penal laws, acts of Congress generally do not have extraterritorial effect unless Congress so intends. Here, § 2244(a)(3) expressly invokes the "special maritime and territorial jurisdiction of the United States." This special jurisdiction is defined as including, to the extent permitted by international law, any foreign vessel during a voyage having a scheduled departure from or arrival in the United States with respect to an offense committed by or against a national of the United States. The criminal sexual contact between Neil (D) and the victim occurred on a foreign vessel that departed from and arrived in the United States, and the victim was a United States national. This conduct thus falls squarely into the definition of special maritime and territorial jurisdiction. The remaining question, therefore, is whether the exercise of jurisdiction by the United States (P) would violate international law. Here, two principles of international law support extraterritorial jurisdiction. The first is the territorial principle, under which the United States (P) may assert jurisdiction when acts performed outside of its borders have detrimental effects within the United States. Here, there were sufficient contacts with the United States to justify application of the territorial principle: the cruise ship departed from and returned to a U.S. port; Neil (D) was arrested in the United States; the victim was a U.S. national; and the victim sought counseling in the United States. The second principle is the passive personality principle, under which a State may assert jurisdiction—in certain cases—over crimes committed against its nationals. Notwithstanding that, generally, the passive personality principle has not been accepted as a sufficient basis for extraterritorial jurisdiction over ordinary torts and crimes, that does not militate against a finding of jurisdiction here, where the statute at issue invokes the passive personality principle by expressly stating that it applies where the victim is a U.S. national. Affirmed.

ANALYSIS

Extraterritorial jurisdiction based on the passive personality principle has been sustained when the victims of the defendant's failure to make child support payments were American citizens, *see, e.g., United States v. Hill, 279 F.3d 731* (9th Cir. 2002), or when a Mexican national assisted in the kidnapping and murder of an American Drug Enforcement Agency agent in Mexico, see, e.g., *United States v. Felix-Gutierrez,* 940 F.2d 1200 (9th Cir. 1991). This principle has been increasingly accepted when applied to terrorist and other organized attacks on a State's nationals that are motivated by those victims' nationality.

Quicknotes

INTERNATIONAL LAW The body of law applicable to dealings between nations.

JURISDICTION The authority of a court to hear and declare judgment in respect to a particular matter.

United States v. Vasquez-Velasco

Federal government (P) v. Foreign drug trafficker (D)

15 F.3d 833 (9th Cir. 1994)

NATURE OF CASE: Appeal of criminal conviction.

FACT SUMMARY: Javier Vasquez-Velasco (D), a member of a drug cartel in Guadalajara, and several other members, beat and killed [John] Walker [an American citizen writing a novel in Mexico] and [Alberto] Radelat [a photographer and U.S. legal resident]. He was convicted under U.S. law. On appeal, Vasquez-Velasco (D) argued that U.S. penal laws do not apply extraterritorially.

RULE OF LAW

Extraterritorial application of a penal statute to the murder of a U.S. citizen mistaken for a federal agent is consistent with principles of international law.

FACTS: *United States v. Felix-Gutierrez,* 940 F.2d 1200 (9th Cir. 1991), *cert. denied,* 508 U.S. 906 (1993), a case in which a defendant was convicted of kidnapping and murdering Enrique Camarena, an American Drug Enforcement Agency (DEA) agent, and Alfredo Zavala, a DEA informant, was the basis for the appeal by the defendant in this case, Javier Vasquez-Velasco (D). Vasquez-Velasco (D), a member of a drug cartel in Guadalajara, and several other members, beat and killed [John] Walker [an American citizen writing a novel in Mexico] and [Alberto] Radelat [a photographer and U.S. legal resident]. At trial, the Government (P) argued that Vasquez-Velasco (D) and his three co-defendants committed the crimes to further their positions in a Guadalajara drug cartel. The murders Vasquez-Velasco (D) was charged with were allegedly retaliatory actions against a DEA crackdown. Vasquez-Velasco (D) was convicted in a jury trial of committing violent crimes in aid of a racketeering enterprise in violation of 18 U.S.C. § 1959. On appeal, Vasquez-Velasco (D) argued that U.S. penal laws do not apply extraterritorially.

ISSUE: Is the extraterritorial application of a penal statute to the murder of a U.S. citizen mistaken for a federal agent consistent with principles of international law?

HOLDING AND DECISION: (Fletcher, J.) Yes. Extraterritorial application of a penal statute to the murder of a U.S. citizen mistaken for a federal agent is consistent with principles of international law. International law generally permits the exercise of extraterritorial jurisdiction under the objective territorial principle, under which jurisdiction is asserted over acts performed outside the United States that produce detrimental effects within the United States, and the protective principle, under which jurisdiction is asserted over foreigners for an act committed outside the United States that may impinge on the territorial integrity, security, or political independence of the United States. Extraterritorial application of 18 U.S.C. § 1959 to violent crimes associated with drug trafficking is reasonable under international law principles, since it is a serious and universally condemned offense. Despite the fact the crimes in this case did not involve the murder of a DEA agent, extraterritorial jurisdiction is still appropriate because, according to the Government's (P) theory, the cartel members mistook Walker and Radelat for DEA agents. As in *Felix-Gutierrez,* the crime was directed against the United States. Affirmed.

ANALYSIS

The objective territorial and protective principles apply because the defendant in this case murdered the two U.S. citizens on the mistaken belief they were Drug Enforcement Agency (DEA) agents, and their murders might intimidate the DEA and local police and drug agencies, who might otherwise cooperate with the DEA. The case therefore turns on the defendant's subjective beliefs; if the Government had been unsuccessful in its argument that the murders were committed as retaliation against the DEA, extraterritorial jurisdiction would be harder to apply.

Quicknotes

INTERNATIONAL LAW The body of law applicable to dealings between nations.

JURISDICTION The authority of a court to hear and declare judgment in respect to a particular matter.

RACKETEERING A conspiracy organized for the commission or attempted commission of extortion or coercion.

Regina v. Bartle, Bow Street Stipendiary Magistrate and Commissioner of Police, Ex Parte Pinochet

Government (P) v. Alleged torturer (D)

U.K. House of Lords, 2 W.L.R. 827, 38 I.L.M. 581 (1999)

NATURE OF CASE: Appeal from arrest and extradition order.

FACT SUMMARY: Pinochet (D) claimed that he could not be extradited because he was not guilty of any crime under English law.

RULE OF LAW
Torture is an international crime.

FACTS: An English magistrate issued an arrest warrant for Pinochet (D), the former head of state of Chile, at the request of a Spanish investigating judge for extradition. The House of Lords found that Pinochet (D) could not claim immunity in regard to torture that had been made a universal crime by the International Convention Against Torture and other Cruel, Inhuman, or Degrading Treatment or Punishment of 1984. Pinochet (D) claimed torture was not strictly an international crime in the highest sense.

ISSUE: Is torture an international crime?

HOLDING AND DECISION: (Lord Browne-Wilkinson, J.) Yes. Torture is an international crime. The Torture Convention was agreed not in order to create an international crime that had not previously existed but to provide an international system under which the international criminal—the torturer—could find no safe haven. All State parties are required to prohibit torture on their territory and to take jurisdiction over any alleged offender who is found within their territory. Torture is to be treated as an extraditable offense and will be considered to have been committed not only in the place where it occurred but also in the State where either the alleged offender or victim is a national.

ANALYSIS

The Torture Convention created an exception to the otherwise applicable immunity of present and former heads of state from criminal process. Pinochet (D) ultimately was found to be too sick to stand trial. He was allowed to return to Chile.

Quicknotes

EXTRADITION The surrender by one state or nation to another of an individual allegedly guilty of committing a crime in that area.

IMMUNITY Exemption from a legal obligation.

United States v. Yousef

Federal government (P) v. Convicted terrorist (D)

327 F.3d 56 (2d Cir. 2003)

NATURE OF CASE: Appeal from conviction of bombing a foreign airplane.

FACT SUMMARY: [Yousef (D) and another co-defendant (D) appealed from their conviction in federal district court on charges of bombing a Philippine airplane outside the United States (P) that carried no U.S. citizens, on the grounds the court lacked jurisdiction.]

RULE OF LAW

Universal jurisdiction arises under customary international law only where crimes (1) are universally condemned by the community of nations, and (2) by their nature occur either outside of a State or where there is no State capable of punishing, or competent to punish, the crime.

FACTS: [Yousef (D) and another co-defendant (D), who were not United States nationals, appealed from their conviction in federal district court on charges of bombing a Philippine airplane outside the United States (P) that carried no U.S. citizens, on the grounds the court lacked jurisdiction. The district court held it had jurisdiction, on the principle of universal jurisdiction, since it concluded the defendants' conduct qualified as terrorist acts. The court of appeals granted review.]

ISSUE: Does universal jurisdiction arise under customary international law only where crimes (1) are universally condemned by the community of nations, and (2) by their nature occur either outside of a State or where there is no State capable of punishing, or competent to punish, the crime?

HOLDING AND DECISION: [Judge not stated in casebook excerpt.] Yes. Universal jurisdiction arises under customary international law only where crimes (1) are universally condemned by the community of nations, and (2) by their nature occur either outside of a State or where there is no State capable of punishing, or competent to punish, the crime. Universal jurisdiction historically was restricted to piracy, and, in more recent times, has been expanded to include war crimes, and crimes against humanity. Unlike those offenses, "terrorism" does not have a precise definition and has not achieved universal condemnation. In fact, the nations of the world are divisively split on the legitimacy of such aggression. Given such a lack of international consensus on the definition of terrorism or even its proscription, labeling acts as acts of terrorism does not provide a basis for universal jurisdiction. Reversed.

ANALYSIS

The court of appeals, while concluding universal jurisdiction was unavailable, nevertheless ruled extraterritorial jurisdiction could be based on the protective principle of jurisdiction, since the bombing of the Philippine aircraft was part of a larger plot to attack U.S. aircraft, as well as on the Montreal Convention for the Suppression of Unlawful Acts Against the Safety of Civil Aviation (the Montreal Convention), the purpose of which is to ensure individuals who attack airlines cannot take refuge in a country because its courts lack jurisdiction over someone who committed such an act against a foreign-flag airline in another nation.

Quicknotes

INDICTMENT A formal written accusation made by a prosecutor and issued by a grand jury, charging an individual with a criminal offense.

INTERNATIONAL LAW The body of law applicable to dealings between nations.

JURISDICTION The authority of a court to hear and declare judgment in respect to a particular matter.

TREATY An agreement between two or more nations for the benefit of the general public.

Wilson v. Girard

U.S. Secretary of Defense (P) v. U.S. soldier (D)

354 U.S. 524 (1957)

NATURE OF CASE: Appeal from an injunction against extradition.

FACT SUMMARY: Girard (D), a Specialist Third Class in the United States Army, wounded a Japanese woman during a military exercise in Japan. Japan indicted Girard (D) for causing death by wounding, but Girard (D) was granted an injunction against his delivery to the Japanese authorities.

RULE OF LAW

A sovereign nation has exclusive jurisdiction to punish offenses against its laws committed within its borders, unless it expressly or impliedly consents to surrender its jurisdiction.

FACTS: Girard (D), a Specialist Third Class in the United States Army, wounded a Japanese woman during a military exercise in Japan. A security treaty between Japan and the United States authorized the making of administrative agreements between the two governments concerning the conditions that would govern the disposition of the United States Armed Forces in Japan. Such an agreement provided that the United States might waive its jurisdiction over offenses committed in Japan by members of its armed forces. Subsequently, another protocol agreement was signed by the two governments, pursuant to the North Atlantic Treaty Organization (NATO) agreement. It authorized that in criminal cases where the right to jurisdiction is concurrent, the military authorities of the United States would have the primary right to exercise jurisdiction over members of the armed forces for offenses arising out of any act or omission done in the performance of official duty. The United States (P) claimed the right to try Girard (D) on the ground that his act was done in the performance of official duty giving the United States primary jurisdiction. Japan insisted that Girard's (D) action was not within the scope of his official duty and therefore it had the primary right of jurisdiction. The United States ultimately waived whatever jurisdiction it might have. Girard (D) sought a writ of habeas corpus that was denied, but he was granted an injunction against delivery to the Japanese authorities. Wilson (P), Secretary of Defense, appealed.

ISSUE: Does a sovereign nation have exclusive jurisdiction to punish offenses against its laws committed within its borders, unless it expressly or impliedly consents to surrender its jurisdiction?

HOLDING AND DECISION: (Per curiam) Yes. A sovereign nation has exclusive jurisdiction to punish offenses against it committed within its borders, unless it expressly or impliedly consents to surrender its jurisdiction. Japan's cession to the United States of jurisdiction to try American military personnel for conduct constituting an offense against the laws of both countries was conditioned by the protocol agreement, which provided that "the authorities of the State having the primary right shall give sympathetic consideration to a request from the authorities of the other State for a waiver of its right in cases where that other State considers such a waiver to be of particular importance." Furthermore, there has been no prohibition against this under the Constitution or legislation subsequent to the security treaty. In the absence of such statutory or constitutional barriers, the wisdom of the arrangement is exclusively for the determination of the Executive and Legislative Branches. These branches have decided to waive jurisdiction and deliver Girard (D) to the Japanese authorities. Therefore, the judgment of the district court is reversed.

ANALYSIS

The trend toward granting limited immunities in cases relating to official acts and activities appears to be on the increase. This is to be distinguished from the normal diplomatic immunities that are part of customary international law. The agreements between the United States and Japan are good examples of the willingness of one nation to grant a special position to foreign government employees.

Quicknotes

EXTRADITION The surrender by one State or nation to another of an individual allegedly guilty of committing a crime in that area.

INJUNCTION A court order requiring a person to do or prohibiting that person from doing a specific act.

TREATY An agreement between two or more nations for the benefit of the general public.

WAIVER Intentional or voluntary forfeiture of a recognized right.

WRIT OF HABEAS CORPUS A proceeding in which a defendant brings a writ to compel a judicial determination of whether he is lawfully being held in custody.

CHAPTER 12

Immunity from Jurisdiction

Quick Reference Rules of Law

CHAPTER 12

12. *Georges v. United Nations.* (1) The fulfillment by the United Nations (UN) of its obligation under Section 29 of the Convention on Privileges and Immunities of the United Nations (CPIUN) to "make provisions for appropriate modes of settlement of" certain disputes is not a condition precedent to its immunity under Section 2 of the CPIUN, which provides that the UN "shall enjoy immunity from every form of legal process except insofar as in any particular case it has expressly waived its immunity." (2) Individuals do not have standing to challenge the United Nation's (UN's) immunity under the Convention on Privileges and Immunities of the United Nations (CPIUN) on the basis of a material breach thereof by the UN. (3) A U.S. citizen's constitutional right to access federal courts is not violated where such access is denied on the basis of an international organization's or sovereign's immunity. *131*

The Schooner *Exchange* v. McFadden

Government (D) v. Claimants (P)

11 U.S. (7 Cranch) 116 (1812)

NATURE OF CASE: Appeal from reversal of dismissal of claim of ownership.

FACT SUMMARY: Two Americans (P) claimed that they owned and were entitled to possession of the schooner *Exchange*.

RULE OF LAW

National ships of war entering the port of a friendly power are to be considered as exempted by the consent of that power from its jurisdiction.

FACTS: Two Americans (P) claimed they had seized the schooner *Exchange* on the high seas and that they now owned it and were entitled to possession of the ship. The United States Attorney (D) claimed that the United States and France were at peace and that a public ship of the Emperor of France had been compelled by bad weather to enter the port of Philadelphia and was prevented by leaving by process of the court. The district court granted the United States' (D) request to dismiss the claims of ownership and ordered that the ship be released. The circuit court reversed, and the United States (D) appealed to the United States Supreme Court.

ISSUE: Are national ships of war entering the port of a friendly power to be considered as exempted by the consent of that power from its jurisdiction?

HOLDING AND DECISION: (Marshall, C.J.) Yes. National ships of war entering the port of a friendly power are to be considered as exempted by the consent of that power from its jurisdiction. The jurisdiction of the nation within its own territory is exclusive and absolute. The *Exchange*, a public armed ship, in the service of a foreign sovereign, with whom the United States is at peace, and having entered an American port open for her reception, must be considered to have come into the American territory, under an implied promise, that while necessarily within it, and demeaning herself in a friendly manner, she should be exempt from the jurisdiction of the country. Reversed and district court judgment affirmed.

ANALYSIS

This case implicated the absolute form of sovereign immunity from judicial jurisdiction. The Court highlighted three principles: the exemption of the person of the sovereign from arrest or detention within a foreign country; the immunity that all civilized nations allow to foreign ministers; that a sovereign is understood to cede a portion of his territorial jurisdiction when he allows troops of a foreign prince to pass through his dominions.

Quicknotes

JURISDICTION The authority of a court to hear and declare judgment in respect to a particular matter.

SOVEREIGN IMMUNITY Immunity of government from suit without its consent.

Argentine Republic v. Amerada Hess Shipping Corp.

Country at war (D) v. Foreign corporations (P)

488 U.S. 428 (1989)

NATURE OF CASE: Review of reversal of dismissal of action seeking damages for property destruction.

FACT SUMMARY: A pair of Liberian corporations (P) sought to sue the Argentine Republic (D) in U.S. courts under the Alien Tort Statute.

RULE OF LAW

The Alien Tort Statute does not confer jurisdiction over foreign States.

FACTS: United Carriers, Inc. (United) (P), a Liberian corporation, chartered a vessel called the *Hercules* to Amerada Hess Shipping Corporation (Amerada) (P), another Liberian corporation. The ship was to be used to transport fuel. While off the South American coast during the 1983 Falkland Islands War, it was irreparably damaged and had to be scuttled. United (P) and Amerada (P) sued Argentina (D) in U.S. District Court. The court dismissed, holding jurisdiction to be absent. The Second Circuit Court of Appeals reversed, holding that jurisdiction existed under the Alien Tort Statute of 1789. The United States Supreme Court granted review.

ISSUE: Does the Alien Tort Statute confer jurisdiction over foreign States?

HOLDING AND DECISION: (Rehnquist, C.J.) No. The Alien Tort Statute does not confer jurisdiction over foreign States. The statute confers jurisdiction in district courts over suits brought by aliens in tort for violations of international law or U.S. treaties. The law, as an initial matter, is silent as to whether it applies to suits against foreign States. More importantly, in 1976, Congress enacted the Foreign Sovereign Immunities Act (FSIA), which dealt in a comprehensive manner with the issue of jurisdiction over foreign States. The law provides that, except as provided in the Act, foreign States shall be immune from U.S. courts' jurisdiction. While the FSIA does not explicitly repeal the Alien Tort Statute to the extent that it may confer jurisdiction over a foreign State, it is clear this was the intent behind the FSIA. This being so, the FSIA can be the only source of jurisdiction over a foreign State. Reversed.

ANALYSIS

The main focus of the Foreign Sovereign Immunities Act (FSIA) appears to be commercial. There are a variety of commercial activities that occur outside the United States that can lead to a foreign State's being sued in a U.S. court. The same is not true in the tort arena.

Quicknotes

DAMAGES Monetary compensation may be awarded by the court to a party who has sustained injury or loss to his person, property, or rights due to another party's unlawful act, omission, or negligence.

JURISDICTION The authority of a court to hear and declare judgment in respect to a particular matter.

TORT A legal wrong resulting in a breach of duty by the wrongdoer, causing damages as a result of the breach.

Siderman de Blake v. Republic of Argentina

Property owner and torture victim (P) v. Sovereign (D)

965 F.2d 699 (9th Cir. 1992)

NATURE OF CASE: Appeal from a judgment dismissing torture claims lodged against the government of another country.

FACT SUMMARY: After the military regime governing Argentina (D) tortured Jose Siderman (P) and threatened his family with death, the Sidermans (P) fled to the United States, later filing this complaint for damages due to the torture and for the expropriation of their property.

RULE OF LAW

The right to be free from official torture is fundamental and universal, a right deserving of the highest status under international law.

FACTS: After the Argentine (D) military regime subjected Jose Siderman (P) to seven days of torture, during which they shouted anti-Semitic epithets at him, they left him in an isolated area, threatening his family with death unless they left Argentina (D) immediately. Forced to sell an interest in 127,000 acres of land at a steep discount in order to finance their flight, the Sidermans (P) came to the United States. Argentine (D) military officials diverted to themselves the profits and revenues from the Sidermans' (P) corporation, INOSA. The Sidermans (P) filed this complaint, alleging torture and expropriation of their property. When Argentina (D) did not appear, the court entered a default judgment for the Sidermans (P) on the torture claim but dismissed the expropriation claims. The district court later vacated the default judgment, dismissing the action on the grounds of Argentina's (D) immunity under the Foreign Sovereign Immunity Act (FSIA). The Sidermans (P) appealed.

ISSUE: Is the right to be free from official torture fundamental and universal, a right deserving of the highest status under international law?

HOLDING AND DECISION: [Judge not stated in casebook excerpt.] Yes. The right to be free from official torture is fundamental and universal, a right deserving of the highest status under international law. The record reveals no ground for shielding Argentina (D) from the Sidermans' (P) claims that their family business was stolen from them by the military junta. It further suggests that Argentina (D) has implicitly waived its sovereign immunity with respect to the Sidermans' (P) claims for torture. Thus, the district court erred in dismissing the Sidermans' (P) torture claims. Reversed.

ANALYSIS

While not all customary international law carries with it the force of a *jus cogens* norm, which is derived from values taken to be fundamental by the international community, the prohibition against official torture has attained that status. Thus, under international law, any State that engages in official torture violates a *jus cogens* norm. The court concluded, however, that if violations of a *jus cogens* norm committed outside the United States were to be exceptions to immunity, Congress must make them so. The fact that there had been a violation of a *jus cogens* norm did not confer jurisdiction under the FSIA.

Quicknotes

***JUS COGENS* NORM** Universally understood principles of international law that cannot be set aside because they are based on fundamental human values.

SOVEREIGN IMMUNITY Immunity of government from suit without its consent.

Republic of Argentina v. Weltover, Inc.

Bond issuer (D) v. Bond holders (P)

504 U.S. 607 (1992)

NATURE OF CASE: Review of denial of dismissal of action for breach of contract.

FACT SUMMARY: Argentina (D) contended that it could not be sued in a U.S. court for defaulting on bonds it had issued.

RULE OF LAW

A foreign government may be amenable to suit in a U.S. court for defaulting on its bonds.

FACTS: Due to currency instability, Argentine businesses often had trouble participating in foreign transactions. The Argentine government (D), to ameliorate this problem, instituted a program wherein it agreed to sell to domestic borrowers U.S. dollars in exchange for Argentine currency. The dollars could be used to pay foreign creditors of Argentine businesses. Argentina (D) issued bonds, called "Bonods," to reflect its obligations. In 1986, Argentina (D), facing a shortage of reserves of U.S. dollars, defaulted on bond payments. Several bondholders (P), who collectively owned $1.3 million worth of bonds payable in New York, sued for breach of contract in federal court in New York. Argentina (D) moved to dismiss, asserting sovereign immunity. The district court denied the motion, and the Second Circuit Court of Appeals affirmed. The United States Supreme Court granted review.

ISSUE: May a foreign government be amenable to suit in a U.S. court for defaulting on its bonds?

HOLDING AND DECISION: (Scalia, J.) Yes. A foreign government may be amenable to suit in a U.S. court for defaulting on its bonds. The Foreign Sovereign Immunities Act of 1976 (FSIA) creates an exception to foreign sovereign immunity "commercial" activities. For purposes of the FSIA, an activity falls within the exception if (1) it occurs outside the United States, (2) is in connection with commerce, and (3) causes a direct effect in the United States. Here, the first element without question has been satisfied. Whether a government's activity is "commercial" must be determined with reference to the nature of the act. The issuing of a bond is a commercial rather than a sovereign act—private concerns can and often do issue bonds; it is not an activity given only to sovereigns. Finally, an effect is "direct" if an effect is the natural and immediate consequence of the activity in question. Here, the effect in the United States was direct because the bonds were payable in New York, so the breach occurred there. In sum, the activities of Argentina (D) with respect to the bonds were commercial in nature, so the commercial activity exception to the FSIA applies. Affirmed.

ANALYSIS

The key to determining if the commercial activity exception applies in any given case is whether the government has entered the marketplace. If it has, it is to be treated, under the Foreign Sovereign Immunities Act of 1976 (FSIA), as a private player. If it undertakes an activity peculiar to a sovereign, the exception does not apply.

Quicknotes

BOND A debt instrument issued by the issuing entity evidencing a promise to repay the loan with a specified amount of interest on a particular date.

BREACH OF CONTRACT Unlawful failure by a party to perform its obligations pursuant to contract.

SOVEREIGN IMMUNITY Immunity of government from suit without its consent.

Permanent Mission of India to the United Nations v. City of New York

Sovereign's permanent mission (D) v. Municipality (P)

551 U.S. 193 (2007)

NATURE OF CASE: Appeal from affirmance of decision denying immunity from declaratory judgment action to establish the validity of tax liens.

FACT SUMMARY: India (D) and Mongolia (D) contended that they were immune under the Foreign Sovereign Immunities Act from New York City's ("the City") (P) action seeking declaratory judgments that tax liens the City (P) had on buildings owned by India (D) and Mongolia (D) were valid to the extent the buildings were used to house diplomatic employees.

RULE OF LAW

The Foreign Sovereign Immunities Act of 1976 does not immunize a foreign government from a lawsuit to declare the validity of tax liens on property held by the sovereign for the purpose of housing its employees.

FACTS: India (D) and Mongolia (D) owned buildings in New York City ("the City") (P) that in part were used to house lower-level diplomatic employees. Under New York law, real property owned by a foreign government is exempt from taxation when used exclusively for diplomatic offices or quarters for ambassadors or ministers-plenipotentiary to the United Nations. For years, the City (P) levied property taxes against India (D) and Mongolia (D) for that portion of their diplomatic office buildings used to house lower-level employees and their families, but the governments (D) refused to pay the taxes. By operation of state law, the unpaid taxes converted into tax liens held by the City (P) against the properties. The City (P) filed a state-court suit seeking declaratory judgments to establish the liens' validity, but the governments (D) removed the cases to federal court, where they argued that they were immune under the Foreign Sovereign Immunities Act of 1976 (FSIA), which is "the sole basis for obtaining jurisdiction over a foreign State in federal court." The district court disagreed, relying on a FSIA exception withdrawing a foreign State's immunity from jurisdiction where "rights in immovable property situated in the United States are in issue." The court of appeals affirmed, holding that the "immovable property" exception applied, and thus the district court had jurisdiction over the City's (P) suits. The United States Supreme Court granted certiorari.

ISSUE: Does the Foreign Sovereign Immunities Act of 1976 immunize a foreign government from a lawsuit to declare the validity of tax liens on property held by the sovereign for the purpose of housing its employees?

HOLDING AND DECISION: (Thomas, J.) No. The the Foreign Sovereign Immunities Act of 1976 (FSIA) does not immunize a foreign government from a lawsuit to declare the validity of tax liens on property held by the sovereign for the purpose of housing its employees. Under the FSIA, a foreign State is presumptively immune from suit unless a specific exception applies. In determining the immovable property exception's scope, the Court begins, as always, with the statute's text. Section 1605(a)(4) of the FSIA does not expressly limit itself to cases in which the specific right at issue is title, ownership, or possession, nor does it specifically exclude cases in which a lien's validity is at issue. Rather, it focuses more broadly on "rights in" property. At the time of the FSIA's adoption, "lien" was defined as a "charge or security or incumbrance upon property," and "incumbrance" was defined as "[a]ny right to, or interest in, land which may subsist in another to the diminution of its value." New York law defines "tax lien" in accordance with these general definitions. A lien's practical effects bear out the definitions of liens as interests in property. Because a lien on real property runs with the land and is enforceable against subsequent purchasers, a tax lien inhibits a quintessential property ownership right—the right to convey. It is thus plain that a suit to establish a tax lien's validity implicates "rights in immovable property." Such an interpretation is supported by two of the FSIA's purposes: adoption of the restrictive view of sovereign immunity and codification of international law at the time of the FSIA's enactment. First, property ownership is not an inherently sovereign function. Moreover, the FSIA was intended to codify the preexisting real property exception to sovereign immunity recognized by international practice. That practice supports the City's (P) view that India (D) and Mongolia (D) are not immune, as does the contemporaneous restatement of foreign relations law. That restatement stated that a foreign sovereign's immunity does not extend to "an action to obtain possession of or establish a property interest in immovable property located in the territory of the State exercising jurisdiction." Restatement (Second) of Foreign Relations Law of the United States § 68(b), p. 205 (1965). Because an action seeking the declaration of the validity of a tax lien on property is a suit to establish an interest in such property, such an action would be allowed under this rule. Affirmed.

DISSENT: (Stevens, J.) The true dispute in this case is over a foreign sovereign's tax liability—not about the validity of the City's (P) lien. Had Congress intended to waive sovereign immunity in tax litigation, it would have said as much.

Continued on next page.

ANALYSIS

Even if the tax liens in this case are declared valid, India (D) and Mongolia (D) would be immune from foreclosure proceedings. Nevertheless, the benefit to the City (P) of having the liens validated is that once a court has declared property tax liens valid, foreign sovereigns traditionally concede and pay. Even if the foreign sovereign fails to pay in the face of a valid court judgment, that country's foreign aid may be reduced by the United States by 110 percent of the outstanding debt. Finally, the liens would be enforceable against subsequent purchasers.

Quicknotes

CERTIORARI A discretionary writ issued by a superior court to an inferior court in order to review the lower court's decisions; the United States Supreme Court's writ ordering such review.

LIEN A claim against the property of another in order to secure the payment of a debt.

SOVEREIGN IMMUNITY Immunity of government from suit without its consent.

Doe v. Federal Democratic Republic of Ethiopia

U.S. citizen (P) v. Foreign nation (D)

851 F.3d 7 (D.C. Cir. 2017)

NATURE OF CASE: Appeal from dismissal, for lack of subject matter jurisdiction, of action against foreign nation for the tort of intrusion-upon-seclusion.

FACT SUMMARY: A U.S. citizen, pseudonymously named Kidane (P), brought suit for an intrusion-upon-seclusion tort against the Federal Democratic Republic of Ethiopia (Ethiopia) (D), contending that Ethiopia (D) had violated his privacy by tricking him into downloading software that it could use to spy on him without his knowledge. Kidane (P) also contended that the U.S. courts had jurisdiction through an exception in the Foreign Sovereign Immunities Act—which otherwise precludes jurisdiction for suits against sovereign nations—for noncommercial torts.

RULE OF LAW

For the noncommercial-torts exception in the Foreign Sovereign Immunities Act to apply to confer jurisdiction on United States courts, the alleged tort must have occurred solely within the United States.

FACTS: John Doe, pseudonymously named Kidane (P), was born in the Federal Democratic Republic of Ethiopia (Ethiopia) (D), but he moved to the United States and became a U.S. citizen. Kidane (P) sought to bring suit for an intrusion-upon-seclusion tort against Ethiopia (D). Kidane (P) claimed he was tricked into downloading a computer program that allegedly enabled Ethiopia (D) to spy on him from abroad. However, foreign States are immune from suit unless an exception to the Foreign Sovereign Immunities Act (FSIA) applies. Kidane (P) invoked the FSIA's exception for noncommercial torts, which abrogates immunity from an action involving "personal injury or death, or damage to or loss of property, occurring in the United States and caused by the tortious act or omission of [a] foreign State or of any official or employee of that foreign State while acting within the scope of his office or employment[.]" 28 U.S.C. § 1605(a)(5). Finding that at least a portion of the alleged tort must have occurred transnationally outside the United States, the district court held that the FSIA's exception for noncommercial torts was inapplicable and dismissed for lack of subject matter jurisdiction. The court of appeals granted review.

ISSUE: For the noncommercial-torts exception in the Foreign Sovereign Immunities Act to apply to confer jurisdiction on United States courts, must the alleged tort have occurred solely within the United States?

HOLDING AND DECISION: (Henderson, J.) Yes. For the noncommercial-torts exception in the Foreign Sovereign Immunities Act (FSIA) to apply to confer jurisdiction on United States courts, the alleged tort must have occurred solely within the United States. The phrase in the FSIA, "occurring in the United States" is no mere surplusage, and it has been established through precedent that the entire tort—including not only the injury but also the act precipitating that injury—must occur in the United States. Ethiopia's (D) alleged digital espionage could not have occurred entirely in the United States. Without the software's initial dispatch or an intent to spy—integral aspects of the final tort that lay solely abroad—Ethiopia (D) could not have intruded upon Kidane's (P) seclusion. Given that Congress's primary purpose in enacting the FSIA exception for noncommercial torts was to eliminate a foreign State's immunity for traffic accidents and other torts committed in the United States, for which liability is imposed under domestic tort law, it is clear that transnational cyberespionage lies beyond the exception's reach. Affirmed.

ANALYSIS

Kidane (P) also argued that when the United States Congress codified the noncommercial-torts exception, it considered—but rejected—the approach of the European Convention on State Immunity. The European Convention abrogated sovereign immunity for certain torts if the facts underlying the torts occurred in the forum nation and if "the author of the injury or damage was present in that territory at the time." European Convention on State Immunity art. 11, reprinted in *Hearings on H.R. 11,315 Before the Subcomm. on Admin. Law & Governmental Relations of the H. Comm. on the Judiciary*, 94th Cong. 39 (1976) (1976 Hearings). Kidane (P) noted the absence of similar language in the exception. However, the court rejected this argument, concluding that Kidane (P) read too much into Congress's silence on this point, especially in light of Congress's purpose in enacting the exception.

Quicknotes

SOVEREIGN IMMUNITY Immunity of government from suit without its consent.

Dole Food Company v. Patrickson

Corporation (D) v. Food worker (P)

538 U.S. 468 (2003)

NATURE OF CASE: Appeal from judgment denying removal to federal district court to foreign corporations impleaded in a state-court tort action.

FACT SUMMARY: Dead Sea Bromine Co. and Bromine Compounds, Ltd. (collectively, the Dead Sea Companies (D)), which were impleaded by Dole Food Company and others (Dole petitioners) (D) in a state-court tort action, contended that as subsidiaries of an instrumentality of Israel they were entitled to remove the case to federal district court under the Foreign Sovereign Immunities Act of 1976.

RULE OF LAW

(1) Under the Foreign Sovereign Immunities Act of 1976, a State must own a majority of the shares of a corporation if the corporation is to be deemed an instrumentality of the State.

(2) Instrumentality status under the Foreign Sovereign Immunities Act of 1976 is determined at the time the complaint is filed.

FACTS: Farm workers (P) filed a state-court action against Dole Food Company and others (Dole petitioners) (D), alleging injury from chemical exposure. The Dole petitioners (D) impleaded Dead Sea Bromine Co. and Bromine Compounds, Ltd. (collectively, the Dead Sea Companies (D)). As to the Dead Sea Companies (D), the court of appeals rejected their claim that they were instrumentalities of a foreign State (Israel) as defined by the Foreign Sovereign Immunities Act of 1976, and that they were therefore entitled to removal to federal district court. The court instead ruled that a subsidiary of an instrumentality is not itself entitled to instrumentality status. The United States Supreme Court granted certiorari.

ISSUE:

(1) Under the Foreign Sovereign Immunities Act of 1976, must a State own a majority of the shares of a corporation if the corporation is to be deemed an instrumentality of the State?

(2) Is instrumentality status under the Foreign Sovereign Immunities Act of 1976 determined at the time the complaint is filed?

HOLDING AND DECISION: (Kennedy, J.)

(1) Yes. Under the Foreign Sovereign Immunities Act of 1976 (FSIA), a State must own a majority of the shares of a corporation if the corporation is to be deemed an instrumentality of the State. Removal of actions against foreign States is governed by 28 U.S.C. § 1441(d). Section 1603(a) of the FSIA defines "foreign State" to include its "instrumentality," which in turn is defined, in part, as any entity "which is a . . . corporat[ion]" whose shares are majority-owned by the foreign State, and that is not a U.S. citizen or created under the laws of a third country. Thus, the issue is whether the Dead Sea Companies (D) were an instrumentality of Israel. Israel did not have any direct ownership of shares in these companies, which were separated from Israel by one or more intermediate corporate tiers. Therefore, the Dead Sea Companies (D) were only indirect subsidiaries of Israel. They do not satisfy the FSIA requirement that the State own "majority" of the shares of the corporation to qualify for instrumentality status. Only direct ownership satisfies the statutory requirement. In issues of corporate law structure often matters. The statutory reference to ownership of "shares" shows that Congress intended coverage to turn on formal corporate ownership. As a corporation and its shareholders are distinct entities, a corporate parent that owns a subsidiary's shares does not, for that reason alone, own or have, legal title to the subsidiary's assets; and, it follows with even greater force, the parent does not own or have legal title to the subsidiary's subsidiaries. The veil separating corporations and their shareholders may be pierced in certain exceptional circumstances, but the Dead Sea Companies (D) refer to no authority for extending the doctrine so far that, as a categorical matter, all subsidiaries are deemed to be the same as the parent corporation. Affirmed as to this issue.

(2) Yes. Instrumentality status under the Foreign Sovereign Immunities Act of 1976 (FSIA) is determined at the time the complaint is filed. The plain language of FSIA § 1603(b)(2), which requires that a corporation show that it is an entity "a majority of whose shares . . . is owned by a foreign State," and is expressed in the present tense, requires that instrumentality status be determined at the time the action is filed. Here, any relationship recognized under the FSIA between the Dead Sea Companies (D) and Israel had been severed before suit was commenced, so the companies would not be entitled to instrumentality status even if their theory that such status could be conferred on a subsidiary were accepted. Affirmed as to this issue.

ANALYSIS

Under corporate law principles, which the Court looked to in this case, the fact that Israel might have exercised

Continued on next page.

considerable control over the Dead Sea Companies (D) would not have changed the outcome of the Court's decision, since control and ownership are distinct concepts, and it is majority ownership by a foreign State, not control, that is the benchmark of instrumentality status.

Quicknotes

CERTIORARI A discretionary writ issued by a superior court to an inferior court in order to review the lower court's decisions; the Supreme Court's writ ordering such review.

IMPLEADER Procedure by which a third party, who may be liable for all or part of liability, is joined to an action so that all issues may be resolved in a single suit.

Rubin v. Islamic Republic of Iran

Judgment creditor (P) v. Foreign terrorism-sponsoring state (D)

138 S. Ct. 816 (2018)

NATURE OF CASE: Appeal from judgment denying judgment creditors from attaching and executing on certain property belonging to a foreign nation against which the judgment award was rendered. [The complete procedural posture of the case is not presented in the casebook extract.]

FACT SUMMARY: Judgment creditors (P), who obtained a judgment award against the Islamic Republic of Iran (Iran) (D) pursuant to the State-sponsor-of-terrorism exception in the Foreign Sovereign Immunity Act of 1976 (FSIA), sought to attach and execute on certain property belonging to Iran (D) held in the United States in satisfaction of the judgment, contending that the property was stripped of the immunity typically afforded to the property of a foreign State where the party seeking to attach and execute holds a judgment pursuant to the terrorist-State exception to the FSIA.

RULE OF LAW

Judgment creditors who have obtained their judgment award under the terrorist-State exception to the Foreign Sovereign Immunities Act of 1976 may not attach and execute on assets of the terrorist State against which they have obtained the judgment where the immunity of those assets from attachment and execution in satisfaction of such a judgment award has not been expressly rescinded by any statutory provision.

FACTS: The Foreign Sovereign Immunities Act of 1976 (FSIA), 28 U.S.C. §§ 1604, 1609, grants foreign States and their agencies and instrumentalities immunity from suit in the United States and grants their property immunity from attachment and execution in satisfaction of judgments against them, but with some exceptions. Judgment creditors (P) held a judgment against the Islamic Republic of Iran (Iran) (D) pursuant to one such exception that applies to foreign States designated as State sponsors of terrorism with respect to claims arising out of acts of terrorism, 28 U.S.C. § 1605A. To enforce that judgment, the judgment creditors (P) sought to attach and execute against certain Iranian assets—a collection of antiquities housed at the University of Chicago (D). The judgment creditors (P) contended that the property was stripped of its immunity by another provision of the FSIA, § 1610(g), which they maintained provides a blanket exception to the immunity typically afforded to the property of a foreign State where the party seeking to attach and execute holds a § 1605A judgment. The court of appeals disagreed with the judgment holders (P), and the United States Supreme Court granted certiorari. [The complete procedural posture of the case is not presented in the casebook extract.]

ISSUE: May judgment creditors who have obtained their judgment award under the terrorist-State exception to the Foreign Sovereign Immunities Act of 1976 attach and execute on assets of the terrorist State against which they have obtained the judgment where the immunity of those assets from attachment and execution in satisfaction of such a judgment award has not been expressly rescinded by any statutory provision?

HOLDING AND DECISION: (Sotomayor, J.) No. Judgment creditors who have obtained their judgment award under the terrorist-State exception to the Foreign Sovereign Immunities Act of 1976 (FSIA) may not attach and execute on assets of the terrorist State against which they have obtained the judgment where the immunity of those assets from attachment and execution in satisfaction of such a judgment award has not been expressly rescinded by any statutory provision. As a default rule under the FSIA, foreign States have immunity from the jurisdiction of U.S. courts, § 1604, but there are express exceptions, including the one at issue here, for State sponsors of terrorism, under § 1605A(a). Similarly, the FSIA provides as a default that "the property in the United States of a foreign State shall be immune from attachment arrest and execution." § 1609. However, § 1610 outlines certain exceptions to this immunity. In 2008, Congress amended the FSIA, adding § 1610(g), which made it clear that agencies and instrumentalities of a foreign State did not have immunity from suit or judgment where a § 1605A judgment holder sought to satisfy a judgment held against the foreign State. The issue thus boils down to whether § 1610(g) does something more, e.g., whether it provides an independent exception to immunity so that it allows a § 1605A judgment holder to attach and execute against any property of the foreign State, regardless of whether the property is deprived of immunity elsewhere in § 1610. Textually, § 1610(g)(1) provides that certain property will be "subject to attachment in aid of execution, and execution, upon [a § 1605A] judgment as provided in this section." The most natural reading is that "this section" refers to § 1610 as a whole, so § 1610(g)(1) will govern the attachment and execution of property that is exempted from the grant of immunity as provided elsewhere in § 1610. Other provisions of § 1610 unambiguously revoke the immunity of property of a foreign State, including specifically where a plaintiff holds a judgment under

Continued on next page.

§ 1605A, provided certain express conditions are satisfied. Unlike those other provisions, § 1610(g) conspicuously lacks the textual markers, "shall not be immune" or "notwithstanding any other provision of law," that would have shown that it serves as an independent avenue for abrogation of immunity. In fact, its use of the phrase "as provided in this section" signals the opposite: A judgment holder seeking to take advantage of § 1610(g)(1) must identify a basis under one of § 1610's express immunity-abrogating provisions to attach and execute against a relevant property. Thus, although § 1610(g) still provides relief to judgment holders who previously would not have been able to attach and execute against property of an agency or instrumentality of a foreign State, it does not provide a freestanding basis for parties holding a judgment under § 1605A to attach and execute against the property of a foreign State, where the immunity of the property is not otherwise rescinded under a separate provision within § 1610. In other instances where Congress wanted to rescind such immunity, it did so expressly. Out of respect for the delicate balance that Congress struck in enacting the FSIA, a blanket abrogation of attachment and execution immunity for § 1605A judgment holders cannot be read into the statute absent a clearer indication of Congress's intent. Affirmed.

ANALYSIS

The Court's interpretation of § 1610(g) arguably is consistent with the historical practice of rescinding attachment and execution immunity primarily in the context of a foreign State's commercial acts. Indeed, the Foreign Sovereign Immunities Act of 1976 (FSIA) expressly provides in its findings and declaration of purpose that "[u]nder international law, States are not immune from the jurisdiction of foreign courts insofar as their commercial activities are concerned, and their commercial property may be levied upon for the satisfaction of judgments rendered against them in connection with their commercial activities." Section 1602. This focus of the FSIA is reflected within § 1610, as subsections (a), (b), and (d) all outline exceptions to immunity of property when that property is used for commercial activity. The Court's reading of § 1610(g) means that individuals with § 1605A judgments against a foreign State must primarily invoke other provisions revoking the grant of immunity for property related to commercial activity, including § 1610(a)(7), unless the property is expressly carved out in an exception that applies notwithstanding any other provision of law. Thus, the Court is in effect saying that if Congress had intended to depart from the history and structure of the FSIA, it should have done so expressly in the text of the statute.

Quicknotes

ATTACHMENT The seizing of the property of one party in anticipation of, or in order to satisfy, a favorable judgment obtained by another party.

IMMUNITY Exemption from a legal obligation.

Jurisdictional Immunities of the State (Germany v. Italy: Greece Intervening)

Perpetrator of atrocities in World War II (P) v. Former ally (D)

2012 I.C.J. 99

NATURE OF CASE: Proceedings before the International Court of Justice alleging violation by one nation of another nation's jurisdictional immunity.

FACT SUMMARY: Germany (P) claimed Italy (D) violated Germany's (P) jurisdictional immunity by permitting Italian citizens to bring claims in Italy (D) against Germany (P) for atrocities committed by the German Third Reich in Italy during World War II.

RULE OF LAW

Customary international law requires that a State be accorded jurisdictional immunity in proceedings for torts allegedly committed on the territory of another State by its armed forces and other organs of State in the course of conducting an armed conflict.

FACTS: In June 1940, Italy (D) entered World War II as an ally of the German Third Reich. In September 1943, following the removal of Italy's (D) leader, Mussolini, from power, Italy (D) surrendered to the Allies and, the following month, declared war on Germany (P). German forces then occupied much of Italian territory and, between October 1943 and the end of the War, perpetrated many atrocities against the population of that territory, including massacres of civilians and deportation of large numbers of civilians for use as forced labor. In addition, German forces took as prisoners, both inside Italy (D) and elsewhere in Europe, several hundred thousand members of the Italian armed forces. Most of these prisoners (the "Italian military internees") were denied the status of prisoner of war and deported to Germany (P) and German-occupied territories for use as forced labor. Starting in 1998, Italian courts permitted Italian claimants to file suits against Germany (P) seeking reparations for the atrocities committed by the Third Reich. Italian courts also declared enforceable in Italy (D) decisions of Greek courts rendered against Germany (P) on the basis of German acts similar to those that gave rise to the claims brought before Italian courts (Greece was, for this reason, a non-party intervenor in the case). Italy (D) further took measures of constraint against Villa Vigoni, German State property located in Italy (D). Based on these acts of various Italian organs, Germany (P) brought proceedings in the International Court of Justice (I.C.J.) alleging Italy (D) had violated Germany's (P) jurisdictional immunity. Italy (D) argued that immunity should be denied under the territorial tort principal because the acts were committed in the territory of the forum State, and that regardless of where the acts occurred, immunity should be denied because the acts involved the most serious violations of the rules of international law of a peremptory character for which no alternative means of redress was available.

ISSUE: Does customary international law require that a State be accorded jurisdictional immunity in proceedings for torts allegedly committed on the territory of another State by its armed forces and other organs of state in the course of conducting an armed conflict?

HOLDING AND DECISION: [Judge not stated in casebook excerpt.] Yes. Customary international law requires that a State be accorded jurisdictional immunity in proceedings for torts allegedly committed on the territory of another State by its armed forces and other organs of state in the course of conducting an armed conflict. Sources of international customary law in this area include the decisions of national courts regarding the immunity of foreign States, State legislation, claims to immunity made by States before foreign courts, and the statements made by States regarding this subject. *Opinio juris* in this context is reflected by States' asserting that they are entitled, under international law, to immunity from the jurisdiction of other States. It is also reflected by States that grant such immunity, demonstrating their belief international law imposes upon them an obligation to do so. On the other hand, some States assert a right to exercise jurisdiction over foreign States. The International Law Commission (ILC) also concluded that the rule of State immunity is derived from customary international law, basing its conclusion on State practice. Of note, the ILC stated that the rule of State immunity does not apply in situations of armed conflict, and no State has questioned this interpretation. Moreover, those few States that have ratified the U.N. Convention on the Jurisdictional Immunities of States and Their Property (the Convention) have also declared their understanding that the Convention is inapplicable to armed conflict and military activities. Thus, that Convention cannot be read to support Italy's (D) position that immunity is denied in instances where tortious conduct committed by armed forces of a foreign State in the forum State's territory has resulted in death, personal injury or property damage. Judicial decisions from individual States support Germany's (P) position that immunity inheres in such situations, and this position is supported by *opinio juris*, as demonstrated by the positions taken by States and their jurisprudence. It is also significant that there is a near

Continued on next page.

absence of contrary jurisprudence, or statements by States to the contrary. For all these reasons, Germany (P) has immunity for the acts of its armed forces committed on Italy's (D) territory during World War II. [Judgment for Germany (P) as to this issue.]

ANALYSIS

As this decision illustrates, national courts and tribunals have been highly instrumental to the development of the doctrine of jurisdictional immunities of States, and it has been largely through the application of the principles of jurisdictional immunities of States that such national courts and tribunals typically started dealing with matters governed by international law. On the other hand, the role of national courts in adjudicating cases on the alleged violation of human rights by foreign States, has often been hampered, or even prevented, by the rule of jurisdictional immunity.

Quicknotes

IMMUNITY Exemption from a legal obligation.

JURISDICTION The authority of a court to hear and declare judgment in respect to a particular matter.

OPINIO JURIS An "opinion of law," or belief certain conduct must occur due to legal obligation.

Arrest Warrant of 11 April 2000 (Democratic Republic of the Congo v. Belgium)

Sovereign state (P) v. Sovereign state (D)

2002 I.C.J. 3

NATURE OF CASE: Application claiming violations of international law and seeking order of provisional measures of protection relating to an arrest warrant for a sovereign's foreign minister.

FACT SUMMARY: The Democratic Republic of the Congo (D.R.C.) (P) contended that an international arrest warrant for its foreign minister, issued by Belgium (D), violated international law by purporting to exercise jurisdiction over another State's foreign minister, and the D.R.C. (P) sought an order of provisional measures of protection on the ground that the warrant effectively prevented the foreign minister from leaving the D.R.C. (P).

RULE OF LAW

A State's foreign minister enjoys full immunity from criminal jurisdiction in another State's courts, even where the minister is suspected of humanitarian violations.

FACTS: Under Belgian law, which provided for universal jurisdiction in the case of grave breaches of the Geneva Conventions, crimes against humanity, and other serious offenses, a Belgian judge issued an international arrest warrant for the foreign minister of the Democratic Republic of the Congo (D.R.C.) (P), seeking his extradition on allegations of grave violations of humanitarian law. Belgian law also provided that any immunity conferred by an individual's official capacity did not prevent application of universal jurisdiction. The Belgian warrant was transmitted to the International Criminal Police Organization (Interpol) and was circulated internationally. The D.R.C. (P) brought an application against Belgium (D) in the International Court of Justice (I.C.J.), asserting that the warrant violated international law by purporting to exercise jurisdiction over another State's foreign minister, and that the minister should enjoy immunity equivalent to that enjoyed by diplomats and heads of state. The D.R.C. (P) also sought an order of provisional measures of protection on the ground that the warrant effectively prevented the foreign minister from leaving the D.R.C. (P). The I.C.J. issued its judgment.

ISSUE: Does a State's foreign minister enjoy full immunity from criminal jurisdiction in another State's courts, even where the minister is suspected of humanitarian violations?

HOLDING AND DECISION: [Judge not stated in casebook excerpt.] Yes. A State's foreign minister enjoys full immunity from criminal jurisdiction in another State's courts, even where the minister is suspected of war crimes or crimes against humanity. A foreign minister's duties involve overseeing the State's diplomatic activities, acting as the State's representative in international negotiations and meetings, and traveling internationally. The minister may bind the State, and he or she must be able to be in constant communication with the State and its diplomatic missions around the world, as well as with representatives of other States. Such a minister is recognized under international law as a representative of the State solely by virtue of his or her office. Based on these functions, an acting Minister of Foreign Affairs enjoys full immunity from criminal jurisdiction and inviolability so that he or she may not be hindered in the performance of his or her duties. Such immunity inheres regardless of whether the alleged criminal acts were performed in the minister's "official" capacity or "private" capacity, and regardless of when the conduct occurred. Otherwise, even the mere risk that by traveling to or transiting another State the minister might be exposed to legal proceedings could deter the minister from traveling internationally and fulfilling his or her official functions. Belgium's (D) argument that immunities cannot protect foreign ministers when they are accused of having committed war crimes or crimes against humanity is rejected. Belgium (D) points to instruments creating international criminal tribunals and decisions of national courts that state expressly that an individual's official capacity is not a bar to the exercise by such tribunals or courts of their jurisdiction. As support, it points to a judge's statement that "[i]nternational law cannot be supposed to have established a crime having the character of a *jus cogens* and at the same time to have provided an immunity that is coextensive with the obligation it seeks to impose." It also points to another judge's statement that "no established rule of international law requires State immunity *ratione materiae* to be accorded in respect of prosecution for an international crime." The Democratic Republic of the Congo (D.R.C.) (P), by contrast, points to statements by judges in the cases cited by Belgium (D) that support its assertion that, under international law as it currently stands, there is no exception to absolute immunity from criminal prosecution of an incumbent foreign minister accused of crimes under international law. The D.C.R. (P) also would limit the instruments creating war crimes tribunals to those tribunals and not extend them to other proceedings before

Continued on next page.

national courts. Based on current practice and court decisions of some nations, there is no exception to the rule according immunity from criminal jurisdiction and inviolability to incumbent foreign ministers suspected of having committed war crimes or crimes against humanity. Also, the rules regarding immunity for officials in the instruments creating war crimes tribunals are limited to those tribunals and do not create an exception to customary international law in regard to national courts. Decisions issued by those tribunals have not addressed the issue at bar and therefore do not affect this conclusion. Another consideration is that even if a national court has jurisdiction to prosecute an individual who is acting in an official capacity, such jurisdiction does not negate the individual's immunity under customary international law. Nevertheless, it must be emphasized that immunity from jurisdiction enjoyed by an incumbent foreign minister does not mean that he or she enjoys impunity for crimes he or she may have committed. Jurisdictional immunity is procedural, whereas criminal responsibility is a matter of substantive law, so that jurisdictional immunity does not operate to exonerate the minister, who may, under certain circumstances, be prosecuted for his or her crimes. The minister may be tried in the domestic courts of his or her State and may cease to enjoy immunity if the State that the minister represents waives it. After the minister ceases to hold office, the minister will no longer enjoy all the immunities he or she previously enjoyed, and may be prosecuted for acts committed prior to or subsequent to the time the minister was in office, as well as in respect of acts committed during that period of office in a private capacity. Finally, the minister may be tried by international criminal courts where they have jurisdiction.

ANALYSIS

This case did not decide the tenability of the claim of universal jurisdiction by domestic courts. However, some of the Court's judges, in a separate opinion, expressed the belief that universal jurisdiction is permitted in the case of those crimes considered the most heinous by the international community, so that the warrant for the arrest of the Democratic Republic of the Congo's (P) foreign minister did not as such violate international law. It thus appears that the judges of the International Court of Justice are split on the issue of universal jurisdiction as exercised by local or domestic courts. In any event, a domestic court's exercise of universal jurisdiction is not without precedent: in 1961, Israel claimed universal jurisdiction when it kidnapped the former Nazi Adolf Eichmann from Argentina, tried him in an Israeli court, and executed him.

Quicknotes

INTERNATINAL LAW Body of law applicable to dealings between nations.

JURISDICTION The authority of a court to hear and declare judgment in respect to a particular matter.

JUS COGENS Any principle of law that is recognized by the entire international community as essential to the preservation of human values and is therefore observed by all governments except outlawed governments.

Regina v. Bartle and Commissioner of Police, Ex Parte Pinochet

Government (P) v. Former head of state (D)

U.K. House of Lords, 2 W.L.R. 827, 38 I.L.M. 581 (1999)

NATURE OF CASE: Appeal from extradition proceedings.

FACT SUMMARY: Pinochet (D) claimed that he was immune from prosecution as a former head of state.

RULE OF LAW

The notion of continued immunity for former heads of state is inconsistent with the provisions of the Torture Convention.

FACTS: The House of Lords (P) considered charges that Pinochet (D), the former head of state of Chile, had violated the Torture Convention. Chile, Spain, and the United Kingdom were all parties to the Torture Convention, which became law on December 8, 1988. Pinochet (D) claimed he was immune as a former head of state under principle of international law.

ISSUE: Is the notion of continued immunity for former heads of state inconsistent with the provisions of the Torture Convention?

HOLDING AND DECISION: (Lord Browne-Wilkinson, J.) Yes. The notion of continued immunity for former heads of state is inconsistent with the provisions of the Torture Convention. If, as alleged, Pinochet (D) organized and authorized torture after December 8, 1988, he was not acting in any capacity that gives rise to immunity because such conduct was contrary to international law. The torture proceedings should proceed on the allegation that torture in pursuance of a conspiracy to commit torture was being committed by Pinochet (D) after December 1988 when he lost his immunity.

ANALYSIS

The court discussed the common law as well. Under common law, a former head of state enjoys immunity for official acts done while in office. The purpose of the Torture Convention was to provide that there is no safe haven for torturers.

Quicknotes

EXTRADITION The surrender by one State or nation to another of an individual allegedly guilty of committing a crime in that area.

SOVEREIGN IMMUNITY Immunity of government from suit without its consent.

Georges v. United Nations

Victim of cholera outbreak in Haiti (P) v. International organization (D)

834 F.3d 88 (2d Cir. 2016)

NATURE OF CASE: Appeal from dismissal for lack of subject matter jurisdiction of putative class action asserting various tort and contract claims against the United Nations.

FACT SUMMARY: Citizens of the United States or the Republic of Haiti (Haiti) (P), who claimed that they or their relatives were sickened or died, or would be sickened or would die, as a direct result of the cholera epidemic that ravaged Haiti, brought a putative class action against the United Nations (UN) (D) in U.S. federal district court, asserting that the UN (D) was responsible for the epidemic, and that, because the UN (D) failed to fulfill its obligation under Section 29 of the Convention on Privileges and Immunities of the United Nations (CPIUN) to make provisions for appropriate modes of settlement of certain disputes, the UN (D) was not immune from suit in U.S. courts.

RULES OF LAW

(1) The fulfillment by the United Nations (UN) of its obligation under Section 29 of the Convention on Privileges and Immunities of the United Nations (CPIUN) to "make provisions for appropriate modes of settlement of" certain disputes is not a condition precedent to its immunity under Section 2 of the CPIUN, which provides that the UN "shall enjoy immunity from every form of legal process except insofar as in any particular case it has expressly waived its immunity."

(2) Individuals do not have standing to challenge the United Nation's (UN's) immunity under the Convention on Privileges and Immunities of the United Nations (CPIUN) on the basis of a material breach thereof by the UN.

(3) A U.S. citizen's constitutional right to access federal courts is not violated where such access is denied on the basis of an international organization's or sovereign's immunity.

FACTS: In 2010, the United Nations (UN) (D) sent personnel from Nepal to the Republic of Haiti (Haiti). It was known that cholera was endemic to Nepal. A cholera epidemic ensued in Haiti, affecting thousands. Citizens of the United States or Haiti (P), who claimed that they or their relatives were sickened or died, or would be sickened or would die, as a direct result of the cholera epidemic that ravaged Haiti, brought a putative class action against the UN (D) in U.S. federal district court, asserting that the UN (D) was responsible for the epidemic. They alleged that not only did the UN (D) fail to test or screen these Nepalese personnel prior to their deployment, allowing them to carry into Haiti the strain of cholera that was the epidemic's source, but also stationed them at a base on the banks of a water source that, through the spread of untreated human waste, affected the drinking waters of tens of thousands of Haitians, which resulted in massive outbreaks of cholera throughout the entire country. Section 2 of the Convention on Privileges and Immunities of the United Nations (CPIUN) provides that the UN (D) "shall enjoy immunity from every form of legal process except insofar as in any particular case it has expressly waived its immunity." Section 29 of the CPIUN requires the UN (D) to "make provisions for appropriate modes of settlement of" certain disputes. The plaintiffs alleged that the UN (D) had disregarded its obligations under Section 29, and that such disregard vitiated the UN's (D) immunity under Section 2, contending principally that the UN's (D) fulfillment of its Section 29 obligation was a condition precedent to its Section 2 immunity. The UN (D) did not make an appearance, but the U.S. Executive Branch submitted a statement of interest in the case, taking the position that the UN (D) retained its immunity. The district court agreed with the Executive Branch, concluded that the UN (D) was immune from legal process and suit, and dismissed for lack of subject matter. On appeal, the plaintiffs reiterated their argument that fulfillment of the UN's (D) Section 29 obligation was a condition precedent to its Section 2 immunity. They also argued that the UN's (D) material breach of the CPIUN, by failing to fulfill its Section 29 obligation, also rendered it no longer entitled to the benefit of immunity under Section 2, and that the district court's application of the CPIUN to dismiss their action violated their constitutional right of access to the federal courts. The court of appeals granted review.

ISSUE:

(1) Is the fulfillment by the United Nations (UN) of its obligation under Section 29 of the Convention on Privileges and Immunities of the United Nations (CPIUN) to "make provisions for appropriate modes of settlement of" certain disputes a condition precedent to its immunity under Section 2 of the CPIUN, which provides that the UN "shall enjoy immunity from every form of legal process except insofar as in any particular case it has expressly waived its immunity?"

(2) Do individuals have standing to challenge the United Nation's (UN's) immunity under the Convention on Privileges and Immunities of the United Nations

Continued on next page.

(CPIUN) on the basis of a material breach thereof by the UN?

(3) Is a U.S. citizen's constitutional right to access federal courts violated where such access is denied on the basis of an international organization's or sovereign's immunity?

HOLDING AND DECISION: (Cabranes, J.)

(1) No. The fulfillment by the United Nations (UN) of its obligation under Section 29 of the Convention on Privileges and Immunities of the United Nations (CPIUN) to "make provisions for appropriate modes of settlement of" certain disputes is not a condition precedent to its immunity under Section 2 of the CPIUN, which provides that the UN "shall enjoy immunity from every form of legal process except insofar as in any particular case it has expressly waived its immunity." As a matter of textual construction, Section 2 of the CPIUN provides that the UN (D) "shall enjoy immunity from every form of legal process except insofar as in any particular case it has expressly waived its immunity." Especially when coupled with the compulsory "shall"—which is universally understood to indicate an imperative or mandate"—Section 2's express mention of the UN's (D) express waiver as a circumstance in which the UN (D) "shall [not] enjoy immunity" negatively implies that all other circumstances, including the UN's (D) failure to fulfill its Section 29 obligation, are excluded. It necessarily follows that the UN's (D) fulfillment of its Section 29 obligation is not a condition precedent to its Section 2 immunity. This conclusion is buttressed by the Executive Branch's interpretation of the CPIUN, which is entitled to great weight. The Executive Branch found nothing in Section 29 that states, either explicitly or implicitly, that compliance with its terms is a precondition to the UN's immunity under Section 2. The plaintiffs' arguments to the contrary are unconvincing. In pointing out that the UN (D) has previously stated that an assertion of its immunity does not leave a plaintiff without redress, since the plaintiff must be afforded an appropriate means of settlement under Section 29, the plaintiffs merely suggest that, at most, the UN (D) views Section 29 as more than merely aspirational, as obligatory and perhaps enforceable, but this does not in any way suggest that the UN (D) views Section 29 as a condition precedent to Section 2. Also unconvincing is the argument that foreign signatories to the CPIUN have repeatedly held that the availability of alternative dispute settlement is a material condition to international organizations' entitlement to immunity, and that these foreign courts' views provide persuasive authority for this case, per the direction of the United States Supreme Court. This argument is misleading. The Court has indeed held that in interpreting any treaty, the opinions of sister signatories are entitled to considerable weight, but in so holding, the Court was obviously referring to the opinions of States that are parties to the treaty that is being interpreted regarding that same treaty, not the opinions of States that happen to have ratified the treaty at issue regarding another treaty entirely. Most of the plaintiffs' examples fall into the latter category. They are cases from the courts of States that have ratified the CPIUN, but they pertain to unrelated agreements, most of which do not contain language that is even comparable—much less identical—to that found in Sections 2 and 29 of the CPIUN. Thus, the plaintiffs' reliance on cases interpreting those agreements is misplaced. Affirmed as to this issue.

(2) No. Individuals do not have standing to challenge the United Nation's (UN's) immunity under the Convention on Privileges and Immunities of the United Nations (CPIUN) on the basis of a material breach thereof by the UN. According to the plaintiffs, the UN's (D) material breach of its Section 29 obligation means that it is no longer entitled to the performance of duties owed to it under the CPIUN, including its Section 2 immunity. The merits of this argument, however, do not need to be reached, because the plaintiffs lack standing to raise it. Absent protest or objection by an offended sovereign, an individual has no standing to raise the violation of international law as an issue. Here, the plaintiffs have not identified any sovereign that has objected to the UN's (D) alleged material breach. To the contrary, the United States has asserted its position that the UN (D) has not waived its immunity, and no other country has expressed an interest in this litigation. Affirmed as to this issue.

(3) No. A U.S. citizen's constitutional right to access federal courts is not violated where such access is denied on the basis of an international organization's or sovereign's immunity. The plaintiffs' argument that the district court erred because it violated the U.S. citizen plaintiffs' constitutional rights to access the federal courts by applying immunity in this case, amount to questioning "why immunities in general should exist." *Brazak v. United Nations*, 597 F.3d 107, 114 (2d Cir. 2016). However, legislatively and judicially crafted immunities of one sort or another have existed since well before the framing of the Constitution, have been extended and modified over time, and are firmly embedded in American law. Thus, if the plaintiffs' argument were correct, it would seem to defeat not only the UN's (D) immunity, but also judicial immunity, prosecutorial immunity, and legislative immunity. In other words, the plaintiffs have not persuasively differentiated the quotidian and constitutionally permissible application of these doctrines from application of Section 2 of the CPIUN. Affirmed as to this issue.

Continued on next page.

ANALYSIS

This case illustrates principles of treaty construction. The interpretation of a treaty, like the interpretation of a statute, begins with its text, and, where the language of a treaty is plain and unambiguous, a court must refrain from amending it because to do so would be to make, not construe, a treaty. Additionally, because, as a general matter, a treaty is a contract between nations, it is to be interpreted according to the principles that govern the interpretation of written contracts between individuals. Applying these principles, the court determined that the Convention on Privileges and Immunities of the United Nations (CPIUN) contained no language that stated, either explicitly or implicitly, that compliance with its terms and Section 29 in particular, is a precondition to the UN's (D) immunity under Section 2. Further, conditions precedent to most contractual obligations, and, therefore, treaty obligations, are not favored and must be expressed in plain, unambiguous language. Here, the court found no such language linking Sections 2 and 29 in the CPIUN.

Quicknotes

CONDITION PRECEDENT The happening of an uncertain occurrence which is necessary before a particular right or interest may be obtained or an action performed.

IMMUNITY Exemption from a legal obligation.

CHAPTER 13

Human Rights

Quick Reference Rules of Law

Dakir v. Belgium

Muslim female national (P) v. Nation (D)

Eur. Ct. H.R. (App. No. 4619/12, Second Section, July 11, 2017)

NATURE OF CASE: Application complaining that a ban on wearing in public places clothing designed to conceal the face deprived the applicant of the possibility of wearing a full-face veil (niqab) in accord with her religious beliefs, and resulted in a violation of Articles 8, 9, and 10 of the Convention for the Protection of Human Rights and Fundamental Freedoms.

FACT SUMMARY: Dakir (P), a Muslim woman and a national of the Kingdom of Belgium (Belgium) (D), complained that Belgium's (D) ban on wearing in public places clothing designed to conceal the face deprived her of the possibility of wearing a full-face veil (niqab) in accord with her religious beliefs, and, therefore, resulted in a violation of Articles 8, 9, and 10 of the Convention for the Protection of Human Rights and Fundamental Freedoms. Belgium (D) justified the ban on grounds of public safety, gender equality, and the furtherance of societal "living together."

RULE OF LAW

A nation's ban on the wearing of any clothing entirely or substantially concealing the face does not violate the Convention for the Protection of Human Rights and Fundamental Freedoms' guarantee of the right to respect for one's private life (Article 8) or the right to freedom to manifest one's religion or beliefs (Article 9).

FACTS: The Kingdom of Belgium (Belgium) (D) enacted a law prohibiting the wearing of any clothing entirely or substantially concealing the face. The law's purpose was to promote public safety, gender equality, and the furtherance of societal "living together," by endorsing a societal model where the individual takes precedence over his or her philosophical, cultural, or religious ties. The ban was also believed to further the "protection of the rights and freedoms of others." Dakir (P), a Muslim woman and a national of Belgium (D), lodged an application with the European Court of Human Rights, complaining that the ban on wearing in public places clothing designed to conceal the face deprived her of the possibility of wearing a full-face veil (niqab) in accord with her religious beliefs, and, therefore, resulted in a violation of Articles 8, 9, and 10 of the Convention for the Protection of Human Rights and Fundamental Freedoms by violating her right to respect for her private life, her right to freedom to manifest her religion or beliefs, and her right to freedom of expression.

ISSUE: Does a nation's ban on the wearing of any clothing entirely or substantially concealing the face violate the Convention for the Protection of Human Rights and Fundamental Freedoms' guarantee of the right to respect for one's private life (Article 8) or the right to freedom to manifest one's religion or beliefs (Article 9)?

HOLDING AND DECISION: [Judge not stated in casebook extract.] No. A nation's ban on the wearing of any clothing entirely or substantially concealing the face does not violate the Convention for the Protection of Human Rights and Fundamental Freedoms' (the Convention's) guarantee of the right to respect for one's private life (Article 8) or the right to freedom to manifest one's religion or beliefs (Article 9). Although Belgium's (D) ban implicates the right to respect for private life of women who wish to wear the full-face veil for reasons related to their beliefs, and in terms of their freedom to manifest those beliefs, where, as here, the ban is challenged on grounds that the applicant is prevented from wearing in public places clothing that the practice of her religion requires her to wear, it mainly raises an issue with regard to the freedom guaranteed by Article 9 of the Convention to manifest one's religion or beliefs. As a matter of precedent, as found in *S.A.S. v. France* [GC] (no. 43835/11, §§ 35-52, ECHR 2014), Belgium's (D) goal of ensuring the observance of the minimum requirements of life in society may be regarded as an element of the "protection of the rights and freedoms of others," and the ban may be regarded as justified in its principle solely insofar as it seeks to guarantee the conditions of "living together." In determining whether the ban violates the Convention, it must be emphasized that the role of the Convention system is subsidiary to a nation's legislative authorities, who, by virtue of their direct and continuous contact with the vital forces of their countries, are in principle better placed than an international court to evaluate local needs and conditions. Thus, in matters of general policy, on which opinions within a democratic society may reasonably differ widely, the role of the domestic policymaker is to be given special weight. With regard to Article 9 a nation should be granted a wide degree of deference in deciding whether and to what extent a limitation of the right to manifest one's religion or beliefs is "necessary." However, such deference is limited by what is at stake in a given case and whether the nations that are parties to the Convention have reached a consensus or share common values regarding the challenged law. Here, the ban runs the risk of contributing to the consolidation of the stereotypes that affect certain segments of the population and of encouraging the expression of intolerance. Also, the ban, even if it is not based on the

Continued on next page.

religious connotation of the garment in question, mainly affects Muslim women who wish to wear the niqab. Moreover, by imposing a ban on wearing in public places a garment designed to conceal the face, a nation restricts to a certain extent the reach of pluralism, since the ban prevents certain women from expressing their personality and their beliefs by wearing the full-face veil in public. On the other hand, Belgium's (D) ban sought to address a practice that was deemed incompatible, in Belgian society, with the ground rules of social communication, and, more broadly, the establishment of human relations that are essential for living together. In doing so, Belgium (D) sought to protect a form of interaction between individuals that was essential, in its view, to the functioning of a democratic society. Thus, the question whether it should be permitted to wear the full-face veil in public places in Belgium (D) constitutes a choice of society. Finally, there is still no consensus within the member States of the Council of Europe as to whether there should be a blanket ban on the wearing of the full-face veil in public places, which justifies affording Belgium (D) a very wide margin of deference. Accordingly, the ban can be regarded as proportionate to the aim pursued, namely the preservation of the conditions of "living together" as an element of the "protection of the rights and freedoms of others," and, therefore, the ban may be regarded as "necessary in a democratic society." For these reasons, there has been no violation of Articles 8 or 9 of the Convention. [Judgment for Belgium (D).]

CONCURRENCE: (Spano, J.) The Court relies on the precedent of *S.A.S. v. France,* where the Grand Chamber accepted that the imposition of a measure banning the wearing of a full-face veil can be justified in its principle solely insofar as it seeks to guarantee the conditions of "living together." However, the Grand Chamber's conclusion was case-specific, and should not be extended to other cases. First, Articles 8 § 2 and 9 § 2 of the Convention do not provide for an explicit textual basis for this so-called "living together" principle as a legitimate aim that could justify an interference with Convention rights. It is not self-evident that it can be legally tenable to interpret the legitimate aim of the rights and freedoms of others to include the concept of "living together" in other factual situations where a nation wishes to regulate human behavior through laws that restrict Convention rights. Second, the "living together" concept is vague and malleable, so that it can potentially serve as a rhetorical tool for regulating any human interaction or behavior purely on the basis of a particular view of what constitutes the "right way" for people to interact in a democratic society. That is anathema to the fundamental values of the autonomy of self, human dignity, tolerance, and broadmindedness that are the foundations of the Convention system. Third, the "living together" principle has its ideological basis in a kind of societal consensus or a majoritarian morality of how individuals should act in the public space. This is tantamount to government-imposed assimilation of human interaction and behavior. An aim invoked for restricting human rights that is in fact based on a transient majority's opinion of what is suitable and right, and without the majority being required to define in concrete terms particular harms or mischiefs that need clearly to be addressed, cannot in principle form the basis of justifiable restrictions of Convention rights in a democratic society. History has shown that even in democracies there is a risk that majority sentiments that are translated into law may threaten fundamental human rights. In such instances, insular and vulnerable groups may be left only with recourse to the courts—whether national or international—which have a duty to review and detect, if possible, whether the imposition of measures, although widely accepted in the legislative forum, are triggered by animus or intolerance towards a particular idea, view, or religious faith. In *S.A.S.,* the Grand Chamber concluded that the ban on full-face coverings could justifiably be enforced by criminal sanctions. However, in that case, the penalties were extremely light (a fine of 150 Euros, and possibly the requirement to take a citizenship course), whereas under Belgium's (D) ban, the penalty could be considerably harsher insofar as it can entail imprisonment for up to seven days. Thus, any deprivation of liberty in the enforcement of Belgium's (D) ban, even in repetitive cases, would implicate a strong presumption of disproportionality of the interference with Convention rights. Governments are not free to base their attempts at restricting Convention rights on any aim whatsoever. The legitimacy of an aim must be based on objective, identifiable factors that are directly conducive to alleviating certain harms that flow from the exercise of the human right that is restricted. It follows that public animus and intolerance towards a particular group of persons can never justifiably restrict Convention rights.

ANALYSIS

Those that oppose bans on clothing and masks that completely cover the face in public spaces, which have been enacted in several countries, argue that the bans violate the rights of Muslim women to practice their religion, are not necessary or proportionate to their putative aims insofar as they restrict religious freedoms, and ultimately are discriminatory against Muslim women. The Court, aware of such objections, noted that a general policy or measure that has disproportionate prejudicial effects on a group of individuals can be regarded as discriminatory even if it does not specifically target the group and there is no discriminatory intent, but only if such policy or measure has no "objective and reasonable" justification, i.e., if it does not pursue a "legitimate aim" or if there is not a "reasonable relationship of proportionality" between the means employed and the aim sought to be

Continued on next page.

achieved. In the case at bar, the Court concluded that although the ban had more restrictive consequences for the exercise by certain Muslim women of some of their fundamental liberties, the measure had an objective and reasonable justification. Likewise, Belgium (D) maintained that the ban was not discriminatory, as it did not specifically target the full-face veil and applied to any person who wore an item concealing the face in public, whether a man or a woman, and whether for religious or other reasons.

Quicknotes

OBJECTIVE STANDARD A standard that is not personal to an individual but is dependent on some external source.

Lawless Case

[Parties not identified.]

Eur. Ct. of H.R., Ser. A. no. 1 (1961)

NATURE OF CASE: Case before the European Court of Human Rights to determine whether derogation of the European Convention for the Protection of Human Rights and Fundamental Freedoms was proper.

FACT SUMMARY: Lawless, a member of the Irish Republican Army (IRA) who was arrested and placed in an internment camp without trial, asserted his detention by Ireland violated the European Convention for the Protection of Human Rights and Fundamental Freedoms (Convention). Ireland contended it had properly derogated from the Convention because it faced a public emergency insofar as IRA members staged terrorist attacks.

RULE OF LAW

A nation may take measures that derogate from treaty obligations where the nation is faced with a public emergency that threatens the life of the nation and where the measures are strictly limited to the exigencies of the situation and do not conflict with other obligations under international law.

FACTS: The Irish Republican Army (IRA), operating out of the Republic of Ireland (Ireland), staged cross-border attacks in Northern Ireland on various government and private buildings and institutions. In response, Ireland arrested certain IRA activists and placed them in an internment camp without trial. Ireland did so pursuant to a statute that permitted such detentions for the preservation of public peace and security of the state, as long as certain conditions were met. The statute, the Offences against the State (Amendment) Act, provided such detentions could occur as long as the government exercised its powers to detain pursuant to a proclamation, and safeguards to ensure the detainees well-being were followed. Lawless, one of the detainees, filed suit before the European Court of Human Rights asserting his detention violated Articles 5 and 6 of the European Convention for the Protection of Human Rights and Fundamental Freedoms (Convention). Those Articles guaranteed, inter alia, a fair trial for a detainee. Ireland claimed the detentions were proper under Article 15, which permits derogation from the Convention in time of war or public emergency. The European Commission on Human Rights, which investigated the matter, concluded Ireland's derogation was justified. The European Court of Human Rights ruled on the standards to be applied in determining whether the derogation was proper.

ISSUE: May a nation take measures that derogate from treaty obligations where the nation is faced with a public emergency that threatens the life of the nation and where the measures are strictly limited to the exigencies of the situation and do not conflict with other obligations under international law?

HOLDING AND DECISION: [Judge not stated in casebook excerpt.] Yes. A nation may take measures that derogate from treaty obligations where the nation is faced with a public emergency that threatens the life of the nation and where the measures are strictly limited to the exigencies of the situation and do not conflict with other obligations under international law. Here, there existed a public emergency that threatened the life of the nation of Ireland, as the situation created by the IRA affected the entire population and constituted a threat to the State. The IRA was a secret, non-governmental army that used violence to attain its goals, and it carried out terrorist activities in Ireland's neighbor, Northern Ireland, thus seriously jeopardizing the relations of those two nations. Moreover, there was an alarming increase in those activities. Thus, Ireland was justified in issuing a proclamation pursuant to the Offences against the State (Amendment) Act, and taking measures derogating from its obligations under the Convention. Additionally, the measures taken were strictly required by the exigencies of the situation. The exercise of the nation's criminal law was unable to check the growing danger posed by the IRA, as the nature of the IRA made it extremely difficult to amass evidence that would result in convictions, and, closing the border with Northern Ireland, where the IRA carried out its attacks, would have had extreme repercussions for the populations of both nations. Accordingly, the detentions without trials of suspected IRA activists, was warranted under the circumstances, and sufficient safeguards were implemented to prevent abuses of detainees. One of these safeguards was the creation of a commission that could require the release of any detainee. Another was the government had publicly announced it would release any detainee who gave an undertaking to respect the nation's constitution and laws and not to engage in any illegal activity. Given these circumstances and safeguards, the detention without trial was a measure that was strictly required by the exigencies of the situation, so Ireland was in compliance with Article 15 of the Convention, both as to all the detainees in general, and as to Lawless in particular. [Judgment for Ireland as to this issue.]

ANALYSIS

This case is of historical importance, as well as an important legal precedent regarding the law of derogations, as it

Continued on next page.

was the first international court case decision that involved the interpretation of international human rights law and the first one filed against a country. It was also the first case decided by the European Court of Human Rights.

Quicknotes

EXIGENT CIRCUMSTANCES Circumstances requiring an extraordinary or immediate response; an exception to the prohibition on a warrantless arrest or search when police officers believe probable cause to exist and there is no time for obtaining a warrant.

Legal Consequences of the Construction of a Wall in the Occupied Palestinian Territory

[Parties not identified.]

I.C.J., Advisory Opinion, 2004 I.C.J. 136

NATURE OF CASE: Advisory opinion of the International Court of Justice, addressing, inter alia, whether certain treaties had extraterritorial application.

FACT SUMMARY: [Facts not stated in casebook excerpt.]

RULE OF LAW

The International Covenant on Civil and Political Rights is applicable in respect of acts done by a State in the exercise of its jurisdiction outside its own territory.

FACTS: [Facts not stated in casebook excerpt.]

ISSUE: Is the International Covenant on Civil and Political Rights applicable in respect of acts done by a State in the exercise of its jurisdiction outside its own territory?

HOLDING AND DECISION: [Judge not stated in casebook excerpt.] Yes. The International Covenant on Civil and Political Rights (Covenant) is applicable in respect of acts done by a State in the exercise of its jurisdiction outside its own territory. The scope of the Covenant's application is defined by Article 2, paragraph 1, which provides that "Each State Party to the present Covenant undertakes to respect and to ensure to all individuals within its territory and subject to its jurisdiction the rights recognized in the present Covenant . . . ." This language can be interpreted to mean only individuals in a State's territory and subject to its jurisdiction are covered by the Covenant. However, it can also be interpreted as covering both individuals present in a State's territory and those outside the territory, but subject to the State's jurisdiction. A State's jurisdiction is primarily territorial but may in certain cases also be exercised extraterritorially. Given the Covenant's goals and purpose, it seems natural this latter interpretation should apply. This is in keeping with the practice of the Human Rights Committee, which has found the Covenant applicable where the State exercises jurisdiction on foreign territory. The Covenant's history, found in the *travaux préparatoires* (preparatory work), confirms such an interpretation by showing the drafters did not intend to permit states to escape their obligations when they exercise jurisdiction outside their national territory, but only intended to prevent persons residing abroad from asserting, *vis-à-vis* their state of origin, rights that do not fall within the competence of that State, but of the State of residence.

ANALYSIS

Contrary to the International Court of Justice's (I.C.J.'s) view in this Advisory Opinion, the history of the International Covenant on Civil and Political Rights (Covenant) seems to support the plain meaning of Article 2, paragraph 1, namely only individuals in a State's territory and subject to its jurisdiction are covered by the Covenant. As originally drafted, the Covenant would have required each State party to ensure Covenant rights to everyone "within its jurisdiction." The United States, however, amended this to "within its territory." The Covenant was passed with the amendment. Thus, the original intent of the drafters and the practice of the ratifying States is at odds with the I.C.J.'s opinion.

Quicknotes

JURISDICTION The authority of a court to hear and declare judgment in respect to a particular matter.

CHAPTER 14

Injury to Aliens and Foreign Investors

Quick Reference Rules of Law

PAGE

1. *Fireman's Fund Insurance Co. v. Mexico.* An expropriation of property under the North American Free Trade Agreement includes the following elements: a taking (which includes destruction) that is permanent and either de jure or de facto, direct or indirect, in the form of a single measure or several measures over time; tangible or intangible property; a substantially complete deprivation of the economic use and enjoyment of the rights to the property; usually a transfer of ownership, but not always; as measured by the effect of the State's measures, not the underlying intent; as possibly determined by the investor's reasonable "investment-backed expectations;" and the compensability of which is determined by whether the measure is within the State's recognized police powers, the public purpose and effect of the measure, the measure's discriminatory nature, the proportionality between the means used and the goals intended to be realized, and the bona fide nature of the measure. *144*

2. *Tecnicas Medioambientales Tecmed S.A. ("TECMED") v. Mexico.* (1) The denial by a State of a permit to a non-national to operate property for its only intended use is an expropriation of the property where the denial is prompted by political considerations that do not constitute a social emergency. (2) The duty of fair and equitable treatment is violated where a State's conduct frustrates an investor's fair expectations, deprives the investor of clear guidelines as to the investor's required actions, and fails to provide the investor with any alternatives other than a complete loss of its investment. (3) A State does not violate a guarantee of full protection and security where it neither participates in nor promotes adverse actions against an investor and reacts to such adverse actions reasonably in accord with the parameters inherent in a democratic State. *146*

3. *Texaco Overseas Petroleum Co. v. Libya.* The reference to general principles of law in the international arbitration context is always regarded to be a sufficient criterion for the internationalization of a contract. *149*

4. *Ahmadou Sadio Diallo (Guinea v. Democratic Republic of the Congo).* The possibility of reconsideration by an administrative authority of an administrative decision as a matter of grace does not constitute a local remedy that must be exhausted before the decision can be challenged in an international proceeding. *150*

5. *Ahmadou Sadio Diallo (Guinea v. Democratic Republic of the Congo).* (1) A State has standing to bring a diplomatic protection claim on behalf of its national who is a shareholder in a company organized under the laws of a host State where it alleges that internationally wrongful acts by the host State have caused injury to the national's rights as a shareholder. (2) There is no exception in the customary international law of diplomatic protection that permits "substitution" of a shareholder for a company in exceptional circumstances. *152*

6. *Tecnicas Medioambientales Tecmed S.A. ("TECMED") v. Mexico.* (1) An award for compensatory money damages for expropriated property may include amounts proven to constitute the market value of the property, including amounts for projections of increased revenue and goodwill. (2) An award for compensatory money damages for expropriated property may include compound interest. (3) Moral damages will not be awarded where there is no evidence of injury to reputation. (4) Arbitration expenses and counsel fees will not be awarded to a claimant who has been only partially successful. *154*

Fireman's Fund Insurance Co. v. Mexico

Debentures owner (P) v. Sovereign state (D)

Intl. Centre for Settlement of Investment Disputes, ICSID Case No. ARB(AF)/02/1, Award, July 17, 2006

NATURE OF CASE: Arbitration of claims by a debentures-owner alleging violations of the North American Free Trade Agreement and expropriation of property.

FACT SUMMARY: Fireman's Fund Insurance Company (Fireman's Fund) (P), a U.S. insurance company that owned debentures issued by a Mexican financial services company, pursued an arbitration against Mexico (D) for expropriation of its property.

RULE OF LAW

An expropriation of property under the North American Free Trade Agreement includes the following elements: a taking (which includes destruction) that is permanent and either de jure or de facto, direct or indirect, in the form of a single measure or several measures over time; tangible or intangible property; a substantially complete deprivation of the economic use and enjoyment of the rights to the property; usually a transfer of ownership, but not always; as measured by the effect of the State's measures, not the underlying intent; as possibly determined by the investor's reasonable "investment-backed expectations;" and the compensability of which is determined by whether the measure is within the State's recognized police powers, the public purpose and effect of the measure, the measure's discriminatory nature, the proportionality between the means used and the goals intended to be realized, and the bona fide nature of the measure.

FACTS: Fireman's Fund Insurance Company (Fireman's Fund) (P), a U.S. insurance company that owned debentures issued by a Mexican financial services company, pursued an arbitration against Mexico (D) for expropriation of its property, claiming that Mexico (D) had helped to facilitate the purchase of debentures issued at the same time by the same company that were denominated in Mexican pesos and owned by Mexican investors, but did not facilitate the purchase of the debentures denominated in U.S. dollars owned by Fireman's Fund (P). The tribunal determined that Mexico's (D) acts did not constitute an expropriation. However, in doing so, it delineated the contours of what "expropriation" means.

ISSUE: Does an expropriation of property under the North American Free Trade Agreement include the following elements: a taking (which includes destruction) that is permanent and either de jure or de facto, direct or indirect, in the form of a single measure or several measures over time; tangible or intangible property; a substantially complete deprivation of the economic use and enjoyment of the rights to the property; usually a transfer of ownership, but not always; as measured by the effect of the State's measures, not the underlying intent; as possibly determined by the investor's reasonable "investment-backed expectations;" and the compensability of which is determined by whether the measure is within the State's recognized police powers, the public purpose and effect of the measure, the measure's discriminatory nature, the proportionality between the means used and the goals intended to be realized, and the bona fide nature of the measure?

HOLDING AND DECISION: [Judge not stated in casebook excerpt.] Yes. An expropriation of property under the North American Free Trade Agreement (NAFTA) includes the following elements: a taking (which includes destruction) that is permanent and either de jure or de facto, direct or indirect, in the form of a single measure or several measures over time; tangible or intangible property; a substantially complete deprivation of the economic use and enjoyment of the rights to the property; usually a transfer of ownership, but not always; as measured by the effect of the State's measures, not the underlying intent; as possibly determined by the investor's reasonable "investment-backed expectations;" and the compensability of which is determined by whether the measure is within the State's recognized police powers, the public purpose and effect of the measure, the measure's discriminatory nature, the proportionality between the means used and the goals intended to be realized, and the bona fide nature of the measure. NAFTA does not define "expropriation." In ten or so cases in which Article 1110(1) of NAFTA has been considered the definitions vary. Considering those cases and customary international law, the present Tribunal retains the following elements:

(a) Expropriation requires a taking (which may include destruction) by a government-type authority of an investment by an investor covered by NAFTA.
(b) The covered investment may include intangible as well as tangible property.
(c) The taking must be a substantially complete deprivation of the economic use and enjoyment of the rights to the property, or of identifiable distinct parts thereof (i.e., it approaches total impairment).
(d) The taking must be permanent, and not ephemeral or temporary.
(e) The taking usually involves a transfer of ownership to another person (frequently the government

Continued on next page.

authority concerned), but that need not necessarily be so in certain cases (e.g., total destruction of an investment due to measures by a government authority without transfer of rights).

(f) The effects of the host State's measures are dispositive, not the underlying intent, for determining whether there is expropriation.
(g) The taking may be de jure or de facto.
(h) The taking may be direct or indirect.
(i) The taking may have the form of a single measure or a series of related or unrelated measures over a period of time (the so-called "creeping" expropriation).
(j) To distinguish between a compensable expropriation and a noncompensable regulation by a host State, the following factors (usually in combination) may be taken into account: whether the measure is within the recognized police powers of the host State; the (public) purpose and effect of the measure; whether the measure is discriminatory; the proportionality between the means employed and the aim sought to be realized; and the bona fide nature of the measure.
(k) The investor's reasonable "investment-backed expectations" may be a relevant factor whether (indirect) expropriation has occurred.

ANALYSIS

The Restatement (Third) of Foreign Relations Law of the United States provides that for compensation for a taking by a State of a foreign national's property to be just, it must, in the absence of exceptional circumstances, be in an amount equal to the value of the taken property and be paid at the time of the taking, or within a reasonable time thereafter with interest from the date of taking, and in a form economically usable by the foreign national whose property has been taken.

Quicknotes

ARBITRATION An alternative resolution process where a dispute is heard and decided by a neutral third party, rather than through legal proceedings.

BONA FIDE In good faith.

DEBENTURES Long-term unsecured debt securities issued by a corporation.

DE FACTO In fact; in reality; actually. Existing in fact but not officially approved or engendered.

DE JURE By right; lawful.

TAKING A governmental action that substantially deprives an owner of the use and enjoyment of his property, requiring compensation.

Tecnicas Medioambientales Tecmed S.A. ("TECMED") v. Mexico

Foreign company (P) v. Sovereign state (D)

Intl. Centre for Settlement of Investment Disputes, ICSID Case No. ARB(AF)/00/2, Award, 43 I.L.M. 133 (2004)

NATURE OF CASE: Arbitration of claims by foreign company against sovereign state for damages from expropriation of investment.

FACT SUMMARY: Tecnicas Medioambientales Tecmed S.A. (Claimant) (P) a Spanish company, claimed that Mexico (D) had expropriated its investment in Tecmed, Tecnicas Medioambientales de Mexico, S.A. de C.V. (Tecmed), a Mexican company, which in turn owned Cytrar, S.A. de C.V. (Cytrar), also a Mexican company, by refusing to renew Cytrar's annual license to run a hazardous industrial waste landfill (the "Landfill").

RULE OF LAW

(1) The denial by a State of a permit to a non-national to operate property for its only intended use is an expropriation of the property where the denial is prompted by political considerations that do not constitute a social emergency.

(2) The duty of fair and equitable treatment is violated where a State's conduct frustrates an investor's fair expectations, deprives the investor of clear guidelines as to the investor's required actions, and fails to provide the investor with any alternatives other than a complete loss of its investment.

(3) A State does not violate a guarantee of full protection and security where it neither participates in nor promotes adverse actions against an investor and reacts to such adverse actions reasonably in accord with the parameters inherent in a democratic State.

FACTS: Tecnicas Medioambientales Tecmed S.A. (Claimant) (P) a Spanish company, owned over 99 percent of the shares of Tecmed, Tecnicas Medioambientales de Mexico, S.A. de C.V. (Tecmed), a company incorporated under Mexican law. Tecmed in turn held over 99 percent of the stock of Cytrar, S.A. de C.V. (Cytrar), also a Mexican company, that Tecmed had organized for the purpose of running a hazardous industrial waste landfill ("the Landfill") in the municipality of Hermosillo, located in the state of Sonora, Mexico. In 1996, at Tecmed's request, the Mexican agency for hazardous waste management, INE, issued Cytrar a license to operate the Landfill. This license had to be renewed annually at the applicant's request, and it was renewed by INE at Cytrar's request until 1998, when INE, pursuant to a resolution ("the Resolution") refused to renew the license and instead sought to have Cytrar close the Landfill. INE's changed position allegedly was the result primarily of political circumstances associated with a change in government of the municipality of Hermosillo. Whereas the municipality had previously supported Cytrar's running of the Landfill, in 1998 new authorities encouraged a movement of citizens against the Landfill, which sought the non-renewal of the Landfill's operating permit and its closure. The community engaged in demonstrations and disruptive conduct, including blocking access to the Landfill. The Claimant (P) claimed that the denial of the license constituted expropriation and sought damages, including compensation for damage to reputation, and interests in connection with damage alleged to have accrued as of the date INE rejected the application for renewal. The Claimant (P) also sought the granting of permits that would enable it to operate the Landfill until the end of its useful life. It brought a claim for arbitration before the International Centre for Settlement of Investment Disputes (ICSID) under its Rules and under the Agreement on the Reciprocal Promotion and Protection of Investments ("the Agreement") between Spain and Mexico (D). The Claimant (P) alleged that the Agreement protected foreign investors and their investments from direct and indirect expropriation, such as measures tantamount to direct expropriation. Because the denial of the permit effectively deprived Cytrar of its rights to use and enjoy the real and personal property constituting the Landfill in accordance with its sole intended purpose, the Claimant (P) claimed it was denied the benefits and economic use of its investment. Without the permit, the property had no market value and the Landfill's existence as an ongoing business was completely destroyed. Mexico (D) countered INE had the discretionary powers required to grant and deny permits, and that such issues, except in special cases, are exclusively governed by domestic and not international law. It also asserted INE's Resolution was neither arbitrary nor discriminatory and constituted a regulatory measure issued in compliance with the State's police power.

ISSUE:

(1) Is the denial by a State of a permit to a non-national to operate property for its only intended use an expropriation of the property where the denial is prompted by political considerations that do not constitute a social emergency?

(2) Is the duty of fair and equitable treatment violated where a State's conduct frustrates an investor's fair expectations, deprives the investor of clear guidelines

Continued on next page.

as to the investor's required actions, and fails to provide the investor with any alternatives other than a complete loss of its investment?

(3) Does a State violate a guarantee of full protection and security where it neither participates in nor promotes adverse actions against an investor and reacts to such adverse actions reasonably in accord with the parameters inherent in a democratic state?

HOLDING AND DECISION: [Judge not stated in casebook excerpt.]

(1) Yes. The denial by a State of a permit to a non-national to operate property for its only intended use is an expropriation of the property where the denial is prompted by political considerations that do not constitute a social emergency. The term "expropriation" is not defined in the Agreement. Generally expropriation means a forcible taking by the government of property owned by private persons, although it can also cover a de facto taking, where Government actions or laws transfer assets to third parties, or where such actions or laws deprive persons of their ownership over such assets, without transfer to third parties or the government. It is this last meaning of expropriation that is referred to in the applicable sections of the Agreement, and it is sometimes referred to as "indirect" or "creeping" expropriation. Creeping expropriation, however, must be distinguished from de facto expropriation, since the former occurs gradually or stealthily, whereas the latter can occur through a single action or several sequential or simultaneous actions. In any event, to determine whether there has been an indirect expropriation, the actions must be examined on a case-by-case basis. Here, the first step of the analysis is to determine whether the Resolution deprived the Claimant (P) of the economical use and enjoyment of its investments to the point where the rights related thereto ceased to exist. Ordinarily, a regulatory measure that is made pursuant to the State's police power entails only a decrease in assets or rights, whereas a de facto expropriation is a complete deprivation of those assets or rights. Thus, the effect of the Resolution is important in determining whether there was an indirect expropriation by Mexico (D), and the Agreement says as much. In addition to interpreting the Agreement, the tribunal must also apply international law. Under customary international law, it is understood that the measures adopted by a State, whether regulatory or not, are an indirect de facto expropriation if they are irreversible and permanent and destroy the owner's assets or rights. Additionally, under international law, the owner is also deprived of property where the use or enjoyment of benefits related thereto is exacted or interfered with to a similar extent, even where legal ownership over the assets in question is not affected, and so long as the deprivation is not temporary. As under the Agreement, the key is the measure's effect, rather than the intent behind it. Here, the Resolution meets these characteristics of an indirect expropriation: it has provided for the non-renewal of the permit and the closing of the Landfill permanently and irrevocably and thereafter, based on INE regulations, the Landfill will not be useable for its intended purpose, so that Cytrar's economic and commercial operations in the Landfill after such denial have been fully and irrevocably destroyed. Moreover, the Landfill could not be used for a different purpose, and therefore could not be sold. The Claimant (P) invested in the Landfill only to engage in hazardous waste landfill activities and to profit therefrom; it is now deprived of that investment. Under the Agreement's plain meaning, regulatory administrative actions are not per se excluded from the Agreement's scope, even if they are beneficial to society, if they neutralize an investment's economic value without compensation. This includes environmental measures such as the one at issue. The next step in the analysis is to determine whether the measures are proportional to the public interest and to the protection legally granted to investments. In other words, there must be proportionality between the means employed and the aim sought to be realized. The measure will not be deemed proportional if the investor bears an undue burden under it. Here, the factors motivating INE's Resolution were political, not environmental, and the community's desires were not so great as to lead to social crisis or public unrest, so that the public interest did not outweigh the Claimant's (P) loss of value, and therefore the Resolution was not proportionate to the deprivation of rights sustained by the Claimant (P). Accordingly, the Resolution and its effects amounted to an expropriation in violation of the Agreement and international law.

(2) Yes. The duty of fair and equitable treatment is violated where a State's conduct frustrates an investor's fair expectations, deprives the investor of clear guidelines as to the investor's required actions, and fails to provide the investor with any alternatives other than a complete loss of its investment. The requirement of fair and equitable treatment in the Agreement is an expression of the bona fide principle of international law, under which States must provide to international investments treatment that does not affect the foreign investor's basic expectations used in making the investment. The foreign investor expects the host State to act in a consistent manner, free from ambiguity and totally transparently in its relations with the foreign investor, so that it may know beforehand any and all rules and regulations that will govern its investments, as well as the goals of the relevant policies and administrative practices or directives, to be able to plan its investment and comply with such regulations. The expectation of

Continued on next page.

consistency applies to the revocation of preexisting decisions or permits that were relied on by the investor; and the State must not use the legal instruments that govern the investor's actions or the investment in a manner that does not conform to their usual function, or to deprive the investor of its investment without compensation. Compliance with these principles is necessary for the State to be compliant with both the bona fide principle and with the fair and equitable treatment principle. So as not to be deemed arbitrary, the State's actions must not shock, or at least not surprise, a sense of juridical propriety. Applying these principles here, INE's behavior frustrated Cytrar's fair expectations and negatively affected the generation of clear guidelines that would allow the Claimant (P) or Cytrar to direct its actions or behavior to prevent the non-renewal of the permit, or weakened its position to enforce rights or explore ways to maintain the permit by relocating. Despite Cytrar's good faith expectation that the permit would be renewed at least until Cytrar's relocation of the Landfill to a new site had been completed, INE did not consider Cytrar's proposals in that regard, and not only did it deny the renewal of the permit, even though the relocation had not yet taken place, but it also did so in the understanding that this would lead Cytrar to relocate. This behavior, attributable to Mexico (D), resulted in losses and damages to the Claimant (P) and constituted a violation of the duty to accord fair and equitable treatment to the Claimant (P) and its investment.

(3) No. A State does not violate a guarantee of full protection and security where it neither participates in nor promotes adverse actions against an investor and reacts to such adverse actions reasonably in accord with the parameters inherent in a democratic State. The Claimant (P) asserts that Mexican government officials at all levels of government failed to act as quickly, efficiently, and thoroughly as they should have to prevent or eliminate the community's adverse conduct toward the Landfill and Cytrar's staff, and therefore, Mexico (D) breached the guarantee of full protection and security provided in the Agreement. First, there is insufficient evidence that Mexican government officials encouraged, fostered, or contributed support to those who conducted the demonstrations and other adverse activities against the Landfill, or that they participated in such activities. Thus, there is insufficient evidence to attribute the activities to Mexico (D) under international law. In any event, the guarantee of full protection and security is not absolute and does not impose strict liability on a State that grants it. Furthermore, there was insufficient evidence that the Mexican officials or judiciary reacted unreasonably to the adverse activities in a manner that was not in accordance with the parameters inherent in a democratic State.

ANALYSIS

Non-nationals are more vulnerable to domestic legislation, since unlike nationals, they will generally have played no part in the election or designation of its authors nor have been consulted on its adoption. Thus, according to the European Court of Human Rights, although a taking of property must always be effected in the public interest, different considerations may apply to nationals and non-nationals and there may well be legitimate reason for requiring nationals to bear a greater burden in the public interest than non-nationals. Thus, as demonstrated by this case, interference with a non-national's property rights that is an indirect expropriation rather than an outright taking will require compensation. In this case, the tribunal awarded the Claimant (P) such compensation (over $5.5 million plus interest).

Quicknotes

ARBITRATION An alternative resolution process where a dispute is heard and decided by a neutral third party, rather than through legal proceedings.

BONA FIDE In good faith.

DAMAGES Monetary compensation that may be awarded by the court to a party, who has sustained injury or loss to his person, property, or rights due to another party's unlawful act, omission or negligence.

SOVEREIGN A State or entity with independent authority to govern its affairs.

Texaco Overseas Petroleum Co. v. Libya

Oil company (P) v. Country (D)

Intl. Arbitral Award, 104 J. Droit Intl. 350 (1977), *translated in* 17 I.L.M. 1 (1978)

NATURE OF CASE: Arbitration decree.

FACT SUMMARY: Libya (D) promulgated a decree attempting to nationalize all of Texaco's (P) rights, interest, and property in Libya.

RULE OF LAW

The reference to general principles of law in the international arbitration context is always regarded to be a sufficient criterion for the internationalization of a contract.

FACTS: Libya (D) promulgated a decree attempting to nationalize all of Texaco's (P) rights, interest, and property in Libya (D). Texaco (P) requested arbitration and Libya (D) refused to arbitrate. The International Court of Justice appointed a sole arbitrator pursuant to Texaco's (P) request, who found Libya (D) in breach of its obligations under the Deeds of Concessions and legally bound to perform in accordance with their terms.

ISSUE: Is the reference to general principles of law in the international arbitration context always regarded to be a sufficient criterion for the internationalization of a contract?

HOLDING AND DECISION: [Judge not stated in casebook excerpt.] Yes. The reference to general principles of law in the international arbitration context is always regarded to be a sufficient criterion for the internationalization of a contract. The recourse to general principles is justified by the lack of adequate law in the State considered and the need to protect the private contracting party against unilateral and abrupt modifications of law in the contracting State. Legal international capacity is not solely attributable to a State; international law encompasses subjects of a diversified nature. Unlike a State, however, a private contracting party has only a limited capacity and it is entitled to invoke only those rights that it derives from its contract.

ANALYSIS

One conflict here was whether to apply Libyan law or international law in the arbitration proceedings. While the contract itself deferred to Libyan law, the Court notes that Libyan law does not preclude the application of international law, but that the two must be combined in order to verify that Libyan law complies with international law. Furthermore, even though international law recognizes the right of a state to nationalize, that right in itself is not a sufficient justification to disregard its contractual obligations.

Quicknotes

ARBITRATION Attempted resolution of a dispute by a neutral third party rather than through legal proceedings.

CONTRACTUAL OBLIGATION A duty agreed to be performed pursuant to a contract.

NATIONALIZATION Government acquisition of a private enterprise.

Ahmadou Sadio Diallo (Guinea v. Democratic Republic of the Congo)

Sovereign state (P) v. Sovereign state (D)

2007 I.C.J. 582, 599-601

NATURE OF CASE: A State responsibility, diplomatic protection case before the International Court of Justice.

FACT SUMMARY: The Republic of Guinea (Guinea) (P) filed a State responsibility, diplomatic protection case on behalf of its national, Diallo, against the Democratic Republic of Congo (D.R.C.) (D) for its alleged violations of Diallo's rights; the D.R.C. (D) contended that the claims were inadmissible because local remedies had not been exhausted.

RULE OF LAW

The possibility of reconsideration by an administrative authority of an administrative decision as a matter of grace does not constitute a local remedy that must be exhausted before the decision can be challenged in an international proceeding.

FACTS: The Republic of Guinea (Guinea) (P) filed a State responsibility, diplomatic protection case on behalf of its national, Diallo, against the Democratic Republic of Congo (D.R.C.) (D) in the International Court of Justice. Guinea (P) claimed that Diallo, who had resided in the D.R.C. (D) for 32 years, had been unlawfully arrested and imprisoned without trial by D.R.C.'s (D) authorities, detained in violation of his human rights, and his investments, property, and businesses unlawfully expropriated. After Diallo, in local proceedings, unsuccessfully attempted to recover sums owed to him by D.R.C.'s (D) companies, the D.R.C. (D) effectively expelled him by refusing him entry into the country. Such "refusal of entry" is not appealable under D.R.C.'s (D) law. Guinea (P) claimed that Diallo's arrest, detention, and expulsion violated international law, for which violation the D.R.C. (D) was responsible. The D.R.C. (D) contended that the claims were inadmissible because local remedies had not been exhausted, including reconsideration by its Prime Minister, so that Diallo did not meet the requirement for the exercise of diplomatic protection, which includes exhaustion of local remedies.

ISSUE: Does the possibility of reconsideration by an administrative authority of an administrative decision as a matter of grace constitute a local remedy that must be exhausted before the decision can be challenged in an international proceeding?

HOLDING AND DECISION: [Judge not stated in casebook excerpt.] No. The possibility of reconsideration by an administrative authority of an administrative decision as a matter of grace does not constitute a local remedy that must be exhausted before the decision can be challenged in an international proceeding. The rule that local remedies must be exhausted before international proceedings may be instituted is a well-established rule of customary international law that provides the State against whom the claim is made the opportunity to redress any wrongs by its own means and within the framework of its own legal system. The issue posed by this case is whether the Democratic Republic of Congo's (D.R.C.'s) (D) legal system actually provided local remedies that Diallo could have exhausted. The Republic of Guinea (Guinea) (P) must prove either that local remedies were exhausted or that there were exceptional circumstances that excused such exhaustion. The D.R.C. (D), however, must prove that its legal system offered effective remedies that were not exhausted. Guinea (P) did not present evidence as to remedies for the arrest and detention, and the D.R.C. (D) did not address exhaustion of remedies regarding these alleged illegal acts. The D.R.C. (D) only addressed the issue of expulsion, saying that remedies for expulsion were institutionally provided by its legal system. The Court, therefore, will only address the issue of local remedies in respect of expulsion. The expulsion, which was characterized as a "refusal of entry," is not appealable under the D.R.C.'s (D) law, so that the D.R.C. (D) cannot now rely on an error allegedly made by its administrative agencies at the time Diallo was "refused entry," to claim that he should have treated the measure as an expulsion. Instead, Diallo was justified in relying on the D.R.C.'s (D) authorities when they informed him that he could not appeal the refusal of entry, including for purposes of the local remedy rule. Even if the D.R.C.'s (D) action in fact constituted an expulsion, the D.R.C. (D) has failed to show that there is any means of legal redress against expulsion decisions under its law. Although Diallo could request reconsideration by the appropriate administrative authority of its decision, such reconsideration does not qualify as a local remedy. Remedies that must be exhausted include legal and administrative remedies, but administrative remedies can only be considered for purposes of the local remedies rule if they are aimed at vindicating a right and not at obtaining a favor, unless they constitute an essential prerequisite for the admissibility of subsequent contentious proceedings. Here, the possibility of having the administrative authority—the D.R.C. (D) Prime Minister—retract his decision as a matter of grace does not constitute a local remedy to be exhausted. Because the D.R.C. (D) has failed to show, at

Continued on next page.

least regarding to expulsion, that it provides effective remedies to be exhausted, the D.R.C.'s (D) objection to the expulsion claim must be dismissed.

ANALYSIS

The "rule of local remedies" at issue in this case originally developed in the area of diplomatic protection, but has been extended to the area of human rights as well, and is primarily designed to ensure respect for the sovereignty of the host State, which is permitted to resolve the dispute by its own means before international mechanisms are invoked.

Quicknotes

REMEDY Compensation for violation of a right or for injuries sustained.

Ahmadou Sadio Diallo (Guinea v. Democratic Republic of the Congo)

Sovereign state (P) v. Sovereign state (D)

2007 I.C.J. 582, 603-615

NATURE OF CASE: A state responsibility, diplomatic protection case before the International Court of Justice.

FACT SUMMARY: The Republic of Guinea (Guinea) (P) filed a State responsibility, diplomatic protection case on behalf of its national, Diallo, against the Democratic Republic of Congo (D.R.C.) (D) for its alleged violations of Diallo's rights, including his rights as a shareholder ("associé") of limited companies (SPRLs) incorporated in the D.R.C. (D). The D.R.C. (D) contended that Guinea (P) did not have standing to protect Diallo.

RULE OF LAW

(1) A State has standing to bring a diplomatic protection claim on behalf of its national who is a shareholder in a company organized under the laws of a host State where it alleges that internationally wrongful acts by the host State have caused injury to the national's rights as a shareholder.

(2) There is no exception in the customary international law of diplomatic protection that permits "substitution" of a shareholder for a company in exceptional circumstances.

FACTS: The Republic of Guinea (Guinea) (P) filed a State responsibility, diplomatic protection case on behalf of its national, Diallo, against the Democratic Republic of Congo (D.R.C.) (D) for its alleged violations of Diallo's rights, including his rights as a shareholder ("associé") of two limited companies (SPRLs) incorporated in the D.R.C. (D)—Africom-Zaire and Africontainers-Zaire. Diallo was also a manager ("gérant") of these companies. Guinea (P) claimed that its diplomatic protection claim was viable because it was claiming that D.R.C.'s (D) acts infringed on Diallo's rights as a shareholder, rather than just on the companies' rights. Guinea (P) also contended it could bring a claim on a "theory of substitution" based on the companies' rights. The D.R.C. (D) objected to the admissibility of these claims, arguing that Guinea (P) lacked standing to bring them.

ISSUE:

(1) Does a State have standing to bring a diplomatic protection claim on behalf of its national who is a shareholder in a company organized under the laws of a host State where it alleges that internationally wrongful acts by the host State have caused injury to the national's rights as a shareholder?

(2) Is there an exception in the customary international law of diplomatic protection that permits "substitution" of a shareholder for a company in exceptional circumstances?

HOLDING AND DECISION: [Judge not stated in casebook excerpt.]

(1) Yes. A State has standing to bring a diplomatic protection claim on behalf of its national who is a shareholder in a company organized under the laws of a host State where it alleges that internationally wrongful acts by the host State have caused injury to the national's rights as a shareholder. In support of its diplomatic protection claim on behalf of Diallo as associé, the Republic of Guinea (Guinea) (P) refers to the judgment in the Court's *Barcelona Traction* case [1970 I.C.J. 3], where the Court ruled that "an act directed against and infringing only the company's rights does not involve responsibility toward the shareholders, even if their interests are affected" but added that "[t]he situation is different if the act complained of is aimed at the direct rights of the shareholder as such." Guinea (P) also asserts that a similar position was taken up in Article 12 of the International Law Commission's (ILC) draft Articles on Diplomatic Protection, which provides that: "To the extent that an internationally wrongful act of a State causes direct injury to the rights of shareholders as such, as distinct from those of the corporation itself, the State of nationality of any such shareholders is entitled to exercise diplomatic protection in respect of its nationals." Guinea (P) asserts that under the Decree of 27 February 1887 on commercial corporations, Diallo is entitled to property rights, including dividends, from the companies, as well as "functional rights," encompassing the right to control and manage the companies. It further claims that the Democratic Republic of Congo's (D.R.C.'s) (D) investment code also entitles Diallo additional shareholder rights, including the right to share in the companies' profits and the right of ownership of the companies. Guinea (P) has standing to assert these rights because it is essentially asserting a diplomatic protection claim on behalf of a natural or legal person. An internationally wrongful act against a shareholder is the violation by the host State of the shareholder's direct rights in relation to a legal person that are defined by the domestic law of the host State. Thus, diplomatic protection of the direct rights of shareholders of a public limited company is not an exception to the general legal régime of diplomatic protection for natural or legal persons, as derived from customary international law. At this point

Continued on next page.

in the proceedings, the Court need not determine which of Diallo's rights appertain to his status as a shareholder versus his status as a manager, as the Court will define the precise nature of those rights at the merits stage. Accordingly, the D.R.C.'s (D) objections to standing are rejected and dismissed as to Diallo's direct rights as a shareholder.

(2) No. There is no exception in the customary international law of diplomatic protection that permits "substitution" of a shareholder for a company in exceptional circumstances. The Court considers whether Republic of Guinea (Guinea) (P) may advance a claim encompassing harm to the companies themselves based on a "theory of substitution." Such a theory deviates from the normal rules of State responsibility. The Court, in dictum, has hinted that such a theory might be available in exceptional circumstances. However, State practice and decisions of international courts and tribunals in this area of diplomatic protection do not support such a theory. The role of diplomatic protection has been minimized in the area of the protection of rights of shareholders and of companies because disputes in this area are largely governed by agreement and recourse is made to diplomatic protection for shareholders only rarely where such an agreement does not govern nor has proved inoperative. It is in this relatively limited context that protection by substitution might be raised, but it would appear to constitute the very last resort for the protection of foreign investments. At present, such an exception does not exist in customary international law, and Guinea (P) may not assert a claim based on such an exception.

ANALYSIS

In contemporary international law, the protection of the rights of companies and the rights of their shareholders, and the settlement of the associated disputes, are essentially governed by bilateral or multilateral agreements for the protection of foreign investments. Examples of such agreements are the treaties for the promotion and protection of foreign investments, and the Washington Convention of 18 March 1965 on the Settlement of Investment Disputes between States and Nationals of Other States, which created an International Centre for Settlement of Investment Disputes (ICSID), and also by contracts between States and foreign investors.

Quicknotes

DIPLOMATIC PROTECTION The act by which a State, on behalf of one of its citizens who is an injured party, intervenes when a rule of international law has been violated.

Tecnicas Medioambientales Tecmed S.A. ("TECMED") v. Mexico

Foreign company (P) v. Sovereign state (D)

Intl. Centre for Settlement of Investment Disputes, ICSID Case No. ARB(AF)/00/2, Award, 43 I.L.M. 133 (2004)

NATURE OF CASE: Award of damages in arbitration for expropriation of investment.

FACT SUMMARY: After determining that Mexico (D) had expropriated Tecnicas Medioambientales Tecmed S.A.'s (Claimant's) (P) property by refusing to issue a permit for the operation of a landfill ("the Landfill") owned by the Claimant's (P) subsidiary [for the facts of the case and the tribunal's findings and ruling, see the brief at page 130, supra], the arbitral tribunal awarded the Claimant (P) money damages and interest, but not moral damages or litigation expenses and attorneys' fees.

RULE OF LAW

(1) An award for compensatory money damages for expropriated property may include amounts proven to constitute the market value of the property, including amounts for projections of increased revenue and goodwill.
(2) An award for compensatory money damages for expropriated property may include compound interest.
(3) Moral damages will not be awarded where there is no evidence of injury to reputation.
(4) Arbitration expenses and counsel fees will not be awarded to a claimant who has been only partially successful.

FACTS: An arbitral tribunal determined that Mexico (D) had expropriated Tecnicas Medioambientales Tecmed S.A.'s (Claimant's) (P) property by refusing to issue a permit for the operation of a landfill ("the Landfill") owned by the Claimant's (P) subsidiary [for the facts of the case and the tribunal's findings and ruling, see the brief at page 146, supra]. The tribunal then had to determine the appropriate damages. The Claimant (P) primarily requested money damages and secondarily restitution in kind. It also requested interest, moral damages, litigation expenses, and attorneys' fees. The tribunal explained its decision regarding each of these items.

ISSUE:
(1) May an award for compensatory money damages for expropriated property include amounts proven to constitute the market value of the property, including amounts for projections of increased revenue and goodwill?
(2) May an award for compensatory money damages for expropriated property include compound interest?
(3) Will moral damages be awarded where there is no evidence of injury to reputation?
(4) Will arbitration expenses and counsel fees be awarded to a claimant who has been only partially successful?

HOLDING AND DECISION: [Judge not stated in casebook excerpt.]
(1) Yes. An award for compensatory money damages for expropriated property may include amounts proven to constitute the market value of the property, including amounts for projections of increased revenue and goodwill. Based on the Landfill's acquisition value of $4,028,788, capital investments and profits for the two years in which the Landfill was operational, the market value of the Landfill is $5,553,017.12. The Claimant's (P) expert witness assessed the value of additional investments at $1,951,473,237, but there is no evidence supporting that value, whereas Mexico (D) claims that amount is $439,000, based on accounting data. The tribunal accepts Mexico's (D) value of this item. The tribunal also finds, based on the Landfill's growing revenues and profits and increasing goodwill, that profits were $1,085,229.12. Moreover, to provide an integral compensation for the damage inflicted, the amount of closing the Landfill will not be deducted from such amount, since the decision forcing such closure was in violation of the Agreement between Spain and Mexico (D).
(2) Yes. An award for compensatory money damages for expropriated property may include compound interest. Compound—versus simple—interest has been awarded in other expropriation cases and is at present deemed the appropriate standard of interest in international law for expropriation cases. Here, compound interest at a rate of 6 percent is justified.
(3) No. Moral damages will not be awarded where there is no evidence of injury to reputation. There is no evidence that the actions attributable to Mexico (D) caused injury to the Claimant's (P) reputation and therefore caused it to lose business opportunities. Any adverse press coverage of the Claimant's (P) companies cannot be attributed to Mexico (D).
(4) No. Arbitration expenses and counsel fees will not be awarded to a claimant who has been only partially successful. Here, the Claimant (P) has been successful only with respect to some of its claims; and some of Mexico's (D) defenses and challenges were admitted. Therefore, each party will bear its own costs, expenses, and legal counsel fees. The costs incurred by the tribunal and the ICSID will be shared equally between the parties. After Mexico (D) pays the amounts required by this award,

Continued on next page.

the Claimant (P) will take all necessary steps to transfer the Landfill to Mexico (D).

ANALYSIS

This damages award illustrates that in respect of expropriated or nationalized property, tribunals tend to value the expropriated business on a going concern basis, rather than on a liquidation basis, and that, therefore, they will include measures of goodwill and profitability in the value determination. As with other measures of value, those indicia must be based on reliable data and projections.

Quicknotes

ARBITRATION An alternative resolution process where a dispute is heard and decided by a neutral third party, rather than through legal proceedings.

CHAPTER 15

Use of Force

Quick Reference Rules of Law

Judgment of the International Military Tribunal

[Parties not identified.]

Nuremberg, Sept. 30, 1946, reprinted in 41 A.J.I.L. 186-218 (1946)

NATURE OF CASE: Indictment for war crimes.

FACT SUMMARY: Officials of Hitler's Third Reich were indicted for instigating wars of aggression against neighboring countries.

RULE OF LAW

The planning or waging of war that is a war of aggression or a war in violation of international treaties is a crime.

FACTS: Officials of Hitler's Third Reich were indicted for instigating wars of aggression against neighboring countries.

ISSUE: Is the planning or waging of war that is a war of aggression or a war in violation of international treaties a crime?

HOLDING AND DECISION: [Judge not stated in casebook excerpt.] Yes. The planning or waging of war that is a war of aggression or a war in violation of international treaties is a crime. The legal effect of the Kellogg-Briand Pact is that the nations who signed it or adhered to it unconditionally condemned recourse to war as an instrument of policy and expressly renounced it. War for the solution of international controversies undertaken as an instrument of national policy includes a war of aggression, and such war is therefore outlawed by the Pact.

ANALYSIS

This trial involved the indictment of German officials for the seizure of Austria and Czechoslovakia and the war against Poland, as part of Germany's foreign policy. The Tribunal concluded that Germany planned wars against 12 separate nations and therefore was guilty of violating the Charter of the International Military Tribunal's prohibition against wars of aggression and wars in violation of international treaties (namely, the Treaty of Versailles).

Quicknotes

KELLOGG-BRIAND PACT A treaty between the United States and other powers, ratified in 1929, which provided for the renunciation of war as an instrument of national policy.

TREATY OF VERSAILLES An agreement produced in 1919 by the League of Nations (or "the Allies," headed up by Britain, France, Italy and the United States), which, following World War I, levied restrictive military sanctions against Germany, divested Germany of its colonies, and gave over German land to other countries. Poland, Lithuania, Latvia, Estonia, and Finland were formed by the treaty from land lost by Russia, and a multi-party system was imposed on German politics to inhibit any one group from taking power.

Legality of the Threat or Use of Nuclear Weapons

[Parties not identified.]

I.C.J., Advisory Opinion, 1996 I.C.J. 226

NATURE OF CASE: Advisory opinion of the International Court of Justice, addressing, inter alia, whether the mere possession of nuclear weapons constitutes an unlawful threat to use force.

FACT SUMMARY: [The United Nations General Assembly and World Health Organization requested an advisory opinion from the International Court of Justice as to whether the threat or use of nuclear weapons is permitted under any circumstances.]

RULE OF LAW

The possession of nuclear weapons, including for the purpose of deterrence, would constitute an unlawful threat to use force where a threatened use of the weapons itself would be illegal.

FACTS: [The United Nations (U.N.) General Assembly and World Health Organization requested an advisory opinion from the International Court of Justice (I.C.J.) as to whether the threat or use of nuclear weapons is permitted under any circumstances. One of many issues the I.C.J. addressed was whether the mere possession of nuclear weapons, including for deterrence purposes, constitutes an unlawful threat to use force.]

ISSUE: Would the possession of nuclear weapons, including for the purpose of deterrence, constitute an unlawful threat to use force where a threatened use of the weapons itself would be illegal?

HOLDING AND DECISION: [Judge not stated in casebook excerpt.] Yes. The possession of nuclear weapons, including for the purpose of deterrence, would constitute an unlawful threat to use force where a threatened use of the weapons itself would be illegal. Whether a signaled intention by a State to use force in the face of certain eventualities is or is not a "threat" under Article 2, para. 4, of the U.N. Charter, depend on whether the envisaged use of force itself is unlawful. If such use would be illegal, then the State's signaled intention to make such use would likewise be illegal. For the declared readiness of a State to use force to be legal, the ultimate use would have to conform to the Charter. The mere possession of nuclear weapons may be a signal of a State's readiness to use those weapons. Again, however, the legality of such readiness of use depends on whether the intended use itself would be legal or not. If the intended use were for self-defense, such use would have to comply with the principle of necessity and proportionality; if the intended use did not comply with this principle, both the threat of the use, and the use itself, would be illegal.

ANALYSIS

Under the International Court of Justice's analysis, it would be unlawful for a State possessing nuclear weapons to threaten to use them for the purpose of securing territory from another State, or to cause another State to follow, or not follow, a certain economic or political path. It would also be unlawful for the State to threaten a use that would be contrary to the purposes of the United Nations.

Quicknotes

DETERRENT Something that prevents an individual from undertaking certain conduct or behavior.

Arbitral Award Between Guyana and Suriname

Neighboring state (P) v. Neighboring state (D)

Arbitral Panel Convened under the U.N. Convention on the Law of the Sea, 2008, Sept. 17, 2007, 47 I.L.M. 166 (2008)

NATURE OF CASE: Arbitration of disputed maritime boundary, and to determine if unlawful threats or uses of forces had occurred.

FACT SUMMARY: Guyana (P) and Suriname (D) sought an arbitration of their maritime boundary, over which they had a longstanding dispute, and Guyana (P) asserted Suriname (D) had unlawfully threatened or used force when a Surinamese (D) patrol boat ordered an oil rig to depart from the disputed area.

RULE OF LAW

A State makes an unlawful threat of force where its threat of force is more akin to a military action, rather than law enforcement activity, and such action is not a lawful countermeasure to another State's actions, regardless whether the other State's actions are themselves unlawful.

FACTS: Guyana (P) and Suriname had a longstanding dispute over their maritime boundary. Guyana (P) granted to CGX, a Canadian company, a concession for oil exploration in the disputed area. Suriname (D) demanded Guyana (P) cease oil exploration and ordered CGX to cease its operations there. Subsequently, a Surinamese patrol boat ordered the CGX oil rig to depart from the disputed area within 12 hours, or face certain, unspecified consequences. The two nations sought an arbitration of their disputed maritime boundary under the U.N. Convention on the Law of the Sea, 2008 (Convention), and Guyana (P) asked the reviewing tribunal to find Suriname (D) had unlawfully threatened or used force. Suriname (D) countered it had engaged in lawful enforcement actions taken in its territory. The tribunal found Suriname (D) had not used force in the situation, and then it considered the issue of whether Suriname (D) had made an unlawful threat of force.

ISSUE: Does a State make an unlawful threat of force where its threat of force is more akin to a military action, rather than law enforcement activity, and such action is not a lawful countermeasure to another State's actions, regardless whether the other State's actions are themselves unlawful?

HOLDING AND DECISION: [Judge not stated in casebook excerpt.] Yes. A State makes an unlawful threat of force where its threat of force is more akin to a military action, rather than law enforcement activity, and such action is not a lawful countermeasure to another State's actions, regardless whether the other State's actions are themselves unlawful. The patrol boat's order constituted an explicit threat that force might be used in the absence of compliance. While force may be used in law enforcement activities, such force must be unavoidable, reasonable, and necessary to be lawful. Here, Suriname's (D) action seemed more like a threat of military action than mere law enforcement activity. Therefore, it constituted a threat of the use of force that contravened the Convention, the U.N. Charter, and general international law. It was not a lawful response to a wrongful act by Guyana (P), as a threatened use of force was not a lawful countermeasure to Guyana's (P) grant of an oil exploration concession.

ANALYSIS

Although the arbitral tribunal decided in favor of Guyana (P) on the issue of threat of force, it nevertheless only rendered a declaratory judgment, finding that there was no evidence of damage, so monetary compensation was not warranted.

Quicknotes

ARBITRATION An alternative resolution process where a dispute is heard and decided by a neutral third party, rather than through legal proceedings.

DECLARATORY JUDGMENT A judgment of the court establishing the rights of the parties.

Military and Paramilitary Activities in and Against Nicaragua (Nicaragua v. United States)

Country aiding subversives (P) v. Military intervenor (D)

1986 I.C.J. 14, 126

NATURE OF CASE: Proceedings before the International Court of Justice alleging unlawful military and paramilitary acts.

FACT SUMMARY: [Nicaragua (P) asserted that the United States (D) had unlawfully intervened militarily against it.]

RULE OF LAW

Intervention by a nation in and against another nation is not justified where such intervention is requested by an opposition group in the other nation.

FACTS: [The United States (D) provided aid to the Contras, who were fighting the Marxist Sandinistas in Nicaragua (P). The United States (D) supplied financial, political, and military assistance to the Contras, who pursued their war against the Sandinistas from bases in neighboring Honduras and Costa Rica. In addition, U.S. military personnel or their agents covertly mined Nicaragua's (P) harbors and carried out numerous attacks against Nicaraguan ports and military installations. Nicaragua (P) sued the United States (D) for its actions against it. The United States (D) claimed its actions were justified based on the principle of collective self-defense insofar as it was aiding El Salvador stave off military aid from Nicaragua (P) to El Salvador opposition groups.]

ISSUE: Is intervention by a nation in and against another nation justified where such intervention is requested by an opposition group in the other nation?

HOLDING AND DECISION: [Judge not stated in casebook excerpt.] No. Intervention by a nation in and against another nation is not justified where such intervention is requested by an opposition group in the other nation. Nonintervention is a principle of customary international law that would lose its effectiveness if intervention were justifiable by a mere request for assistance made by a group opposing the government in another nation. Given intervention is already permitted when requested by the government of another State, allowing intervention at the request of an opposition group would effectively permit a State to intervene in the internal affairs of another State at any time. Such is not the present state of customary international law.

ANALYSIS

As this portion of the International Court of Justice's opinion suggests, a State is generally entitled to provide military assistance to another State when the government of the other State requests such assistance for the purpose of maintaining public order and security. In such instances, the State providing military assistance is not considered to being using force in violation of Article 2(4) of the U.N. Charter, which prohibits the threat or use of force and calls on all members to respect the sovereignty, territorial integrity, and political independence of other States.

Quicknotes

INTERVENTION The method by which a party, not an initial party to the action, is admitted to the action in order to assert an interest in the subject matter of a lawsuit.

Military and Paramilitary Activities in and Against Nicaragua (Nicaragua v. United States)

Country aiding subversives (P) v. Military intervenor (D)

1986 I.C.J. 14, 103-23

NATURE OF CASE: Proceedings before the International Court of Justice alleging unlawful military and paramilitary acts.

FACT SUMMARY: [The United States (D) provided aid to the Contras, who were fighting the Marxist Sandinistas in Nicaragua (P). The United States (D) supplied financial, political, and military assistance to the Contras, who pursued their war against the Sandinistas from bases in neighboring Honduras and Costa Rica. In addition, U.S. (D) military personnel or their agents covertly mined Nicaragua's (D) harbors and carried out numerous attacks against Nicaraguan ports and military installations. Nicaragua (P) brought proceedings in the International Court of Justice against the United States (D) for its actions against it. The United States (D) claimed its actions were justified based on the principle of collective self-defense insofar as it was aiding El Salvador stave off military aid from Nicaragua (P) to El Salvador opposition groups.]

RULE OF LAW

An assisting State's actions will not be considered justified collective self-defense against a purported armed attack where the "attack" consists merely of the provision of arms from the allegedly attacking State to the opposition in a third State and the third State has not officially declared itself the victim of an armed attack and has not asked for help from the assisting State.

FACTS: [The United States (D) between 1979 and 1983 provided aid to the Contras, who were fighting the Marxist Sandinistas in Nicaragua (P). The United States (D) supplied financial, political, and military assistance to the Contras, who pursued their war against the Sandinistas from bases in neighboring Honduras and Costa Rica. In addition, U.S. military personnel or their agents covertly mined Nicaragua's (P) harbors and carried out numerous of attacks against Nicaraguan ports and military installations. Nicaragua (P) brought proceeding in the International Court of Justice (I.C.J.) against the United States (D) for its actions against it, asserting the U.S. (D) actions violated Article 2(4) of the U.N. Charter and corresponding principles of international law. The United States (D) withdrew from the proceedings after the I.C.J. ruled against it on jurisdictional issues. However, the U.S. (D) claimed in public its actions were justified based on the principle of collective self-defense insofar as it was aiding El Salvador stave off military aid from Nicaragua (P) to El Salvador opposition groups. The I.C.J. proceeded to the merits and adjudicated them on principles of customary international law. One of the issues it addressed was whether U.S. (D) conduct was justified as collective self-defense.]

ISSUE: Will an assisting State's actions be considered justified collective self-defense against a purported armed attack where the "attack" consists merely of the provision of arms from the allegedly attacking State to the opposition in a third State and the third State has not officially declared itself the victim of an armed attack and has not asked for help from the assisting State?

HOLDING AND DECISION: [Judge not stated in casebook excerpt.] No. An assisting State's actions will not be considered justified collective self-defense against a purported armed attack where the "attack" consists merely of the provision of arms from the allegedly attacking State to the opposition in a third State and the third State has not officially declared itself the victim of an armed attack and has not asked for help from the assisting State. The U.S. (D) actions were not justified in terms of self-defense because the provision of arms going to the opposition in El Salvador from Nicaragua (P) between 1979 and 1981 is not considered an armed attack, which necessarily must occur for the right of self-defense to arise. While an armed attack may occur where armed bands or groups invade another State's territory to such an extent the invasion is tantamount to an attack executed by armed forces, the mere provisions of weapons or logistical support to an opposition force does not qualify as an armed attack. Under customary international law, the concept of "armed attack" does not include assistance to rebels in the form of the provision of weapons or logistical or other support. Instead, such assistance may be regarded as a threat or use of force, or amount to intervention in the internal or external affairs of other States. It is also clear that it is the State that is the victim of an armed attack that must form and declare the view it has been so attacked. There is no rule permitting the exercise of collective self-defense in the absence of a request from the State that considers itself the victim of an armed attack, and there is also no rule that permits a non-victim State to exercise collective self-defense based solely on its own assessment of the situation. Further, when one State uses force against another, on the ground the second State has committed a wrongful act of force against a third State, such use of force may be regarded as lawful, by way

Continued on next page.

of exception, only when the wrongful act provoking the response was an armed attack. Thus, the use of force by a State in response to a wrongful act of which it has not itself been the victim is not lawful when the wrongful act is not an armed attack. Thus, States do not have a right of collective self-defense in the form of an armed response when the acts being responded to are not armed attacks—and it is an indication of *opinio juris* that the United States (D) has not claimed such a right exists. The acts of the United States (D) were comprised mostly of the actual use of force, and such acts were prohibited unless there was some justification that rendered them lawful. Absent such a justification—such as self-defense—the United States (D) committed prima facie violations of the principle of the non-use of force. However, not all the U.S.'s (D) acts could be construed as use of force, e.g., supplying funds to the Contras, which could, however, be considered unlawful intervention in Nicaragua's (P) internal affairs. To find the U.S. (D) exercised collective self-defense, there must be a preliminary finding that Nicaragua (P) engaged in an armed attack against El Salvador, Honduras, or Costa Rica. While there was a flow of arms to the El Salvadoran opposition from Nicaragua (P), this flow cannot be equated with an armed attack. As to Honduras and Costa Rica, while there were incursions into those countries that are imputable to Nicaragua (P), there is insufficient evidence to support a finding that those incursions constituted armed attacks. Moreover, none of those nations declared themselves victims of Nicaraguan attacks during the time period at issue (1979–1983). It was not until 1984 that El Salvador officially declared itself the victim of an armed attack and asked the United States (D) to exercise the right of collective self-defense, which tends to prove there was no armed attack in 1981 by Nicaragua (P). At the time, Honduras and Costa Rica also did not claim they were victims of armed attacks, or indicate they requested U.S. (D) assistance. Additionally, the United States (D) did not file a report, as required by Article 51 of the U.N. Charter, in respect of measures a State believes itself bound to take when it exercises the right of individual or collective self-defense. This shows the United States (D) did not believe it was acting in collective self-defense. For all these reasons, there were no armed attacks that provide a justification for the exercise of collective self-defense. Since there was no justification for the U.S. (D) actions, even if they were in strict compliance with the requirement of necessity and proportionality, they would still be unlawful. If those actions did not comport with those requirements, however, those would be additional grounds of wrongfulness. As to necessity, the U.S. (D) measures were taken several months after the armed opposition in El Salvador had carried out its major offensives and had been repulsed. Thus, it was possible to eliminate the main threats to the El Salvadoran government without the United States (D) engaging in activities in and against Nicaragua (P). As to proportionality, the U.S. (D) use of force—mining ports and attacking ports and oil installations—was disproportionate to whatever aid was being given to the opposition in El Salvador. In sum, the U.S. (D) collective self-defense justification must be rejected. Similarly, the challenged U.S. (D) conduct cannot be viewed as legitimate countermeasures responsive to intervention. That is because there were no armed attacks by Nicaragua (P). Whatever actions can be imputed to Nicaragua (P) would have justified only proportionate countermeasures to be taken by the States that purportedly were victims of those acts, i.e., El Salvador, Honduras, and Costa Rica. They could not justify countermeasures taken by a third State (like the United States (D)), and particularly could not justify intervention involving the use of force. [Judgment for Nicaragua (P) as to this issue.]

ANALYSIS

The key to the Court's conclusion was the premise that Nicaragua's (P) uses of force did not amount to armed attacks. A dissenting opinion by Judge Schwebel disagreed with this premise, arguing Nicaragua's (P) support of the El Salvadoran opposition was sufficiently extensive and pervasive to constitute an armed attack that justified collective self-defense by the United States (D). The opinion and dissent thus illustrate the line between use of force and armed attack is not clearly demarcated in customary international law.

Quicknotes

NECESSITY A defense to liability for unlawful activity where the conduct is unavoidable and is justified by preventing an injury to life or health.

Legality of the Threat or Use of Nuclear Weapons

[Parties not identified.]

I.C.J., Advisory Opinion, 1996 I.C.J. 226

NATURE OF CASE: Advisory opinion of the International Court of Justice, addressing, inter alia, whether humanitarian law may restrict the types of weapons States may use.

FACT SUMMARY: [The United Nations General Assembly and World Health Organization requested an advisory opinion from the International Court of Justice as to whether the threat or use of nuclear weapons is permitted under any circumstances.]

RULE OF LAW

Humanitarian law serves to restrict the choice of weapons States may use.

FACTS: [The United Nations General Assembly and World Health Organization requested an advisory opinion from the International Court of Justice (I.C.J.) as to whether the threat or use of nuclear weapons is permitted under any circumstances. One of many issues the I.C.J. addressed was whether humanitarian law may restrict the types of weapons states may use.]

ISSUE: Does humanitarian law serve to restrict the choice of weapons States may use?

HOLDING AND DECISION: [Judge not stated in casebook excerpt.] Yes. Humanitarian law serves to restrict the choice of weapons States may use. A core principle of humanitarian law is States must never make civilians the object of attack, and, therefore, may never use weapons that are incapable of distinguishing between civilian and military targets. A second principle is States may not inflict unnecessary suffering on combatants. Hence, States may not use weapons that cause excessive harm or uselessly aggravate suffering. Moreover, the international community has accepted and largely complied with these principles, starting with the formalization of these principles in the Martens Clause included in the Hague Convention II with Respect to the Law and Customs of War on Land of 1899, and in subsequent treaties and protocols. It is undoubtedly because these humanitarian law principles are regarded as fundamental to the respect of the human person that there has been great accession to the Hague and Geneva Conventions. Moreover, all States are obligated to observe these fundamental laws, because they constitute intransgressible principles of international customary law.

ANALYSIS

In applying its analysis regarding humanitarian law to nuclear weapons, the I.C.J. unanimously concluded a threat or use of nuclear weapons must be compatible with the requirements of international law applicable in armed conflict, particularly the principles and requirements of international humanitarian law.

Quicknotes

ADVISORY OPINION A decision rendered at the request of an interested party as to how the court would rule should the particular issue arise.

Western Front, Aerial Bombardment and Related Claims, Partial Award—Eritrea's Claims

State formerly at war [Eritrea (P)] v. State formerly at war [Ethiopia (D)]

Eritrea-Ethiopia Claims Commission, 2005, Dec. 19, 2005, 45 I.L.M. 396 (2006)

NATURE OF CASE: Claims for compensation for certain acts of war brought before a claims commission.

FACT SUMMARY: Eritrea (P) claimed its Hirgigo Power Station, which was bombed by Ethiopia (D) during the war between those two countries, was not a legitimate military objective.

RULE OF LAW

An object of a military attack is a legitimate military objective where the object's nature, location, purpose, or use makes it an effective contribution to military action, and its total or partial destruction, or capture or neutralization, offers a definite military advantage under the circumstances.

FACTS: During the war between Ethiopia (D) and Eritrea (P), Ethiopia (D) bombed Eritrea's (P) Hirgigo Power Station. This power plant, although not fully operational, was completed and in its testing and commissioning phase, as was most of the transmission infrastructure. The plant was close to a key Eritrean (P) port and naval base located in Massawa, and was protected by antiaircraft missiles, but those missiles had been in that location prior to commencement of the plant's construction. The plant was built at great expense and was expected to contribute to Eritrea's (P) economy and to provide electricity for civilian purposes. It was to replace an old and outdated plant that was "on its last legs." That old plant was not bombed by Ethiopia (D), nor was the naval base. Ethiopia (D) also stated it had not planned the bombing of the Hirgigo plant. After the war, the nations requested a claims commission settle their war-related claims. The Eritrea Ethiopia Claims Commission, which was established for this purpose, considered, inter alia, Eritrea's (P) claim seeking compensation for Ethiopia's (D) bombing of the Hirgigo Power Station on the grounds the plant was not a legitimate military objective.

ISSUE: Is an object of a military attack a legitimate military objective where the object's nature, location, purpose, or use makes it an effective contribution to military action, and its total or partial destruction, or capture or neutralization, offers a definite military advantage under the circumstances?

HOLDING AND DECISION: [Judge not stated in casebook excerpt.] Yes. An object of a military attack is a legitimate military objective where the object's nature, location, purpose, or use makes it an effective contribution to military action, and its total or partial destruction, or capture or neutralization, offers a definite military advantage under the circumstances. The applicable law is found in Article 52, paragraph 2, of Geneva Protocol I, which defines the objects that are legitimate military objectives. It provides "military objectives are limited to those objects which by their nature, location, purpose or use make an effective contribution to military action and whose total or partial destruction, capture or neutralization, in the circumstances ruling at the time, offers a definite military advantage." This provision, while not binding on the parties as a treaty provision, is an expression of customary international law. Also, the term "military advantage" must be assessed in the context of the military operations between the parties taken as a whole, not simply in the context of a specific attack. Here, the plant was an object that by its nature, location, purpose, or use made an effective contribution to military action at the time it was attacked. Whereas electric power stations are generally recognized to be of sufficient importance to a State's capacity to meet its wartime needs of communication, transport, and industry so as usually to qualify as military objectives during armed conflicts, not all such power stations qualify as military objectives, for example, where they are segregated from a general power grid and are limited to supplying power for humanitarian purposes, such as medical facilities, or other uses that could have no effect on the State's ability to wage war. Eritrea (P) asserted the Hirgigo plant was not yet producing power for use in Eritrea (P) and its military forces had their own electric generating equipment and were not dependent on general power grids in the country. Eritrea (P) also submitted evidence supporting its assertion its Defense Ministry used no more than four percent of Eritrea's (P) non-military power supply and Eritrean manufacturing companies did not produce significant military equipment. Nevertheless, the plant had potential wartime value to Eritrea (P). Moreover, although the mere fact there were anti-aircraft guns in the vicinity of the power station does not, by itself, make the power station a military objective, it indicated Eritrean military authorities themselves viewed the station as having military significance. The port and naval base at Massawa were unquestionably legitimate military objectives, so it follows the generating facilities providing the electric power needed to operate them were objects that made an effective contribution to military action. The question then is whether the intended replacement for power generation capacity also

Continued on next page.

made an effective contribution to military action. Ethiopia (D) argues a State at war should not be obligated to wait until an object is, in fact, put into use when the purpose of that object is such it will make an effective contribution to military action once it has been tested, commissioned, and put to use. That argument is accepted. The final question, then, is whether the plant's destruction offered a military advantage to Ethiopia (D). In general, a large power plant being constructed to provide power for an area including a major port and naval facility certainly would seem to be an object the destruction of which would offer a distinct military advantage. Moreover, the fact the power station was of economic importance to Eritrea (P) is evidence that damage to it, given Ethiopia (D) was trying to force Eritrea (P) to agree to end the war, offered a definite advantage, since the purpose of any military action must always be to influence the political will of the adversary. The infliction of economic losses from attacks against military objectives is a lawful means of achieving a definite military advantage. For these reasons, the Hirgigo Power Station was a legitimate military objective, and Eritrea's (P) claim is dismissed. [Judgment for Ethiopia (D)]

SEPARATE OPINION: (Van Houtte, President). First, as to the requirement the object of attack must be effective militarily: such effectiveness must be shown to be actual effectiveness, not effectiveness in the abstract. Otherwise, every object potentially of use to enemy troops could become a military objective. Similarly, more is required than a mere contribution to the "war-fighting capability" of the enemy. Likewise, regarding the second requirement, the effect of the destruction of the object attacked must be shown to have a definite, concrete—rather than speculative or hypothetical—military advantage. The infliction of economic loss or the undermining of morale through the destruction of a civilian object, or the probability that the destruction may bring the decision-makers to the negotiation table, do not make that object a military objective. If these two requirements are not met, an object is entitled to full protection afforded to civilian objects, and, if there is any doubt as to the military nature of the object, under customary international law the presumption is the object is not being used militarily. Applying these principles here, the Hirgigo Power Station clearly had a civilian purpose, and Ethiopia (D) failed to make a specific showing as to how this plant satisfied the requirements of Article 52, paragraph 2 and customary international law for being a legitimate military objective. Ethiopia's (D) general statement "cutting off the power to Massawa would have presented Ethiopia with a clear military advantage of interrupting power to the military offices in Massawa" is insufficient. Moreover, the presence of anti-aircraft missiles in the vicinity of the Hirgigo station did not indicate by itself, that the station had military significance, especially as missiles were already located in the area long before the construction of the station had started. Furthermore, military action must be proportional, i.e., the military advantage must outweigh the damage to civilians and civilian objects. Because Ethiopia (D) had not planned the bombing of the plant, it follows it did not investigate beforehand whether the concrete and direct military advantage of this bombing outweighed the damage to civil society; international law does not permit bombing first and justification later. Furthermore, the fact that neither the port of Massawa itself nor the old power station (which effectively supplied power to the Massawa port) were ever bombed is also relevant. Indeed, if different means are available to block harbor activities, the method that is most effective and that causes the least damage to civilians must be chosen. Finally, the expected benefits of the Hirgigo power station to civilians and the expense and time required to repair the damage caused by the attack should also be considered. For all these reasons, the potential military advantage caused by the bombing was disproportionate to the damage to civilian objects and the civilian population.

ANALYSIS

In contrast to its rulings as to the Hirgigo Power Station, the Commission concluded Ethiopia (D) had violated customary international humanitarian law when it bombed Eritrea's (P) Harsile water reservoir. In this regard, the Commission found the provisions of Article 54 of Geneva Protocol I, which prohibit attack against drinking water installations and supplies that are indispensable to the survival of the civilian population for the specific purpose of denying them for their sustenance value to the adverse party, had become customary international humanitarian law by the time of the bombings. However, because no damage to the Harsile water reservoir had been shown, the Commission awarded no monetary damages to Eritrea (P) for this violation.

Central Front Partial Award—Ethiopia's Claims

State formerly at war [Eritrea (P)] v. State formerly at war [Ethiopia (D)]

Eritrea-Ethiopia Claims Commission, 2004, Apr. 28, 2004, 43 I.L.M. 1275 (2004)

NATURE OF CASE: Claims for compensation for certain acts of war brought before a claims commission.

FACT SUMMARY: Eritrea (P) and Ethiopia (D), which had been at war, both claimed the other's military troops had engaged in acts of rape against civilian women.

RULE OF LAW

A State may be liable for failing to prevent rape by its armed forces where there is evidence of several incidents of rape of civilian women by its troops.

FACTS: [Eritrea (P) and Ethiopia (D) had been at war. After the war, the nations requested a claims commission settle their war-related claims. The Eritrea Ethiopia Claims Commission, which was established for this purpose, considered, inter alia, both parties' claims that the other party's military forces had raped civilian women, for which acts both parties sought compensation.]

ISSUE: May a State be liable for failing to prevent rape by its armed forces where there is evidence of several incidents of rape of civilian women by its troops?

HOLDING AND DECISION: [Judge not stated in casebook excerpt.] Yes. A State may be liable for failing to prevent rape by its armed forces where there is evidence of several incidents of rape of civilian women by its troops. Rape of civilians by opposing or occupying forces is a violation of customary international law, as reflected in the Geneva Conventions. Under Common Article 3(1), States are obliged to ensure women civilians are granted fundamental guarantees. Article 27 of the 1949 Geneva Convention relative to the Protection of Civilian Persons in Time of War provides: "Women shall be especially protected against any attack on their honor, in particular against rape, enforced prostitution or any form of indecent assault." Further, Article 76.1 of Protocol I states: "Women shall be the object of special respect and shall be protected in particular against rape, forced prostitution and any other form of indecent assault." Here, there was evidence of frequent rape of women by soldiers. In the cultures of both parties, rape is such a sensitive matter, victims are extremely unlikely to come forward, and, when victims or other witnesses do present testimony, the evidence available is likely to be far less detailed and explicit than for non-sexual offenses. Because of these heightened cultural sensitivities, as well as the relatively secret and unwitnessed nature of rape, evidence of a pattern of frequent or pervasive rapes is not necessary to establish liability. The Commission is not seeking to impose liability for individual instances of rape, but, rather, is attempting to determine State liability for serious violations of international law that likely affected significant numbers of victims. Rape need not be frequent to support State liability, since it involves intentional and grievous harm. Thus, what is looked for is clear and convincing evidence of several rapes in specific geographical areas under specific circumstances. Such evidence exists for areas (the Central Front regions) where large numbers of opposing troops were in closest proximity to civilian populations for the longest periods of time. Knowing, as they must, such areas posed the greatest risk of opportunistic sexual violence by troops, both parties were obligated to impose effective measures, as required by international humanitarian law, to prevent rape of civilian women. The clear and convincing evidence of several incidents of rape in these areas shows, at a minimum, they failed to do so. As for other areas, where there was evidence of occasional rape, there was insufficient evidence that would support State liability for failing to protect women from rape by their armed forces.

ANALYSIS

The Commission, which was gratified there was no suggestion, much less evidence, either Eritrea (P) or Ethiopia (D) used rape, forced pregnancy, or other sexual violence as an instrument of war, or engaged in strategically systematic sexual violence against civilians, nonetheless found both parties liable for failing to prevent the rape of civilian women by their respective troops. The Commission awarded $2 million to each party for these findings of liability, noting it believed that these serious violations of international humanitarian law demanded serious relief, and that nominal or symbolic damages would not suffice in the face of the physical, mental, and emotional harm known to be suffered by rape victims.

Quicknotes

CLEAR AND CONVINCING EVIDENCE An evidentiary standard requiring a demonstration that the fact sought to be proven is reasonably certain.

INTENTIONAL INFLICTION OF EMOTIONAL DISTRESS Intentional and extreme behavior on the part of the wrongdoer with the intent to cause the victim to suffer from severe emotional distress, or with reckless indifference, resulting in the victim's suffering from severe emotional distress.

CHAPTER 16

International Criminal Law

Quick Reference Rules of Law

PAGE

1. *United States v. Alvarez-Machain.* The presence of an extradition treaty between the United States and another nation does not necessarily preclude obtaining a citizen of that nation through abduction. *170*

2. *"The Justice Case" (Case 3), United States v. Josef Altstoetter et al.* (1) The military tribunal draws its power and jurisdiction to punish violations of international law from the Control Council, as an international body temporarily governing Germany. (2) International law recognizes more than violations of laws and customs of war as offenses. (3) The *ex post facto* rule does not apply to international law, so that the principle *nullum crimen sine lege* cannot be used as a defense to international crimes. *171*

United States v. Alvarez-Machain

Federal government (P) v. Foreign national (D)

504 U.S. 655 (1992)

NATURE OF CASE: Review of dismissal of federal indictment.

FACT SUMMARY: Alvarez-Machain (D), abducted from Mexico for trial in the United States (P) by United States Drug Enforcement Agency agents, contended that his abduction was illegal because of an extradition treaty between the United States (P) and Mexico.

RULE OF LAW

The presence of an extradition treaty between the United States and another nation does not necessarily preclude obtaining a citizen of that nation through abduction.

FACTS: Alvarez-Machain (D) was abducted from his office in Mexico by persons working for the United States Drug Enforcement Agency (DEA). He was wanted in the United States (P) for alleged complicity in the torture-murder of a DEA agent. Alvarez-Machain (D) moved to dismiss the indictment, contending that his abduction violated a U.S.-Mexico extradition treaty. The district court agreed and dismissed the indictment. The court of appeals affirmed, and the United States Supreme Court granted review.

ISSUE: Does the presence of an extradition treaty between the United States and another nation necessarily preclude obtaining a citizen of that nation through abduction?

HOLDING AND DECISION: (Rehnquist, C.J.) No. The presence of an extradition treaty between the United States (P) and another nation does not necessarily preclude obtaining a citizen of that nation through abduction. It has long been the rule that abduction, in and of itself, does not invalidate a prosecution against a foreign national. The only question, therefore, is whether the abduction violates any extradition treaty that may be in effect between the United States (P) and the nation in which the abductee was to be found. Here, the U.S.-Mexican authorities presumably were aware of the United States' (P) long-standing law regarding abductions and did not insist on including a prohibition against abductions. Alvarez-Machain (D) argued that since international law prohibits abductions, the drafters of the treaty had no reason to consider a prohibition thereof necessary. However, this body of law only applies to situations where no extradition treaty exists, so it is irrelevant here. Consequently, since the extradition treaty does not prohibit abduction such as occurred here, it was not illegal. Reversed and remanded.

DISSENT: (Stevens, J.) The majority opinion fails to distinguish between acts of private citizens, which do not violate any treaty obligations, and conduct expressly authorized by the Executive Branch, which undoubtedly constitutes a fragrant violation of international law and a breach of the U.S. (P) treaty obligations.

ANALYSIS

Alvarez-Machain (D) lost this battle but won the war. He was tried in Los Angeles in 1993. At the close of the prosecution's case, the trial judge, Edward Rafeedie, dismissed the case for lack of evidence. The judge used some harsh language in his order, apparently believing the case should never have been brought.

Quicknotes

EXTRADITION The surrender by one State or nation to another of an individual allegedly guilty of committing a crime in that area.

INDICTMENT A formal written accusation made by a prosecutor and issued by a grand jury, charging an individual with a criminal offense.

TREATY An agreement between two or more nations for the benefit of the general public.

"The Justice Case" (Case 3), United States v. Josef Altstoetter et al.

Allied country (P) v. Nazi judges (D)

Trials of Individuals Before the Nuremberg Military Tribunals Under Control Council Law No. 10, 1946-1949, Vol. III (1951). Opinion and Judgment, at 954-84

NATURE OF CASE: Post-World War II trial of Nazi judges by a U.S. military tribunal in Germany.

FACT SUMMARY: Judges (D) who were part of the Nazi regime were charged with various crimes, including crimes against humanity, conspiracy to commit war crimes, and "judicial murder," on the grounds that they had destroyed law and justice in Germany and then utilized the emptied forms of legal process for persecution, enslavement, and extermination on a large scale.

RULE OF LAW

(1) The military tribunal draws its power and jurisdiction to punish violations of international law from the Control Council, as an international body temporarily governing Germany.

(2) International law recognizes more than violations of laws and customs of war as offenses.

(3) The *ex post facto* rule does not apply to international law, so that the principle *nullum crimen sine lege* cannot be used as a defense to international crimes.

FACTS: After World War II, a series of trials took place at Nuremberg and other locations in Germany under Control Council Law No. 10 (C.C. Law 10). The Control Council governed occupied Germany and was made up of representatives from the United States (P), the U.S.S.R (P), France (P), and Great Britain (P). In U.S. occupied zones, trials were held before U.S. judges. In 1947, the U.S. Military Government for Germany created Military Tribunal III to try what was called the "Justice Case," where the Defendants (D) were judges in the Nazi regime. They were charged with "judicial murder and other atrocities, which they committed by destroying law and justice in Germany, and then utilizing the emptied forms of legal process for the persecution, enslavement, and extermination on a large scale," and were accused of conspiracy to commit war crimes against civilians in German-occupied territories (including German civilians and nationals) and against soldiers of countries at war with Germany. They were also accused of crimes against humanity. In addition, some were charged with being members of the SS, SD, and Nazi Party leadership corps, all of which had been declared criminal organizations. All the Defendants (D) pled not guilty. Military Tribunal III rendered its judgment.

ISSUE:

(1) Does the military tribunal draw its power and jurisdiction to punish violations of international law from the Control Council, as an international body temporarily governing Germany?

(2) Does international law recognize more than violations of laws and customs of war as offenses?

(3) Does the *ex post facto* rule apply to international law, so that the principle *nullum crimen sine lege* can be used as a defense to international crimes?

HOLDING AND DECISION: [Judge not stated in casebook excerpt.]

(1) Yes. The military tribunal draws its power and jurisdiction to punish violations of international law from the Control Council, as an international body temporarily governing Germany. It has always been recognized that a State with a functioning government may punish war crimes of perpetrators that come within the State's jurisdiction, but at the State's discretion. The situation here is different, since there is no functioning German government. Thus, the power to punish violations of international law in Germany is not solely dependent on the enactment of rules of substantive criminal law that are applicable only in Germany. Instead, the military tribunal may punish violations of the common international law because Germany is under the temporary control of the Control Council, an international body that has assumed and exercised the power to establish judicial machinery for the punishment of such violations. Such an international body could not, without consent, assume or exercise such power in a State that had a functioning national government that could exercise its sovereignty.

(2) Yes. International law recognizes more than violations of laws and customs of war as offenses. Violations of laws and customs of war are no longer the only offenses recognized by common international law. Given the "force of circumstance, the grim fact of worldwide interdependence, and the moral pressure of public opinion," crimes against humanity committed by the Nazis have also been recognized as violations of international law. One such crime is genocide, which has been confirmed as a crime under international law by the U.N. General Assembly. The commission of genocide is punishable regardless of whether those who committed it were private individuals, public officials, or statesmen, and regardless of whether it was committed on religious, racial, political, or any other grounds. Whether the crime against humanity is the product of statute, international law, or both, it is not unjust to try the

Continued on next page.

perpetrators, who are chargeable with the knowledge that their acts were wrong and punishable when committed. The Defendants' (D) contention that they should not be found guilty because they acted within the authority and by the command of German laws must be rejected, since Control Council Law 10 provides for punishment regardless of whether the acts were in accord with or in violation of domestic laws at the time. The Nuremberg Tribunals are not German courts and are not enforcing German law, nor are the charges based on violations of German law. Instead, they are international tribunals enforcing international law as superior to any German statute or decree. Although German courts during the Nazi regime were required to follow German law (i.e., Hitler's will) even though it was contrary to international law, no such limitation may be applied to the tribunal here. In fact, the very essence of the case here is that German law—the Hitlerian decrees and corrupt and perverted Nazi judicial system—itself constituted the substance of war crimes and crimes against humanity. Thus, the participation in the enactment and enforcement of that law amounts to complicity in crime. Moreover, governmental participation is a material element of the crime against humanity, since only when public officials participate in atrocities and persecutions do those crimes assume international proportions. Because governmental participation is an element of the crime, it cannot also be a defense thereto.

(3) No. *The ex post facto* rule does not apply to international law, so that the principle *nullum crimen sine lege* cannot be used as a defense to international crimes. The *ex post facto* rule, which under written constitutions condemns statutes that define as criminal those acts committed before the law was enacted, cannot apply to international law, which is not the product of statute, but of multipartite treaties, conventions, judicial decisions, and customs. It is "sheer absurdity" to suggest that the rule can be applied to a treaty, custom, or decision of an international tribunal. If the rule were applied to these, there would be no common international law—it would have been strangled at birth. Thus, the principle of *nullum crimen sine lege* does not limit the tribunal's power to punish violations of international law when committed. Not only is this principle not a limitation of sovereignty, it is a principle of justice, so that to assert that it is unjust to punish those who defy treaties and international assurances is untrue, since the perpetrators must know that what they have done is wrong and it would be unjust to allow the perpetrators to go unpunished.

ANALYSIS

A basic precept of criminal law prohibits *ex post facto* prosecutions (*nullum crimen sine lege; nulla poena sine lege*). Arguably, since many of the crimes against humanity, such as genocide and mass killing, were already crimes under every legal system, it would not be unjust under *ex post facto* principles to prosecute and punish perpetrators of such crimes, since arguably the crimes were merely "internationalized" by the Charter of the International Military Tribunal.

Quicknotes

EX POST FACTO After the fact; a law that makes subsequent activity criminal or increases the punishment for a crime that occurred or eliminates a defense that was available to the defendant prior to its passage.

JURISDICTION The authority of a court to hear and declare judgment in respect to a particular matter.

NULLA POENA SINE LEGE No punishment without law.

NULLUM CRIMEN SINE LEGE No crime without law.

CHAPTER 17

Law of the Sea

Quick Reference Rules of Law

Corfu Channel Case (United Kingdom v. Albania)

Nation claiming innocent passage (P) v. Nation denying innocent passage (D)

1949 I.C.J. 4

NATURE OF CASE: Proceedings before the International Court of Justice to determine, inter alia, whether a nation had a right of innocent passage through the territorial waters of another nation that included straits used for international navigation.

FACT SUMMARY: The United Kingdom (P) claimed it had a right of innocent passage to send its warships through straits used for international navigation that encompassed Albania's (D) territorial waters. Albania (D) denied this right.

RULE OF LAW

(1) The criteria for determining whether a channel is subject to the right of innocent passage are that it geographically connects two parts of the high seas, and that it is being used for international navigation.

(2) A passage of warships during peace time comports with the principle of innocent passage where the warships are not in combat formation and their guns are in the line of the ships and their antiaircraft guns are pointing outwards and up in the air.

FACTS: Warships of the United Kingdom (P) sailing through the Corfu Channel, which connects two parts of the Mediterranean Sea, were fired upon by Albanian forces. The United Kingdom (P) protested to Albania (D), which asserted foreign ships had no right to pass through Albanian territorial waters without prior notification to, and the permission of, Albanian authorities. The United Kingdom (P) claimed the right of innocent passage, i.e., in time of peace States can send their ships for innocent purposes through straits used for international navigation. Albania (D) claimed this channel did not belong to the class of international highways as to which a right of innocent passage existed, and the United Kingdom's (P) ships had therefore trespassed on its territorial waters, because the channel was used almost exclusively for local traffic. That channel had also been in dispute because Greece and Albania (D) had both claimed bordering territory, and Albania (D) was afraid of Greek incursions, so Albania (D) claimed a right to regulate the channel. The United Kingdom (P) and Albania (D) agreed to have their dispute resolved by the International Court of Justice (I.C.J.). Two of the issues the I.C.J. addressed were whether the United Kingdom (P) had a right of innocent passage through the Corfu Channel, and, if so, whether it exercised this right properly.

ISSUE:

(1) Are the criteria for determining whether a channel is subject to the right of innocent passage that it geographically connects two parts of the high seas, and that it is being used for international navigation?

(2) Does a passage of warships during peace time comport with the principle of innocent passage where the warships are not in combat formation and their guns are in the line of the ships and their antiaircraft guns are pointing outwards and up in the air?

HOLDING AND DECISION: [Judge not stated in casebook excerpt.]

(1) Yes. The criteria for determining whether a channel is subject to the right of innocent passage are that it geographically connects two parts of the high seas, and that it is being used for international navigation. It is a principle of customary international law that States in time of peace have a right to send warships through straits used for international navigation between two parts of the high seas without previous authorization of a coastal State, provided such passage is innocent. If the passage is innocent, the coastal State may not prohibit the passage. Albania (D) contends the Corfu Channel is not a strait subject to the innocent passage rules because its traffic is primarily local. However, the test for whether the channel is subject to the principles of innocent passage does not depend on the volume of traffic it sees, nor whether the channel is of primary or of lesser importance to international navigation. The key is whether the channel connects two parts of the high seas and is used at all for international navigation. Here, the Corfu Channel has been a useful route for international maritime traffic. Accordingly, it belongs to the class of international highways through which passage cannot be prohibited by a coastal State in time of peace. Given, however, that Albania (D) and Greece dispute the ownership of the straits, Albania (D) would be justified in regulating passage through the straits, but it may not prohibit such passage, nor may it require special authorization for passage. [Judgment for the United Kingdom (P) as to this issue.]

(2) Yes. A passage of warships during peace time comports with the principle of innocent passage where the warships are not in combat formation and their guns are in the line of the ships and their antiaircraft guns are pointing outwards and up in the air. Contrary to

Continued on next page.

Albania's (D) assertions, the evidence shows the United Kingdom's (P) warships were not in combat formation, but rather were in line, one after the other, and were not maneuvering until they were fired upon, and then only to save human life. Also, contrary to Albania's (D) assertions, there were no soldiers aboard the ships, and the main guns were in the line of the ships, and the antiaircraft guns were pointing outwards and up in the air, which is the position of those guns in harbor and at sea. Thus, the position of the guns was not inconsistent with the rules of innocent passage, and the ships made passage consistent with those principles. [Judgment for the United Kingdom (P) as to this issue.]

ANALYSIS

As this case illustrates, the exact meaning of innocent passage has been disputed. An attempt to rectify this situation was made in the Law of the Sea Convention by instituting a right of "transit passage." Article 37 of the Convention applies this right to straits that are used for international navigation between one part of the high seas or an exclusive economic zone and another part of the high seas or an exclusive economic zone. Article 38 provides the right of transit passage applies to all ships and aircraft solely for the purpose of continuous and expeditious transit (with transit passage not being precluded if the purpose of entering the strait is to enter, leave, or return from a State bordering the strait), and Article 39 specifies the duties ships and aircraft must observe, such as proceeding without delay, and refraining from any threat or use of force.

Quicknotes

TERRITORIAL SEA That portion of the sea that is three miles off a nation's coast and over which that nation has jurisdiction.

The "Hoshinmaru" Case (Japan v. Russian Federation)

Sovereign state (P) v. Sovereign state (D)

Intl. Trib. for the Law of the Sea, ITLOS Case No. 14, Judgment (2007)

NATURE OF CASE: Application before the International Tribunal for the Law of the Sea for release of a ship and its crew.

FACT SUMMARY: The *Hoshinmaru*, a Japanese-registered ship, was detained, along with its crew, by the Russian Federation (D), which claimed the *Hoshinmaru* had violated a fishing license issued by the Russian Federation (D). Japan (P) applied for the ship's release.

RULE OF LAW

The amount of security to be posted by a nation seeking the release of a fishing vessel flying its flag that has committed a reporting offense in the context of an otherwise satisfactory cooperative framework must reflect the seriousness of the offense and the degree of cooperation between the detaining nation and the nation seeking release.

FACTS: The *Hoshinmaru* is a fishing ship registered in Japan (P), and its crew is comprised of Japanese nationals. The ship had obtained a fishing license from the Russian Federation (D) that permitted it to fish certain amounts of specified fish in the waters of the exclusive economic zone of the Russian Federation (D), including 101.8 tons of sockeye salmon and 161.8 tons of chum salmon. While fishing in the exclusive economic zone, the ship was boarded by Russian Federation (D) inspectors, who discovered that sockeye salmon were being kept under the chum salmon and that the ship's master had declared 20 tons of sockeye salmon as the cheaper chum salmon. This constituted an offense, since part of the sockeye salmon catch was being concealed and data in the fishing log and vessel report was misleading. Accordingly, the Russian Federation (D) detained the ship and its crew. Japan (P) applied to the International Tribunal for the Law of the Sea for release of the ship and its crew. As part of its judgment, the Tribunal determined the amount of the bond or other financial security that Japan (P) would have to post to secure such release.

ISSUE: Must the amount of security to be posted by a nation seeking the release of a fishing vessel flying its flag that has committed a reporting offense in the context of an otherwise satisfactory cooperative framework reflect the seriousness of the offense and the degree of cooperation between the detaining nation and the nation seeking release?

HOLDING AND DECISION: [Judge not stated in casebook excerpt.] Yes. The amount of security to be posted by a nation seeking the release of a fishing vessel flying its flag that has committed a reporting offense in the context of an otherwise satisfactory cooperative framework must reflect the seriousness of the offense and the degree of cooperation between the detaining nation and the nation seeking release. To determine the appropriate amount, nature, and form of the bond or other financial security to be posted, the Tribunal must apply the rules set forth in the Convention and other rules of international law not incompatible with the Convention. The offense committed is considered by the Russian Federation (D) to be very serious, since if the substitution of one fish for another had not been detected by the inspectors, the 20 tons of sockeye would have been stolen and taken illegally out of the exclusive economic zone. Thus, according to the Russian Federation (D), this is a classic case of illegal, unreported, and unregulated fishing and justifies a bond of 22,000,000 rubles. Japan (P), on the other hand, asserts that the offense is not fishing without a license or overfishing, but falsely recording the catch that the vessel was entitled to take under its license. Also, since the amount of sockeye salmon on board the vessel was well within the license limit, the sockeye salmon stock could not be deemed damaged or endangered. Both sovereigns cooperate closely in respect of fishing in the exclusive economic zone and have an institutional framework for managing and conserving fish, which includes rules for such management and conservation. Japan (P) has indicated that it will continue to endeavor to ensure that crews of vessels flying its flag respect such rules and other local laws and regulations. Although the offense at issue is a transgression within an otherwise satisfactory cooperative framework, it should not be considered a minor or purely technical offense. Monitoring of catches, which requires accurate reporting, is one of the most essential means of managing marine living resources. Not only is it the right of the Russian Federation (D) to apply and implement such measures but the provisions of article 61, paragraph 2, of the Convention should also be taken into consideration to ensure through proper conservation and management measures that the maintenance of the living resources in the exclusive economic zone is not endangered by over-exploitation. Therefore, on basis of these considerations, the amount of security to be posted by Japan (P) should be 10,000,000 rubles, paid to the bank account indicated by the Russian Federation (D), or in the form of a bank guarantee.

ANALYSIS

The Convention at issue in this case is the United Nations Convention on the Law of the Sea (LOS Convention). The

Continued on next page.

LOS Convention, Article 73(2), provides that "Arrested vessels and their crews shall be promptly released upon the posting of reasonable bond or other security." As in this case, the reasonableness of the security to be posted by the flag State seeking prompt release takes into account the depletion of marine life and should serve to deter the plundering of the living resources of the sea. Given available technology, in addition to requiring a bond or other financial security, other sanctions a tribunal could order might include having a satellite tracking device on the detained vessel.

Quicknotes

INTERNATIONAL LAW Body of law applicable to dealings between nations.

SOVEREIGN A State or entity with independent authority to govern its affairs.

South China Sea Arbitration (Philippines v. China)

Sovereign nation (P) v. Sovereign nation (D)

Award, PCA Case No. 2013-19 (July 12, 2016)

NATURE OF CASE: Arbitral award in dispute between sovereign nations over maritime and territorial rights to various geographic features in the South China Sea.

FACT SUMMARY: [Several nations bordering on the South China Sea, including the Philippines (P) and China (D), disputed various maritime and territorial rights in the South China Sea. To settle some of its disputes with China (D), the Philippines (P) brought an arbitration under the 1982 United Nations Convention on the Law of the Sea ("the Convention" or "UNCLOS") before the Permanent Court of Arbitration (PCA). One of the many issues before the Arbitral Tribunal (Tribunal) was whether various geographic features in the South China Sea, known collectively as the Spratly Islands, would entitle whichever nation was sovereign over the features to exclusive economic zones and continental shelves under the Convention. The Tribunal did not resolve—nor was it asked to—the sovereignty over the Spratly Islands features.]

RULE OF LAW

The high-tide features in the Spratly Islands of the South China Sea, in their natural condition, are not capable of sustaining human habitation or economic life of their own within the meaning of Article 121(3) of the 1982 United Nations Convention on the Law of the Sea ("the Convention" or "UNCLOS"), so will not generate entitlements to an exclusive economic zone and continental shelf under the Convention.

FACTS: [Several nations bordering on the South China Sea, including the Philippines (P) and China (D), disputed various maritime and territorial rights in the South China Sea. To settle some of its disputes with China (D), the Philippines (P) brought an arbitration under the 1982 United Nations Convention on the Law of the Sea ("the Convention" or "UNCLOS") before the Permanent Court of Arbitration (PCA). One of the many issues before the Arbitral Tribunal (Tribunal) was whether various geographic features in the South China Sea, known collectively as the Spratly Islands, would entitle whichever nation was sovereign over the features to exclusive economic zones and continental shelves under the Convention. Some of the named features addressed by the Tribunal's analysis included: Itu Aba, Thitu, North Danger Reef, West York, Spratly Island, South-West Cay, and North-East Cay. Under Article 121(3) of the Convention, if a feature is determined to be capable of sustaining either human habitation or economic life on its own, without external resources, it will be considered an island entitled to an economic zone and a continental shelf. If, however, a feature is determined to be a "rock" incapable of sustaining either human habitation or economic life, that feature will not be entitled to an economic zone and continental shelf. The Tribunal did not resolve—nor was it asked to—the sovereignty over the Spratly Islands features.]

ISSUE: Are the high-tide features in the Spratly Islands of the South China Sea, in their natural condition, capable of sustaining human habitation or economic life of their own within the meaning of Article 121(3) of the United Nations Convention on the Law of the Sea, 1982 ("the Convention" or "UNCLOS") so as to generate entitlements to an exclusive economic zone and continental shelf under the Convention?

HOLDING AND DECISION: [Members of Arbitral Tribunal not stated in casebook extract.] No. The high-tide features in the Spratly Islands of the South China Sea, in their natural condition, are not capable of sustaining human habitation or economic life of their own within the meaning of Article 121(3) of the United Nations Convention on the Law of the Sea, 1982 ("the Convention" or "UNCLOS"), so will not generate entitlements to an exclusive economic zone and continental shelf under the Convention. The Tribunal will first set forth its conclusions regarding the interpretation of Article 121(3), then review the different aspects of the conditions on the features, and then apply its understanding of Article 121(3) to those aspects in making its final determination.

Regarding the interpretation of Article 121(3), in light of its text, context, object and purpose, and drafting history, the word "rock" does not limit the provision to features composed of solid rock. Also, the status of a feature is to be determined on the basis of its natural capacity, without external additions or modifications intended to increase its capacity to sustain human habitation or an economic life of its own. With respect to "human habitation," the critical factor is the non-transient character of the inhabitation, such that the inhabitants can fairly be said to constitute the natural population of the feature, for whose benefit the resources of the exclusive economic zone were seen to merit protection. The term "human habitation" should be understood to involve the inhabitation of the feature by a stable community of people for whom the feature constitutes a home and on which they can remain. Such a community need not necessarily be large, and a few individuals or family groups could suffice. Periodic or habitual

Continued on next page.

residence on a feature by a nomadic people could also constitute habitation. The term "economic life of their own" is linked to the requirement of human habitation. Article 121(3) does not refer to a feature having economic value, but to sustaining "economic life," which ordinarily will be the life and livelihoods of the human population inhabiting and making its home on a maritime feature or group of features. Additionally, Article 121(3) makes clear that the economic life in question must pertain to the feature as "of its own." Economic life, therefore, must be oriented around the feature itself and not focused solely on the waters or seabed of the surrounding territorial sea. Economic activity that is entirely dependent on external resources or devoted to using a feature as an object for extractive activities without the involvement of a local population would also fall inherently short with respect to this necessary link to the feature itself. Extractive economic activity to harvest the natural resources of a feature for the benefit of a population elsewhere certainly constitutes the exploitation of resources for economic gain, but it cannot reasonably be considered to constitute the economic life of an island as its own. Additionally, the text of Article 121(3) is disjunctive, so that the ability to sustain either human habitation or an economic life of its own would suffice to entitle a high-tide feature to an exclusive economic zone and continental shelf. However, as a practical matter, the Tribunal considers that a maritime feature will ordinarily only possess an economic life of its own if it is also inhabited by a stable human community. One exception to that view arises in the case of populations sustaining themselves through a network of related maritime features. Further, Article 121(3) is concerned with the capacity of a maritime feature to sustain human habitation or an economic life of its own, not with whether the feature is presently, or has been, inhabited or home to economic life. The principal factors that contribute to the natural capacity of a feature include the presence of water, food, and shelter in sufficient quantities to enable a group of persons to live on the feature for an indeterminate period of time, as well as factors that bear on the conditions for inhabiting and developing an economic life on a feature, including the prevailing climate, the proximity of the feature to other inhabited areas and populations, and the potential for livelihoods on and around the feature. Each feature is to be assessed on a case-by-case basis. However, in some instances, a group of features may be assessed collectively, as where remote island populations make use of a number of islands, sometimes spread over significant distances, for sustenance and livelihoods. Physical conditions on a particular-feature alone may be dispositive in clear-cut cases—the physical conditions clearly will either support or not support habitation—but additional considerations may be necessary for features that fall close to the line. It will be difficult, if not impossible, to determine from the physical characteristics of a feature alone where the capacity merely to keep people alive ends and the capacity to sustain settled habitation by a human community begins. In such circumstances, the most reliable evidence of the capacity of a feature will usually be the historical use to which it has been put. If the historical record of a feature indicates that nothing resembling a stable community has ever developed there, the most reasonable conclusion would be that the natural conditions are simply too difficult for such a community to form and that the feature is not capable of sustaining such habitation. Conversely, if a feature is presently inhabited or has historically been inhabited, the Tribunal will consider whether there is evidence to indicate that habitation was only possible through outside support.

The Tribunal will next consider the evidence regarding the conditions on the features at issue in light of its conclusions for interpreting Article 121(3). Given that the more salient features have been inhabited or occupied militarily or governmentally, and modified, perhaps in an attempt to influence whether they are entitled to exclusive economic zones, the Tribunal will consider historical evidence of conditions on the features prior to the advent of the exclusive economic zone as a concept or the beginning of significant human modification as representing a more reliable guide to the capacity of the features to sustain human habitation or economic life. The physical conditions on the features suggest that the principal high-tide features in the Spratly Islands are capable of enabling the survival of small groups of people, and this is borne out by the fact that small numbers of fishermen have historically been present on Itu Aba and the other more significant features and appear to have survived principally on the basis of the resources at hand. At the same time, the features are not obviously habitable, and their capacity even to enable human survival appears to be distinctly limited. Therefore, the historical evidence of human habitation and economic life on the Spratly Islands and the implications of such evidence for the natural capacity of the features must be considered. In addition to the presence of fishermen, Itu Aba and South-West Cay were the site of Japanese mining and fishing activities in the 1920s and 1930s. The Spratlys were also the site of other, more adventurous activities in the 1950s. More recently, many of the features have been transformed by substantial construction efforts and are now the site of installations hosting significant numbers of personnel, generally of a governmental nature. Human habitation entails the non-transient inhabitation of a feature by a stable community of people for whom the feature constitutes a home on which they can remain. This standard is not met by the historical presence of fishermen, who came from elsewhere and were on the features temporarily, even for extended periods of time. The same is true of commercial activities, including mining guano and capturing sea turtles, as those were undertaken to extract the economic resources of the Spratlys for the

Continued on next page.

benefit of populations of other places, to which the laborers would return. It was not to make a new life for themselves on the islands. Similarly, the groups of military or other governmental personnel presently stationed on the features in the Spratly Islands do not suffice to constitute "human habitation" for the purposes of Article 121(3). These groups are heavily dependent on outside supply, and their presence on any of the features cannot fairly be said to be sustained by the feature itself, rather than by a continuous lifeline of supply and communication from the mainland. In sum, there is no indication that anything fairly resembling a stable human community has ever formed on the Spratly Islands. Moreover, there is no evidence that suggests that the historical absence of human habitation on the Spratly Islands is the product of intervening forces or otherwise does not reflect the limited capacity of the features themselves. Accordingly, the Spratly Islands features are not capable of sustaining human habitation within the meaning of Article 121(3). A similar conclusion must be reached regarding the capacity of the features to support economic life. All of the economic activity in the Spratly Islands that appears in the historical record has been essentially extractive in nature (i.e., mining for guano, collecting shells, and fishing), aimed to a greater or lesser degree at utilizing the resources of the Spratlys for the benefit of populations elsewhere. Because extractive economic activity, without the presence of a stable local community, necessarily falls short of constituting the economic life of the feature, the history of extractive economic activity on the Spratly Islands does not constitute evidence of an economic life of their own. Accordingly, the high-tide features in the Spratly Islands are not capable of sustaining an economic life of their own within the meaning of Article 121(3). The effect of the Tribunal's conclusions is that the Spratly Islands features will not be entitled to an exclusive economic zone or continental shelf.

ANALYSIS

As the Tribunal in this case notes, the introduction of the exclusive economic zone was not intended to grant extensive maritime entitlements to small features whose historical contribution to human settlement is as slight as that. Nor was the exclusive economic zone intended to encourage nations to establish artificial populations in the hope of making expansive claims, precisely what has now occurred in the South China Sea. On the contrary, Article 121(3) was intended to prevent such developments and to forestall a provocative and counterproductive effort to manufacture entitlements. Nevertheless, the effect of Article 121(3) is not to deny nations the benefit of the economic resources of small rocks and maritime features. Such features remain susceptible to a claim of territorial sovereignty and will generate a 12-nautical-mile territorial sea, provided they remain above water at high tide. Rather, the effect of Article 121(3) is to prevent such features—whose economic benefit, if any, to the nation that controls them is for resources alone—from generating a further entitlement to a 200-nautical-mile exclusive economic zone and continental shelf that would infringe on the entitlements generated by inhabited territory or on the area reserved for the common heritage of mankind.

Quicknotes

DISPOSITION A transferring of property; conveyance.

CHAPTER 18

International Environmental Law

Quick Reference Rules of Law

Trail Smelter Arbitration (United States v. Canada)

Sovereign nation (P) v. Sovereign nation (D)

3 U.N. Rep. Intl. Arb. Awards 1905 (1941)

NATURE OF CASE: Arbitral award in action by one nation against another for air pollution damage.

FACT SUMMARY: [The United States (P) and Canada (D) convened a Special Arbitral Tribunal to decide whether sulfur dioxide fumes from a smelter plant located in Canada (D) caused injury in the United States (P), and, if so, whether Canada (D) could be held liable, and what the appropriate remedy should be.]

RULE OF LAW

Where there are no cases by an international tribunal addressing a given legal issue, apposite decisions of the United States Supreme Court may be relied on for guidance by analogy where no contrary rule prevails in international law and no reason for rejecting such precedents can be adduced from the limitations of sovereignty inherent in the Constitution of the United States.

FACTS: [A smelter plant in Trail, Canada (D), owned by a Canadian corporation, spewed sulfur dioxide into the air, which caused damage in the United States (P) from 1925 to 1937. The United States (P) and Canada (D) convened a Special Arbitral Tribunal to decide whether Canada (D) could be held liable for the damage caused by the plant in the United States (P), and what the appropriate remedy should be. The Tribunal determined that Canada (D) was responsible for the air pollution damage and ordered injunctive relief and the payment of an indemnity.]

ISSUE: Where there are no cases by an international tribunal addressing a given legal issue, may apposite decisions of the United States Supreme Court be relied on for guidance by analogy where no contrary rule prevails in international law and no reason for rejecting such precedents can be adduced from the limitations of sovereignty inherent in the Constitution of the United States?

HOLDING AND DECISION: [Members of the Special Arbitral Tribunal not stated in casebook extract.] Yes. Where there are no cases by an international tribunal addressing a given legal issue, apposite decisions of the United States Supreme Court may be relied on for guidance by analogy where no contrary rule prevails in international law and no reason for rejecting such precedents can be adduced from the limitations of sovereignty inherent in the Constitution of the United States. It is well established in international law that a nation has at all times a duty to protect other nations against injurious acts by individuals from within its jurisdiction. This principle, which has been articulated by leading authorities and forms the basis of international decisions addressing various matters, is not disputed by Canada (D). The real difficulty is determining what constitutes an injurious act. No case of air pollution dealt with by an international tribunal has been cited, nor does the Tribunal know of any such case. The nearest analogy is that of water pollution, but here, too, no decision of an international tribunal has been cited or has been found. There are, however, as regards both air pollution and water pollution, certain decisions of the United States Supreme Court that may legitimately be taken as a guide in this field of international law, for it is reasonable to follow by analogy, in international cases, precedents established by that court in dealing with controversies between States of the Union or with other controversies concerning the quasi-sovereign rights of such States, where no contrary rule prevails in international law and no reason for rejecting such precedents can be adduced from the limitations of sovereignty inherent in the Constitution of the United States. Based on these United States Supreme Court precedents, the Tribunal holds that no nation has the right to use or permit the use of its territory in such a manner as to cause injury by fumes in or to the territory of another nation, or the properties or persons therein, when the case is of serious consequence and the injury is established by clear and convincing evidence. [In light of this determination, technical controls are to be imposed on the Trail Smelter, including caps on maximum hourly emissions of sulfur dioxide based on meteorological and emissions records, and the interrelationship between meteorological conditions and emissions impacts.]

ANALYSIS

The *Trail Smelter Arbitration* is considered a landmark international law case, in general, and in global environmental law. It has become the basis for many more decisions regarding transboundary harm and various treaty provisions. Now, Principle 2 of the 1992 Rio Declaration on Environment and Development is the threshold for transboundary harm, codifying the *Trail Smelter Arbitration* decision into a well-settled rule of customary international law. It is now the principle of both treaties and customary law that one country may not cause significant transboundary environmental harm to another. These principles have been applied, for example, to outer space,

Continued on next page.

insofar as the Outer Space Treaty, Jan. 27, 1967, 610 U.N.T.S. 205, makes the earth's orbit a common pool resource, and a nation launching objects into space is liable under the treaty for damages caused from the objects.

Quicknotes

INDEMNITY The duty of a party to compensate another for damages sustained.

INJUNCTIVE RELIEF A court order issued as a remedy, requiring a person to do, or prohibiting that person from doing, a specific act.

SOVEREIGNTY The absolute power conferred to the State to govern and regulate all persons located and activities conducted therein.

Certain Activities Carried Out by Nicaragua in the Border Area (Costa Rica v. Nicaragua) and Construction of a Road in Costa Rica along the San Juan River (Nicaragua v. Costa Rica)

Border nation (P) v. Border nation (D)

2015 I.C.J. 665

NATURE OF CASE: Portion of consolidated actions brought by nations bordering each other addressing claims that one nation (Costa Rica (D)) violated its international law obligations by failing to conduct an environmental impact assessment prior to engaging in activities that could, and did, cause environmental harm to the other nation (Nicaragua (P)), which sought redress for the alleged violations and injuries.

FACT SUMMARY: Costa Rica (D) constructed a road that mostly ran parallel to the southern bank of the San Juan de Nicaragua River, which constituted a border between Costa Rica (D) and Nicaragua (P), and which was under Nicaraguan (P) sovereignty. Nicaragua (P) claimed that Costa Rica (D) had a duty under international law to have determined prior to commencing the road construction whether such activity created a risk of significant adverse transboundary impacts on Nicaragua (P), and if such risk existed, to conduct an environmental impact assessment. Nicaragua (P) also claimed that the road construction in fact caused it significant transboundary harm, so that Costa Rica (D) violated various international obligations, for which Nicaragua (P) sought a remedy.

RULE OF LAW

(1) Prior to engaging in activities that, under the circumstances, could be expected to cause significant transboundary harm, a nation has a duty under general international law to assess the environmental impacts of the activities.

(2) Where a nation alleges that another nation has caused it significant transboundary harm, so that the other nation has breached its substantive obligations under customary international law concerning transboundary harm, but the nation alleging harm fails to adduce convincing evidence of such harm, the nation's claim must be dismissed.

FACTS: Nicaragua (P) and Costa Rica (D) brought claims against each other before the International Court of Justice (I.C.J.) that arose from each other's activities along their mutual border. The I.C.J. consolidated the cases. In the case brought by Nicaragua (P), Costa Rica (D) constructed a road of 160 km that ran parallel, for over 108 km, to the southern bank of the San Juan de Nicaragua River, which constituted a border between Costa Rica (D) and Nicaragua (P), and which was under Nicaraguan (P) sovereignty. Costa Rica (D) did not prepare an environmental impact assessment prior to commencing the construction. Nicaragua (P) claimed that Costa Rica (D) had a duty under international law to have determined prior to commencing the road construction whether such activity created a risk of significant adverse transboundary impacts on Nicaragua (P), and if such risk existed, to conduct an environmental impact assessment. In turn, if the environmental impact assessment confirmed the risk of significant transboundary harm, Costa Rica (D) would have been obligated to notify and consult with Nicaragua (P) in good faith to determine appropriate measures to prevent or mitigate such risk. Nicaragua (P) also claimed that the road construction in fact caused it significant transboundary harm. Thus, Nicaragua (P) claimed that Costa Rica (D) violated international law by causing such harm, by failing to respect the territorial integrity and sovereignty of Nicaragua (P), and by breaching treaty obligations regarding the protection of the environment. Nicaragua (P) sought a remedy for these violations.

ISSUE:

(1) Prior to engaging in activities that, under the circumstances, could be expected to cause significant transboundary harm, does a nation have a duty under general international law to assess the environmental impacts of the activities?

(2) Where a nation alleges that another nation has caused it significant transboundary harm, so that the other nation has breached its substantive obligations under customary international law concerning transboundary harm, but the nation alleging harm fails to adduce convincing evidence of such harm, must the nation's claim be dismissed?

HOLDING AND DECISION: [Judge not stated in casebook extract.]

(1) Yes. Prior to engaging in activities that, under the circumstances, could be expected to cause significant transboundary harm, a nation has a duty under general international law to assess the environmental impacts of the activities. This principle of prevention reflects every nation's obligation not to allow knowingly its territory to be used for acts contrary to the rights of

Continued on next page.

other nations. Thus, to fulfil its obligation to exercise due diligence in preventing significant transboundary environmental harm, a nation must, before embarking on an activity having the potential adversely to affect the environment of another nation, ascertain if there is a risk of significant transboundary harm, which would trigger the requirement to carry out an environmental impact assessment. This is a case-by-case determination and depends on the particular facts and circumstances. If the environmental impact assessment confirms that there is a risk of significant transboundary harm, the nation planning to undertake the activity is required, in conformity with its due diligence obligation, to notify and consult in good faith with the potentially affected nation, where that is necessary to determine the appropriate measures to prevent or mitigate that risk. The parties disagree whether the scope of the road construction project, given its length and location next to the San Juan River, required such an assessment. In the present case, it fell on Costa Rica (D), not on Nicaragua (P), to assess the existence of a risk of significant transboundary harm prior to the construction of the road, on the basis of an objective evaluation of all the relevant circumstances. Costa Rica (D) asserted that a preliminary assessment of the risk posed by the road project was undertaken when the decision to build the road was made, and that pursuant to this assessment, it was concluded that the road posed no risk of significant harm, and that the only possible risk was the contribution of sediment by the road to a river that already carried a heavy sediment load. However, Costa Rica (D) has not adduced any evidence that it actually carried out such a preliminary assessment. Contrary to Costa Rica's (D) assertions, the scale of the road project was substantial, and any harm caused by the road to the surrounding environment could easily affect the river, and therefore Nicaragua's (P) territory. The location of the road, which at many points was in very close proximity to the river, and the fact that the road would often be built on slopes, risked increasing the discharge of sediment into the river. Another relevant factor in assessing the likelihood of sedimentation due to erosion from the road was that almost a quarter of the road was to be built in areas that were previously forested. The possibility of natural disasters in the area caused by adverse events such as hurricanes, tropical storms, and earthquakes, which would increase the risk of sediment erosion, should equally have been taken into consideration. Further, the geographic conditions of the river basin where the road was to be situated should have been taken into account. The road would pass through wetlands of international importance, which heightened the risk of significant damage since the receiving environment was particularly sensitive. The principal harm that could arise was the possible large deposition of sediment from the road, with resulting risks to the ecology and water quality of the river, as well as morphological changes. For these reasons, the construction of the road by Costa Rica (D) carried a risk of significant transboundary harm. Therefore, the threshold for triggering the obligation to evaluate the environmental impact of the road project was met.

The question thus becomes whether Costa Rica (D) met this obligation. Although Costa Rica (D) prepared several studies of the road's environmental impacts, all these studies were *post hoc* assessments of the environmental impact of the stretches of the road that had already been built and did not assess future harms. However, the obligation to conduct an environmental impact assessment requires an *ex ante* evaluation of the risk of significant transboundary harm, so that the environmental impact assessment must be conducted prior to the implementation of a project. Because Costa Rica's (D) assessments occurred years into the project, rather than before it was commenced, Costa Rica (D) failed to meet its international law obligations to carry out an environmental impact assessment concerning the construction of the road.

(2) Yes. Where a nation alleges that another nation has caused it significant transboundary harm, so that the other nation has breached its substantive obligations under customary international law concerning transboundary harm, but the nation alleging harm fails to adduce convincing evidence of such harm, the nation's claim must be dismissed. The parties submitted to the Court a vast amount of factual and scientific material in support of their respective contentions. They also submitted numerous reports and studies prepared by experts and consultants commissioned by each of them on questions such as technical standards for road construction; river morphology; sedimentation levels in the San Juan River and their causes and effects; the ecological impact of the construction of the road; and the status of remediation works carried out by Costa Rica (D). After reviewing this evidence, and testimony by experts relating thereto, the Court concludes that Nicaragua (P) has failed to prove that it suffered any significant harms from Costa Rica's (D) road construction project. First, Nicaragua (P) has not shown that the river's sediment levels are such that additional sediment eroded from the road passes a sort of critical level in terms of its detrimental effects. Moreover, the case does not present a situation where sediment contributed by the road exceeds maximum allowable limits, which have not been determined for the San Juan River. The evidence tends to show that the road is contributing at most two per cent of the river's total sediment load, which does not give rise to an inference of significant harm, particularly taking into account the high natural variability in the river's sediment loads.

Continued on next page.

Similarly, Nicaragua (P) has not presented any evidence of actual harm to fish in the San Juan River, nor has it identified with precision which species of fish have allegedly been harmed by the construction of the road. At best, Nicaragua (P) has shown that the construction of the road has had a localized impact on macro-invertebrate communities and water quality in small Costa Rican (D) streams draining into the San Juan River. This showing, however, cannot be transposed to the San Juan River as a whole. Any differences in macro-invertebrate richness and abundance between the north and the south banks of the river cannot be attributed to the construction of the road alone, as opposed to other factors such as the size of the catchment area and the nutrient levels therein. Therefore, Nicaragua (P) has not proved that the construction of the road caused significant harm to the river's ecosystem and water quality. Likewise, Nicaragua (P) did not substantiate its contentions regarding harm to tourism and health, and its arguments concerning the risk of toxic spills into the river and of further development of the Costa Rican (D) bank of the river were speculative and failed to show any harm. In light of these failed arguments and contentions, Nicaragua (P) has not proved that the construction of the road caused it significant transboundary harm. Therefore, Nicaragua's (P) claim that Costa Rica (D) breached its substantive obligations under customary international law concerning transboundary harm must be dismissed. Because Nicaragua (P) has also failed to show that Costa Rica (D) in any way exercised any authority on Nicaragua's (P) territory or carried out any activity therein, or that the construction of the road impaired its right of navigation on the San Juan River, Nicaragua's (P) claim concerning the violation of its territorial integrity and sovereignty must also be dismissed. Given the dismissal of these claims, the Court's declaration that Costa Rica (D) violated its obligation to conduct an environmental impact assessment is the appropriate measure of satisfaction for Nicaragua (P).

ANALYSIS

Regarding remedies, Nicaragua (P) had asked the Court to order Costa Rica (D) to "[c]ease all its continuing internationally wrongful acts that affect or are likely to affect the rights of Nicaragua" However, the Court determined that Costa Rica's (D) failure to conduct an environmental impact assessment did not, and would not in the future, adversely affect Nicaragua's (P) rights, so the Court concluded there were no grounds to grant the remedy requested. Similarly, Nicaragua (P) had requested the Court order Costa Rica (D) to restore to the extent possible the situation that existed before the road was constructed, and to provide compensation for the damage caused insofar as it was not made good by restitution. In this regard, the Court observed that restitution and compensation are forms of reparation for material injury. The Court noted that, although Costa Rica (D) did not comply with the obligation to conduct an environmental impact assessment, it had not been established that the construction of the road caused significant harm to Nicaragua (P) or was in breach of other substantive obligations under international law. Thus, the Court concluded that restoring the original condition of the area where the road was located would not constitute an appropriate remedy for Costa Rica's (D) breach of its obligation to carry out an environmental impact assessment. For the same reasons, the Court declined to grant Nicaragua's (P) claim for compensation.

Quicknotes

DUE DILIGENCE The standard of care as would be taken by a reasonable person in accordance with the attendant facts and circumstances.

EX ANTE Based on assumption and prediction, rather than actual results.

POST HOC After this moment.

Glossary

Common Latin Words and Phrases Encountered in the Law

A FORTIORI: Because one fact exists or has been proven, therefore a second fact that is related to the first fact must also exist.

A PRIORI: From the cause to the effect. A term of logic used to denote that when one generally accepted truth is shown to be a cause, another particular effect must necessarily follow.

AB INITIO: From the beginning; a condition that has existed throughout, as in a marriage that was void ab initio.

ACTUS REUS: The wrongful act; in criminal law, such action sufficient to trigger criminal liability.

AD VALOREM: According to value; an ad valorem tax is imposed upon an item located within the taxing jurisdiction calculated by the value of such item.

AMICUS CURIAE: Friend of the court. Its most common usage takes the form of an amicus curiae brief, filed by a person who is not a party to an action but is nonetheless allowed to offer an argument supporting his legal interests.

ARGUENDO: In arguing. A statement, possibly hypothetical, made for the purpose of argument, is one made arguendo.

BILL QUIA TIMET: A bill to quiet title (establish ownership) to real property.

BONA FIDE: True, honest, or genuine. May refer to a person's legal position based on good faith or lacking notice of fraud (such as a bona fide purchaser for value) or to the authenticity of a particular document (such as a bona fide last will and testament).

CAUSA MORTIS: With approaching death in mind. A gift causa mortis is a gift given by a party who feels certain that death is imminent.

CAVEAT EMPTOR: Let the buyer beware. This maxim is reflected in the rule of law that a buyer purchases at his own risk because it is his responsibility to examine, judge, test, and otherwise inspect what he is buying.

CERTIORARI: A writ of review. Petitions for review of a case by the United States Supreme Court are most often done by means of a writ of certiorari.

CONTRA: On the other hand. Opposite. Contrary to.

CORAM NOBIS: Before us; writs of error directed to the court that originally rendered the judgment.

CORAM VOBIS: Before you; writs of error directed by an appellate court to a lower court to correct a factual error.

CORPUS DELICTI: The body of the crime; the requisite elements of a crime amounting to objective proof that a crime has been committed.

CUM TESTAMENTO ANNEXO, ADMINISTRATOR (ADMINISTRATOR C.T.A.): With will annexed; an administrator c.t.a. settles an estate pursuant to a will in which he or she is not appointed.

DE BONIS NON, ADMINISTRATOR (ADMINISTRATOR D.B.N.): Of goods not administered; an administrator d.b.n. settles a partially settled estate.

DE FACTO: In fact; in reality; actually. Existing in fact but not officially approved or engendered.

DE JURE: By right; lawful. Describes a condition that is legitimate "as a matter of law," in contrast to the term "de facto," which connotes something existing in fact but not legally sanctioned or authorized. For example, de facto segregation refers to segregation brought about by housing patterns, etc., whereas de jure segregation refers to segregation created by law.

DE MINIMUS: Of minimal importance; insignificant; a trifle; not worth bothering about.

DE NOVO: Anew; a second time; afresh. A trial de novo is a new trial held at the appellate level as if the case originated there and the trial at a lower level had not taken place.

DICTA: Generally used as an abbreviated form of obiter dicta, a term describing those portions of a judicial opinion incidental or not necessary to resolution of the specific question before the court. Such nonessential statements and remarks are not considered to be binding precedent.

DUCES TECUM: Refers to a particular type of writ or subpoena requesting a party or organization to produce certain documents in their possession.

EN BANC: Full bench. Where a court sits with all justices present rather than the usual quorum.

EX PARTE: For one side or one party only. An ex parte proceeding is one undertaken for the benefit of only one party, without notice to, or an appearance by, an adverse party.

EX POST FACTO: After the fact. An ex post facto law is a law that retroactively changes the consequences of a prior act.

EX REL.: Abbreviated form of the term "ex relatione," meaning, upon relation or information. When the state brings an action in which it has no interest against an individual at the instigation of one who has a private interest in the matter.

FORUM NON CONVENIENS: Inconvenient forum. Although a court may have jurisdiction over the case, the action should be tried in a more conveniently located court, one to which parties and witnesses may more easily travel, for example.

GUARDIAN AD LITEM: A guardian appointed by the court to represent a minor or incompetent person in a legal action.

HABEAS CORPUS: You have the body. The modern writ of habeas corpus is a writ directing that a person (body) being detained (such as a prisoner) be brought before the court so that the legality of his detention can be judicially ascertained.

IN CAMERA: In private, in chambers. When a hearing is held before a judge in his or her chambers or when all spectators are excluded from the courtroom.

IN FORMA PAUPERIS: In the manner of a pauper. A party who proceeds in forma pauperis because of his poverty is one who is allowed to bring suit without liability for costs.

INFRA: Below, under. A word referring the reader to a later part of a book. (The opposite of supra.)

IN LOCO PARENTIS: In the place of a parent.

IN PARI DELICTO: Equally wrong; a court of equity will not grant requested relief to an applicant who is in pari delicto, or as much at fault in the transactions giving rise to the controversy as is the opponent of the applicant.

IN PARI MATERIA: On like subject matter or upon the same matter. Statutes relating to the same person or things are said to be in pari materia. It is a general rule of statutory construction that such statutes should be construed together, i.e., looked at as if they together constituted one law.

IN PERSONAM: Against the person. Jurisdiction over the person of an individual.

IN RE: In the matter of. Used to designate a proceeding involving an estate or other property.

IN REM: A term that signifies an action against the res, or thing. An action in rem is basically one that is taken directly against property, as distinguished from an action in personam, i.e., against the person.

INTER ALIA: Among other things. Used to show that the whole of a statement, pleading, list, statute, etc., has not been set forth in its entirety.

INTER PARTES: Between the parties. May refer to contracts, conveyances, or other transactions having legal significance.

INTER VIVOS: Between the living. An inter vivos gift is a gift made by a living grantor, as distinguished from bequests contained in a will, which pass upon the death of the testator.

IPSO FACTO: By the mere fact itself.

JUS: Law or the entire body of law.

LEX LOCI: The law of the place; the notion that the rights of parties to a legal proceeding are governed by the law of the place where those rights arose.

MALUM IN SE: Evil or wrong in and of itself; inherently wrong. This term describes an act that is wrong by its very nature, as opposed to one which would not be wrong but for the fact that there is a specific legal prohibition against it (malum prohibitum).

MALUM PROHIBITUM: Wrong because prohibited, but not inherently evil. Used to describe something that is wrong because it is expressly forbidden by law but that is not in and of itself evil, e.g., speeding.

MANDAMUS: We command. A writ directing an official to take a certain action.

MENS REA: A guilty mind; a criminal intent. A term used to signify the mental state that accompanies a crime or other prohibited act. Some crimes require only a general mens rea (general intent to do the prohibited act), but others, like assault with intent to murder, require the existence of a specific mens rea.

MODUS OPERANDI: Method of operating; generally refers to the manner or style of a criminal in committing crimes, admissible in appropriate cases as evidence of the identity of a defendant.

NEXUS: A connection to.

NISI PRIUS: A court of first impression. A nisi prius court is one where issues of fact are tried before a judge or jury.

N.O.V. (NON OBSTANTE VEREDICTO): Notwithstanding the verdict. A judgment n.o.v. is a judgment given in favor of one party despite the fact that a verdict was returned in favor of the other party, the justification being that the verdict either had no reasonable support in fact or was contrary to law.

NUNC PRO TUNC: Now for then. This phrase refers to actions that may be taken and will then have full retroactive effect.

PENDENTE LITE: Pending the suit; pending litigation underway.

PER CAPITA: By head; beneficiaries of an estate, if they take in equal shares, take per capita.

PER CURIAM: By the court; signifies an opinion ostensibly written "by the whole court" and with no identified author.

PER SE: By itself, in itself; inherently.

PER STIRPES: By representation. Used primarily in the law of wills to describe the method of distribution where a person, generally because of death, is unable to take that which is left to him by the will of another, and therefore his heirs divide such property between them rather than take under the will individually.

PRIMA FACIE: On its face, at first sight. A prima facie case is one that is sufficient on its face, meaning that the evidence supporting it is adequate to establish the case until contradicted or overcome by other evidence.

PRO TANTO: For so much; as far as it goes. Often used in eminent domain cases when a property owner receives partial payment for his land without prejudice to his right to bring suit for the full amount he claims his land to be worth.

QUANTUM MERUIT: As much as he deserves. Refers to recovery based on the doctrine of unjust enrichment in those cases in which a party has rendered valuable services or furnished materials that were accepted and enjoyed by another under circumstances that would reasonably notify the recipient that the rendering party expected to be paid. In essence, the law implies a contract to pay the reasonable value of the services or materials furnished.

QUASI: Almost like; as if; nearly. This term is essentially used to signify that one subject or thing is almost analogous to another but that material differences between them do exist. For example, a quasi-criminal proceeding is one that is not strictly criminal but shares enough of the same characteristics to require some of the same safeguards (e.g., procedural due process must be followed in a parole hearing).

QUID PRO QUO: Something for something. In contract law, the consideration, something of value, passed between the parties to render the contract binding.

RES GESTAE: Things done. In evidence law, this principle justifies the admission of a statement that would otherwise be hearsay when it is made so closely to the event in question as to be said to be a part of it, or with such spontaneity as not to have the possibility of falsehood.

RES IPSA LOQUITUR: The thing speaks for itself. This doctrine gives rise to a rebuttable presumption of negligence when the instrumentality causing the injury was within the exclusive control of the defendant, and the injury was one that does not normally occur unless a person has been negligent.

RES JUDICATA: A matter adjudged. Doctrine which provides that once a court of competent jurisdiction has rendered a final judgment or decree on the merits, that judgment or decree is conclusive upon the parties to the case and prevents them from engaging in any other litigation on the points and issues determined therein.

RESPONDEAT SUPERIOR: Let the master reply. This doctrine holds the master liable for the wrongful acts of his servant (or the principal for his agent) in those cases in which the servant (or agent) was acting within the scope of his authority at the time of the injury.

STARE DECISIS: To stand by or adhere to that which has been decided. The common law doctrine of stare decisis attempts to give security and certainty to the law by following the policy that once a principle of law as applicable to a certain set of facts has been set forth in a decision, it forms a precedent that will subsequently be followed, even though a different decision might be made were it the first time the question had arisen. Of course, stare decisis is not an inviolable principle and is departed from in instances where there is good cause (e.g., considerations of public policy led the Supreme Court to disregard prior decisions sanctioning segregation).

SUPRA: Above. A word referring a reader to an earlier part of a book.

ULTRA VIRES: Beyond the power. This phrase is most commonly used to refer to actions taken by a corporation that are beyond the power or legal authority of the corporation.

Addendum of French Derivatives

CHATTEL: Tangible personal property.

CY PRES: Doctrine permitting courts to apply trust funds to purposes not expressed in the trust but necessary to carry out the settlor's intent.

IN PAIS: Not pursuant to legal proceedings.

PER AUTRE VIE: For another's life; during another's life. In property law, an estate may be granted that will terminate upon the death of someone other than the grantee.

PROFIT A PRENDRE: A license to remove minerals or other produce from land.

VOIR DIRE: Process of questioning jurors as to their predispositions about the case or parties to a proceeding in order to identify those jurors displaying bias or prejudice.